Y0-ARB-609

Historical Dictionaries of Cities of the World
Series Editor: Jon Woronoff

1. *Tokyo,* by Roman Cybriwsky. 1997.
2. *Stockholm*, by Dennis E. Gould. 1997.

Historical Dictionary of TOKYO

ROMAN CYBRIWSKY

Historical Dictionaries of Cities of the World, No. 1

The Scarecrow Press, Inc.
Lanham, Md., & London
1997

SCARECROW PRESS, INC.

Published in the United States of America
by Scarecrow Press, Inc.
4720 Boston Way
Lanham, Maryland 20706

4 Pleydell Gardens, Folkestone
Kent CT20 2DN, England

British Cataloguing-in-Publication Information Available

Library of Congress Cataloging-in-Publication Data

Cybriwsky, Roman A.
    Historical dictionary of Tokyo / Roman Cybriwsky.
        p.   cm. — (Historical dictionaries of cities of the world ;
    no. 1)
    Includes bibliographical references.
    ISBN 0–8108–3234–8 (cloth : alk. paper)
    1. Tokyo (Japan)—Encyclopedias. I. Title. II. Series.
DS896.1.C43   1997
952'.135—dc20   96–38164

ISBN 0–8108–3234–8 (cloth : alk.paper)

To the four nicest people I know
Olga, Adrian, Alex, and Mary
with thanks for their continued support and patience

CONTENTS

EDITOR'S FOREWORD

From not overly auspicious beginnings in the 15th century, Tokyo has grown into one of the largest, richest, and most important cities in the world. More than most others, it dominates the country because in addition to being the capital and thus the political and administrative center, it is also the commercial, educational, and cultural center. And this dominant position has only been reinforced over the years despite sporadic, and not very effective, attempts at decentralization. This means, in short, that to know Japan it is necessary to know Tokyo.

Yet while our knowledge of Japan is expanding rapidly, the same could hardly be said of Tokyo. Though numerous books and articles on Japan appear, rather few deal specifically with Tokyo. True, more foreigners than ever pass through or live there, but their knowledge is often rather superficial. That gap will be partly filled by this informative *Historical Dictionary of Tokyo,* which not only provides essential facts and figures, dates and descriptions but also imparts some of the flavor of this fascinating city in its many entries on significant persons and events, both in early Edo and then modern Tokyo. Since the city grew by incorporating smaller towns and villages, the entries on various neighborhoods are particularly useful. Although the literature on Tokyo in English is still limited, it does exist, and the bibliography is the place to seek further information on subjects of special interest.

Every city has many facets of its history, economy, and geography. The author of this *Historical Dictionary of Tokyo,* Roman Cybriwsky, initially approached Japan's teeming metropolis from this last angle. As a professor of geography and urban studies at Temple University in Philadelphia, he has spent about half of his time over the past decade in Tokyo at Temple University-Japan. There he has become familiar with many other facets of one of the world's greatest cities. In addition to lecturing in Tokyo, Dr. Cybriwsky has written extensively about the city, including his book *Tokyo: The Changing Profile of an Urban Giant.* Now he has gone a step further with a guide that covers many more aspects of the city in a handy and engaging manner.

Jon Woronoff
Series Editor

PREFACE

Tokyo is an enormous city with nearly 12 million residents and an area of 2,168 square kilometers (837 square miles). Its history is more than five centuries old and covers disparate periods from its beginning as a small castle town (1457), to the powerful capital of the Tokugawa *shōguns* (1603-1868), then a western-facing industrial center beginning in the Meiji Period (1868-1912), to a global economic capital today. It has had much more than its fair share of disasters, particularly fires and earthquakes, and has been rebuilt time and again after these destructions. For this reason and many others, the city is a patchwork of hundreds of neighborhoods and other urban districts, and a study in contrasts in urban form and land use. It has copied trends and fashions from around the world and has reproduced them locally on its own terms. At the same time, it has been an innovative city that now attracts creative people from all over the world looking for inspiration in the arts, architecture, city planning, engineering technology, industry, and many other fields. The city's leaders at various times have included powerful personalities and creative geniuses with personal biographies that would hold the attention of all of us and provide lessons, from one direction or the other, about how to live and how to succeed.

In short, Tokyo is a fascinating city with a great many stories to tell about its people, places, and experiences. This book is a reference volume that, I hope, will help readers learn about the city and steer them to further study. Toward this end, there are more than 250 dictionary entries in this volume, including the city's most influential leaders, both past and present, most important districts, and landmark events over the course of its history. The dictionary is the main part of this book. There is also a lengthy bibliography about the city. I believe that it is the most detailed list of sources in English about Tokyo. I have arranged the bibliography according to major topic. Other features of the book are an introductory essay about Tokyo, a chronology of historic events, a table of population and geographic area for each of the wards, cities, towns, and villages that comprise the Tokyo metropolis, and lists of the city's previous mayors and other chief executives, its tallest buildings, and other information.

Tokyo is so big and so complex that a full reference book would be enormous and consist of many volumes. It was a challenge to decide how to limit the number of entries according to some logical criteria. One guideline that I established for myself was that the dictionary should be tailored specifically to readers in the English language about Tokyo or Japan more generally. That is, I decided to emphasize those people, places, historic events, and terms that English-language readers would most likely encounter in their reading of published literature about Tokyo or Japan, and then might want to look up for a definition or more information. Therefore, one step in drawing up the list of entries for this book was to consult the indexes of popular books about Tokyo such as those by Edward Seidensticker, Paul Waley, and Noel Nouet (see the bibliography) for ideas about which people, places, historical events, and terms seemed to be most common and most appropriate. I also systematically went through the newly opened (1993) Edo-Tokyo Museum, a large and outstanding facility operated by Tokyo Metropolitan Government about the history of the city from the earliest times to the modern period, to see what choices were made there about presenting Tokyo to the lay public. I compared the list of entries that I generated on my own with the museum's exhibits and publications to see what I might have missed, as well as to think a second time about topics on my list that the museum omitted. I then decided for myself whether to omit a particular entry or add a new one.

A special problem came up with respect to entries about

individuals. Because Tokyo is the nation's capital and the center of arts, commerce, communications, and many other aspects of life in Japan, the city is (and has been for a long time) both home and workplace for the majority of the most influential personalities in the country as a whole. To focus this volume on Tokyo specifically, I decided to concentrate on those individuals who had the greatest direct impact on shaping the city and guiding its historical development. That is, the fact that a person was a famous Tokyoite was not in itself a criterion for inclusion in the dictionary. Thus, the book does not give biographies for the many artists, writers and musicians who worked *in* Tokyo over the years but whose work was not specifically *about* Tokyo. So, too, I have not included the many politicians and statesmen (and women) who are more properly considered to be figures in Japanese history, even though they were based in Tokyo for most if not all of their lives or professional careers. However, there were a number of individuals, for example Tokugawa Ieyasu (1543-1616) and Gotō Shimpei (1857-1929), who were major actors in the life of the city as well as leaders of Japan. Consequently, this volume includes their biographies but focuses specifically on their roles with respect to Tokyo. Other aspects of their careers, such as their roles in national affairs, are related elsewhere, including the forthcoming *Historical Dictionary of Japan* in Scarecrow's Asian Historical Dictionaries series and the excellent two-volume *Japan: An Illustrated Encyclopedia* published by Kodansha.

Unfortunately, my methodology yielded comparatively few entries about notable women in Tokyo's history. Not just the Edo-Tokyo Museum and the fine history books referred to above, but also other sources, both Japanese and English, have neglected this half of the population, concentrating almost exclusively on men. I have made a point of learning about influential women in Tokyo and have included several entries that are relevant. However, I know that I too have come up short with respect to this necessary goal. This is just the first edition of this volume; I hope that the next edition will show an improvement, perhaps with the advice of readers who are equally concerned about this shortcoming.

Japanese names are given throughout this volume in the usual Japanese order, i.e., the family name first and then the given name. The system of romanization for Japanese words is the modified Hepburn system as used in the *New Japanese-English Dictionary* published by Kenkyūsha. Long vowels, such as the "u" in Kenkyūsha, the second "o" in Gotō, and the "u" and "o" in Chūō Ward, are indicated by the use of macrons. However, Japanese words that are widely known in English are written without macrons, as they usually appear in English. The majority of these words are place names. For example, I write Tokyo instead of the Japanese *Tōkyō*, Osaka instead of *Ōsaka*, and Kyoto instead of *Kyōto*. Differentiating words that are "widely known" in English from those that are not is problematic; I did my best. Japanese words except proper nouns and words that are widely known in English are written in italics. The word *shōgun* is an example of a problematic Japanese word: should it be shogun or *shōgun*? I found examples of both usages in the literature and chose the latter for this volume. In the bibliography the use of macrons follows the practice of the specific works cited.

Entries in the dictionary are arranged alphabetically and are printed in capital letters. English is used for entries that are known by common English terms. Thus, the entry about the high-speed trains that connect Tokyo to other cities is under BULLET TRAINS instead of under SHINKANSEN. Readers who turn first to SHINKANSEN will see the instruction "see BULLET TRAINS." There are also cross-references in capital letters within the bodies of dictionary entries, as well as within the text of the book's introductory essay "Tokyo: An Introduction to the City." Other cross-references employ the abbreviations q.v. (Latin: *quod vide*, "which see") and qq.v. (*quae vide*, "which [things] see"). The former is used to indicate that the person, place, term, or historic event just mentioned has its own entry in the dictionary, while the latter is used after two or more persons, places, terms, or events that have been mentioned to indicate that all of them have entries in the dictionary.

I now turn to the very pleasurable task of acknowledging the exceptionally kind individuals and institutions who have assisted me. Let me say first that I want to assure the people about to be mentioned and the users of this book that I assume personal responsibility for the shortcomings of this volume and any mistakes it might contain. That having been said, I want to thank my employer, Temple University in Philadelphia, Pennsylvania, for allowing me the opportunity to teach for several years at Temple University Japan (TUJ), the University's campus in Tokyo. That opportunity gave me the chance to stay in Tokyo for extended periods and to conduct research that contributed to this book and to other publications. Vice Provost Richard Joslyn and former Associate Dean William J. Young have been especially supportive in this regard. I also want to thank Temple for two small grants that supported travel to Tokyo for short visits and other research expenses. One grant was from the Center for East Asian Studies and the other was awarded by the faculty senate.

In addition, I want to single out several of my colleagues at the university for their help and support with this project: Tom Boardman, director of the library at TUJ; Jeff Kingston (History); Rob Mason (Geography and Urban Studies); Rei Okamoto (Communications and Japanese); and Barbara Thornbury (Japanese). I am also grateful to Mark Mattson, director of Temple's Computer Cartography Laboratory, for making the maps and laying out the text. Without his help this book would still be unfinished. I also acknowledge L. L. Jeng, always an exceptionally creative writer, who contributed an early draft for the "About the Author" page.

From the large world outside Temple, I want to give special thanks to Professor Yasuo Masai of Rissho University, Professor David Edgington of the University of British Columbia, and Mr. Howard Peng, formerly with the research liaison office of Tokyo Metropolitan Government, for their generous help and criticism. I also give heartfelt thanks to three very special former students who were indispensable as unofficial research assistants: Ayumi Nishikawa helped me whenever I was in Tokyo, most recently while carrying her new baby Terumi; Aoi Shimizu was a terrific research partner both in Tokyo and at home base in Philadelphia; and Nobuko Ikue, a recent graduate, aided me with countless library errands, translations and, explanations. All three of you are wonderful! Thanks!

Last but not least, I am obliged to thank to my two sons, Adrian and Alex Cybriwsky, computer geniuses both, who saved their father from that specific eleventh-hour (and 59 minutes!) disaster involving the diskette for the entire book that a "Delete" button brings. Whew!

ABBREVIATIONS

DSP	Democratic Socialist Party *(Minshu Shakaitō)*
GHQ	General Headquarters
JNR	Japan National Railways
JR	Japan Railways
JCP	Japan Communist Party
JSP	Japan Socialist Party
LDP	Liberal Democratic Party *(Jiyū Minshutō)*
MITI	Ministry of International Trade and Industry *(Tsūshō Sangyōshō)*
NRWU	National Railway Workers' Union
NTV	Nippon Television
SCAP	Supreme Commander for the Allied Powers
TMG	Tokyo Metropolitan Government

CHRONOLOGY

628 The Asakusa Kannon (*Sensōji*) temple is founded.

646 Musashi Province is established as part of a new regional administration system in central Japan (the Taika Reform). It covered what is now Tokyo, Saitama, and eastern Kanagawa Prefectures.

733 Jindaiji, a major Buddhist temple now affiliated with the Tendai Sect, is established in what is presently Chōfu City, Tokyo.

741 The first provincial temple (*kokubunji*) is built in Musashi Province at what is now Kokubunji City in Tokyo.

939 Taira-no-Masakado gains control of the Kantō region after a revolt against the central government.

1457 Edo Castle is constructed by Ōta Dōkan.

1590 Tokugawa Ieyasu establishes his headquarters at Edo.

1592 Reconstruction of Edo Castle is begun by Tokugawa Ieyasu.

1603 Tokugawa Ieyasu establishes the Edo Bakufu (Edo Shogunate).

1603 Kanda Mountain is leveled to reclaim marshes at Hibiya Cove on Tokyo Bay (then called Edo Bay).

1624 Nakamuraza, the leading *kabuki* theater and troupe of Edo, is founded by Nakamura Kanzaburō.

1635 The *sankin kōtai* policy is formalized by the third *shōgun*, Tokukawa Iemistu.

1639 The policy of national isolation is implemented.

1654 The Tamagawa Canal is completed.

1657 The Meireki Fire burns most of Edo over two days in March and takes more than 100,000 lives.

1658 A permanent fire-fighting force is established.

1659 Ryōgoku Bridge is completed over the Sumida River.

1673 Echigoya, a kimono shop that evolved into the Mitsukoshi department store empire, is founded by Mitsui Takatoshi.

1682 A great fire occurs.

1685 The Laws on Compassion for Living Things are put into effect by Tokugawa Tsunayoshi, the fifth *shōgun* (abolished in 1709).

1698 Naitō Shinjuku, the first post-station along the Kōshū Kaidō, is established.

1702 The 47 Ronin incident takes place. (Note: Some sources date the incident to January, 1703.)

1707 Eruption of Mount Fuji.

1718 A system of 48 local fire-fighting units is established in Edo.

1721 A large fire in Nihonbashi destroys 140,000 houses.

1722 Development begins in the Musashino area.

1733 A large riot breaks out early in the year in response to a major famine (the Kyōhō Famine) that began in southwestern Japan in 1732.

1772 The great Meiwa fire occurs.

1783 Eruption of Mount Asama.

1787 The Kansei Reforms are enacted.

1791 A law prohibiting mixed bathing is enacted.

1841 The Tempō Reforms are enacted.

1853 Commodore Matthew C. Perry and his squadron of "black ships" arrive in Edo Bay, bringing an end to Japan's self-imposed isolation under the Tokugawa Shogunate.

1855 The Ansei earthquake damages Tokyo.

1867 Restoration of imperial rule.

1868 Edo Castle is surrendered peacefully to imperial forces, ending control of the city by the *shōgun's* forces.

Edo is renamed Tokyo.

Tokyo prefectural government is established; Karasuma Mitsue is named governor.

1869 The emperor takes up residence in Tokyo.

1872 A major fire ravages Ginza, Kyōbashi, Tsukiji, and other sections of the center of Tokyo; Ginza is rebuilt in brick.

Rail service is opened between Shinbashi and Yokohama.

1873 Ueno Park is opened to the public.

1877 Tokyo University is established.

An industrial fair is held in Ueno Park.

1883 The Rokumeikan is opened.

1889 Promulgation of the Meiji Constitution.

A special administrative system for the City of Tokyo is established.

1903 Hibiya Park opens.

1914 Tokyo Station is completed.

1918 Riots break out in Tokyo and in cities and towns throughout Japan because of the high cost of rice and other necessities.

1923 The Great Kantō Earthquake occurs on 1 September.

1925 The Yamanote Loop rail line is completed.

1927 The first subway line in Tokyo is opened, connecting Asakusa and Ueno.

1931 Tokyo International Airport (Haneda Airport) opens.

1932 Tokyo annexes nearby townships, towns, and villages to form Great Tokyo City.

1936 The February 26 Incident takes place, in which junior army officers seize control of the center of Tokyo and assassinate several government officials.

1937 Korakuen Stadium is completed.

1939 The Ginza Line subway connects Asakusa and Shibuya.

1941 The Pacific War commences.

1943 The administrations of *Tōkyō-fu* and the City of Tokyo are merged to form *Tōkyō-to* (Tokyo Metropolis).

1944 Evacuation of schoolchildren from Tokyo begins.

1945 The Great Tokyo Air Raid takes place on 10 March.

The Pacific War ends; U.S. Occupation forces enter Tokyo.

1947 A new constitution for Japan is promulgated.

The Local Autonomy Law, which called for direct elections of Tokyo's governor and ward leaders, is put into effect.

The 23 Wards of Tokyo are established.

1952 The Local Autonomy Law is revised.
The Occupation of Japan ends with the signing of the San Francisco Peace Treaty.

1956 The Capital Region Improvement Act is promulgated.

1958 Tokyo Tower is completed.

1962 Tokyo's population exceeds 10 million.

1964 The high-speed "bullet" train line (*shinkansen*) is inaugurated between Tokyo and Osaka.

Tokyo hosts the summer Olympic Games.

1969 Major confrontation takes place between radical students and police at Yasuda Hall of Tokyo University.

1973 Oil crisis ("oil shock") causes shortages of gasoline and other necessities.

1974 The Local Autonomy Law is revised again.

1977 The U.S. military base at Tachikawa is returned to Japan.

1978 New Tokyo International Airport (Narita Airport) is opened.

1979 Suzuki Shun'ichi is elected governor of Tokyo Metropolis for the first of four consecutive terms.

1986 The Akasaka Roppongi Redevelopment project (ARK Hills) is completed, reflecting the construction boom taking place in the city.

1991 Tokyo Metropolitan Government headquarters moves to Shinjuku.

1995 A terrorist attack releases the nerve gas sarin in the subway system of downtown Tokyo during the morning rush hour of March 20, killing six and injuring more than 3,000. The doomsday cult Aum Shinrikyō is blamed for the attack.

Aoshima Yukio is elected governor of Tokyo Metropolis.

TOKYO: AN INTRODUCTION TO THE CITY

Tokyo is Japan's largest city and its capital. It is also one of the largest cities in the world and a major center of global economic influence. The population is 11,816,703 (estimate of 1 February 1994 for Tokyo Metropolis), and the area is 2,186.61 square kilometers (844.6 square miles). The meaning of the word *Tōkyō* (q.v.) is "eastern capital," referring to the city's political role in Japan and its location relative to Kyoto and other cities of central Japan that had served as capital earlier in history. Before 1868 the city's name was Edo (q.v.).

Tokyo is located at 35 degrees 45 minutes north latitude and 139 degrees 45 minutes east longitude on the Pacific Ocean side of central Honshū, the largest of Japan's four major islands. It is at the head of Tokyo Bay (q.v.), one of the largest inlets of the Pacific Ocean along Japan's coastline in an area where several locally important rivers, namely, the Sumida River (q.v.), the Edo River (q.v.), the Ara River, and the Tama River (q.v.), form deltas and enter the sea. The city occupies much of the southern Kantō Plain (q.v.), one of Japan's largest lowlands, and is mostly flat in topography. However, there are some hilly areas as well, particularly the Tama Hills (see TAMA AREA) and the far western reaches of Tokyo Prefecture (q.v.). The city's highest elevation is Mount Kumotori (q.v.; *Kumotoriyama*), located in a rugged mountain district at the westernmost point of Tokyo Prefecture; the summit reaches 2,018 meters (6,619 feet).

There are four well-defined seasons each year in Tokyo. Summers are generally hot and muggy, while winters are mild. The warmest month is August, with an average monthly temperature of 26.7 degrees C (80.1 degrees F). The coldest month is January (4.7 degrees C; 40.5 degrees F). The total

1

annual precipitation is 1,460 millimeters (57.5 inches). Much
of the rainfall is concentrated in early summer (mid-June to
mid-July), in a rainy season called *baiu* or *tsuyu*. There is also
a rainy period in September and early October called *shūrin*.
Late summer and fall is a time when Tokyo's climate is influenced by typhoons from the South Pacific.

ADMINISTRATION

The City of Tokyo as a formally defined administrative
unit was abolished in 1943. Since then Tokyo has been administered within the framework of the system of Japan's 47 prefectures (*to, do, fu, ken*) as a unit called *Tōkyō-to*, translated
as "Tokyo Metropolis" (q.v.) or, more loosely, "Tokyo
Prefecture" (q.v.). Its area includes the old city, now known as
the "Ward Area," in the eastern sector, plus a much larger
sector known as the "Tama Area" (q.v.) to the west. The Izu
Islands and the Ogasawara Islands (qq.v.), both island chains
to the south of the Ward Area in the Pacific Ocean, are also
included in the administrative structure of Tokyo Metropolis.
The table below compares the geographical areas and population totals for each of the major parts of Tokyo Metropolis.

Tokyo Metropolis: Population Totals and Area
(Estimates, February 1994)

	Population	Area (sq.km.)	Area (sq.miles)
Ward Area	8,019,938	621.0	239.9
Tama Area	3,765,051	1,159.9	448.0
Islands	31,714	405.7	156.7
TOTAL	11,816,703	2,186.6	844.6

The Ward Area of Tokyo Metropolis is divided into 23
Wards (*ku*). Therefore, it is sometimes referred to as the "23

Wards" or the "23 Wards Area." Each of the wards has its own chief and local government structure with responsibilities for local affairs, as well as a main headquarters building. The Tama Area is comprised of 26 cities, five towns, and one village. These units too have their own local governments that oversee local affairs. Local administration of the islands section of Tokyo Metropolis is organized within the framework of two towns and seven villages.

The administration of Tokyo Metropolis as a whole is the responsibility of Tokyo Metropolitan Government (TMG; q.v.). This government body has a dual character and performs functions of a prefecture government as well as those of a municipality or large city within the Ward Area. The structure of Tokyo Metropolitan Government is divided into two branches: (1) a legislative branch represented by the Tokyo Metropolitan Assembly; and (2) an executive branch headed by a governor. The Tokyo Metropolitan Assembly has 127 members who are all elected by direct popular vote for four-year terms of office. It is the fundamental decision-making body in Tokyo Metropolis, and is responsible for passing and amending laws, establishing a budget, and approving or disapproving the governor's appointments of vice-governors. The governor is also elected to a four-year term by direct popular vote. She or he has authority over the bureaus of Finance, Taxation, Waterworks, Transportation, Housing, Public Health, and others; the Tokyo Fire Department; the Central Wholesale Market; the Offices of Policy Planning and Information; and other aspects of the administration of Tokyo Metropolis. The present governor is Aoshima Yukio (q.v.), elected in 1995.

HISTORY

The origins of human settlement in what is today Tokyo are lost in prehistory. However, it is clear from archaeological evidence that the Kantō Plain was inhabited by hunting and gathering civilizations at least as far back as the late Jōmon period (ca 2000 BC–ca 1000 BC). There are shell mounds at Ochanomizu and Yushi in Bunkyō Ward and at Ōmori in Ōta Ward that record details of these early settlements (see ŌMORI SHELL MOUNDS). Other prehistoric settlements are associated with Yayoi culture, a later civilization (ca 300 BC–ca AD 300) that brought rice cultivation, metallurgy, and other technological and social innovations to both Japan as a whole and to the Kantō Plain specifically. Later, the area that is now Tokyo was part of Musashi Province, one of the administrative units that was set up under the Taika Reforms of 646 during Japan's age of warring clans and powerful chieftains. In 939 the warrior Taira-no-Masakado (q.v.) gained control of the Kantō region and used it as a base to challenge central authority.

The development of Tokyo as an urban settlement is traced to the year 1457 when a warrior leader named Ōta Dōkan (q.v.) chose a site near a small village in the Kantō Plain named Edo to build a castle. The fortification was on a low hill near Tokyo Bay, and it came to be the heart of the growing city. Edo Castle (q.v.), as the fortification was called, was one of many castles in Japan at the time. It was not particularly distinguished. Similarly, the city itself (called Edo) was not particularly large or important. Dōkan was killed in 1486, and the castle deteriorated for approximately one century afterward under a succession of different invaders and occupants, the most notable of whom was the powerful Hōjō clan based in the castle town of Odawara.

The history of Edo-Tokyo took a dramatic turn in 1590, when the warlord Toyotomi Hideyoshi vanquished the Hōjō family in a siege of Odawara and awarded Edo and its surroundings to his chief lieutenant, Tokugawa Ieyasu (q.v.). Ieyasu made the city the capital of his fiefdom and the base for expanding control over ever larger territories in Japan. By 1603, after the death of Hideyoshi and three years after the decisive Battle of Sekigahara (q.v.), he had consolidated power over almost all of the country and proclaimed himself *shōgun* (q.v.). The castle was rebuilt and greatly enlarged, and the city grew quickly to become the largest and most influential in the country. The policy of *sankin kōtai* (q.v.), which required feudal lords to alternate residence between their domains and Edo, was instrumental in fueling urban growth. The Tokugawa shogunate (q.v.) ruled Japan from Edo until 1868.

Edo under the *shōguns* was a remarkable city. Its heart was the castle and a clockwise spiral of moats and high walls that protected the *shōgun*, his immediate family, and his closest allies in the center. The most important feudal lords (*daimyō*; q.v.) also resided within fortifications. Many of them had additional residences on higher ground in the city in a section called *yamanote* (q.v.) mostly to the north and west of the castle. Commoners (see CHŌNIN), including growing numbers of merchants and artisans, lived at the base of Edo Castle on the low flatlands at the mouth of the Sumida River and Tokyo Bay. Their area was called *shitamachi* (q.v.). It was an extremely crowded district that consisted of numerous distinct quarters separated by busy canals and other waterways (see GINZA; NIHOMBASHI). There were also many lively amusement quarters (see SAKARIBA). The largest and most famous pleasure district in Edo was Yoshiwara (q.v.). Because of the crowded conditions in the city and the prevalence of wood construction, there were frequent fires that destroyed entire districts and took many lives (see FIRES). The Meireki Fire of 1657 (q.v.) was the most destructive. Because so much of the city was destroyed (including Edo Castle itself), new policies about land use, building construction materials, and firefighting were enacted in its aftermath. In addition, bridges were built to allow the city to expand across the Sumida River and to open escape routes in case of future disasters. (see RYŌGOKU; RYŌGOKU BRIDGE)

The city changed greatly after the shogunate fell in 1868 (see MEIJI PERIOD). Its name was changed to Tokyo, and the emperor relocated his seat of power from Kyoto to the site of Edo Castle (see IMPERIAL PALACE; MEIJI EMPEROR; MEIJI RESTORATION). Many foreign influences came to the city at this time because of Japanese who were traveling abroad to study and because of the many foreign experts who were welcomed to the country as advisers and teachers (see YATOI). The foreign influences were seen in changing fashions in dress, forms of entertainment, new foods, and the architectural styles of landmark buildings such as the Hoterukan, a hotel in the Tsukiji (q.v.) district for foreigners, the Rokumeikan (q.v.) dance hall, and reconstructed commercial streets in the Ginza (q.v.) district (see GINZA BRICK TOWN). Meanwhile, the historic temple district of Asakusa (q.v.; see SENSŌJI) thrived as an entertainment district of a different sort (see ASAKUSA TWELVE STORIES). Tokyo's first modern office district was developed on vacant ground at the foot of the old castle (see LONDON BLOCK; MARUNOUCHI). Heavy industry expanded along the waterfront and along newly built rail corridors.

All of this growth came to a crashing halt just before noon, 1 September 1923, when the Great Kantō Earthquake (q.v.) shook the city and its surroundings, and sparked hundreds of fires that engulfed most of its neighborhoods and took more than 100,000 lives. Rebuilding began almost immediately after the disaster (see C. A. BEARD; BOARD OF RECONSTRUCTION OF THE CAPITAL CITY; GOTŌ SHIMPEI), although at great financial cost. The city soon returned to its pattern of prosperity and expansion. Growth was especially pronounced on the west side of the city, where bustling commercial centers were developed at Shinjuku and Shibuya (qq.v.), as well as at other transportation nodes. New housing developments were constructed along trolley lines and commuter rail corridors that reached ever farther to the urban edge. However, disaster struck the city again in 1945, when Tokyo and many of its suburbs were bombed by U. S. warplanes near the end of World War II (see AIR RAIDS OF 1945). The destruction of buildings and the loss of life were even more widespread, and the city was left in almost total ruin. From the end of the war until 1952 Tokyo was the headquarters for the Occupation of Japan (q.v.) by U.S. forces.

Reconstruction of the city favored rebuilding the economy. By the late 1950s, Tokyo was well on its way to being a dominant commercial and industrial center once again. The opening of Tokyo Tower (q.v.) in December, 1958, was a symbol of postwar progress. In 1964, the city successfully hosted the summer Olympic Games (see TOKYO OLYMPICS), and impressed visitors from around the world with its many improvements: a monorail line to Tokyo International Airport (q.v.), new international hotels, and the *shinkansen*, a newly unveiled, high-speed interurban train line (see BULLET TRAINS). However, the city's air and water were badly polluted, and housing in many residential neighborhoods was congested and poor in quality. As Japan accumulated wealth in the 1970s and 1980s, the city was able to clean up the worst pollution (see ENVIRONMENTAL PROTECTION) as well as greatly increase the amount of land given to parks and recreation (see LEISURE). Housing conditions improved for most residents as well, although the cost was high because land was expensive. One of the most important areas of new housing construction has been in the Tama Area (q.v.) in the western part of Tokyo Prefecture (q.v.). Tama New Town (q.v.), a planned bedroom town started in 1967, now has more than 150,000 residents.

The central business district of Tokyo has continued to expand in recent years, and now covers much of the three central wards, Chūō, Chiyoda, and Minato. Hundreds of thousands of commuters converge here each day by train, subway, bus, taxi, and private automobile to work, shop, attend school, or find entertainment. There has also been spectacular growth at many newer commercial centers closer to the suburban residences of commuters, especially Shinjuku. This district has come to be an especially important office and retailing center. In 1991 the new headquarters of Tokyo Metropolitan Government (q.v.; "City Hall") opened in Shinjuku. The new City Hall, designed by Tange Kenzo (q.v.), is the city's tallest building. Other commercial expansion has taken place on newly reclaimed islands in Tokyo Bay. This was a favorite development project of former Tokyo governor Suzuki Shunichi (q.v.). But his successor, who assumed office in 1995, Aoshima Yukio (q.v.), has promised to slow construction there in favor of improvements to existing residential areas.

The 1990s have seen a general downturn in the economy of Tokyo, and construction has slowed. Office rents have dropped, although they are still the highest in the world (see LAND PRICES), and many newly constructed buildings have vacancies. There has also been increased unemployment. Social problems are evidenced in the growing number of homeless residents living in cardboard boxes near train stations, under bridges, and in public parks. These developments have never been seen before by younger generations of Tokyo residents who grew up during a period of unparalleled prosperity and economic expansion. The deadly nerve gas attack of 14 April 1995 in the city's subway system, attributed to the religious cult Aum Shinrikyō (q.v.; see also ASAHARA SHŌKŌ), has contributed to heightening feelings of uncertainty on the part of Tokyo residents. The city had always been considered safe (q.v.), but this unexpected incident demonstrated that Tokyo is not immune from crime. As a result, public officials and ordinary citizens alike are calling for increased policing, the use of surveillance cameras in public places, and other safety measures that were once thought to be unnecessary in Tokyo.

ECONOMY

During the Edo Period (q.v.) Tokyo was primarily a consumer city. Its many thousands of residents of the *samurai* (q.v.) class were not engaged directly in production, but instead supported huge numbers of merchants and artisans. Both raw materials and the finished goods that were required to sustain the city were brought in from the outside. In the earlier part of the Edo Period (before 1800) many of the textiles, items of clothing, and manufactured articles that were needed in Edo were brought in from the Kamigata region of Japan (the Kyoto and Osaka area). These imports were called *kudarimono* (q.v.), a word meaning "wares that have come down." By the 19th century, there was more focus on local production (see JIMAWARIMONO), particularly in various satellite towns in the Kantō Plain that emerged as specialized manufacturing cities for the Edo market. Chōshi and Noda in present-day Chiba Prefecture, Kiryū and Ashikaga in Gumma Prefecture, and Ōme in what is now Tokyo Prefecture are examples of such towns.

The largest sector of Tokyo's economy is the tertiary sector. This includes the city's roles as national capital, preeminent corporate headquarters center, communications center of Japan, and leading wholesale and retail trade center. The tertiary sector has been expanding in recent times, increasing from 56.2 percent of Tokyo's work force in 1950, to 59.9 percent in 1970 and 69 percent in 1985. The largest concentration of such employment is in the three central wards (Chūō, Chiyoda, and Minato Wards), but there has also been enormous growth of tertiary sector employment in developing office centers such as Shinjuku, Shibuya, and Ikebukuro (qq.v.). The National Diet Building (q.v.) and offices of various ministries of the national government are concentrated in the Nagatachō and Kasumigaseki sections of Chiyoda Ward. The Tokyo Stock Exchange (q.v.) and the offices of many securities companies are in the Kabutochō section (q.v.) of Chūō Ward. The overwhelming importance of Tokyo as a center of tertiary employment within Japan is seen in the fact that even though Tokyo Prefecture has only about 9.8 percent of the nation's population and covers merely 0.6 percent of its land area, it includes 57.8 percent of the country's largest company headquarters, 83.9 percent of all foreign company offices in Japan, 31.6 percent of securities companies, 37.6 percent of advertising companies, 29.9 percent of newspaper companies, and 64.9 percent of publishing companies (as of 1988).

Tokyo is also a major manufacturing center. It first developed this sector of the economy in the late 19th century in connection with Japan's concerted modernization drive (see MEIJI PERIOD). The majority of its industrial establishments were very small and were concentrated in the *shitamachi* (q.v.) area and along the Sumida River. Textiles, lumber, furniture, and leather industries were particularly numerous. There were also larger factories such as the Senju Woolen Mill (q.v.) in the Senju district (q.v.), the Ishikawajima Shipyards at the mouth of the Sumida River, and the Ōji Paper Company in what is today Kita Ward. Industry also spread along the waterfront of Tokyo Bay. By the early 20th century the Keihin Coastal Industrial Region, spanning the Tokyo Bay waterfront east of Tokyo to Yokohama, had developed into a diversified heavy industrial zone, with chemicals factories, machine works, shipbuilding, steel mills, and other factories. Armaments manufacturing, including aircraft industries, developed in the 1930s to the west of Tokyo in Musashino, Mitaka, Tanashi and other emerging industrial suburbs. Other important industries that developed in and around Tokyo included electronic goods, precision instruments, metalworking, and printing and publishing.

From the time of post-World War II reconstruction to the present, Tokyo's industrial production has shifted to neighboring prefectures (Chiba Prefecture, Kanagawa Prefecture and Saitama Prefecture) and the Tama Area. This has been particularly true for larger factories that require considerable space, as well as for newer high-tech industries that grew up after zoning legislation was enacted in 1959 prohibiting the expansion of industry in central Tokyo. Even now, the majority of Tokyo's 90,000-plus factories are small (having less than ten workers). The secondary sector of the economy (mostly manufacturing) has declined in recent times from 37.1 percent of the labor force in 1950 to 29.7 percent in 1985.

A small fraction of Tokyo's labor force is employed in the primary sector, mostly farming and fishing. In 1950 approximately 6.4 percent of the city's labor force worked in these occupations, but that number has declined since then to one percent in 1970 and 0.6 percent in 1985. Much of this decline is attributed to the loss of rice fields and vegetable farms to housing construction at expanding edges of the city, as well as to declines in Tokyo's fishing industry attributed to pollution in Tokyo Bay and redevelopment along the waterfront. (see WATERFRONT DEVELOPMENT)

TRANSPORTATION

Tokyo is served by two major airports. The New Tokyo International Airport (q.v.), commonly called Narita Airport after the town in Chiba Prefecture where it is located, is located approximately 66 kilometers (41 miles) from the center of the city. It handles most international air passenger traffic to Tokyo and other parts of Japan, as well as exports and imports of air freight items ranging from specialty foods to mail. It opened in 1978 and now processes more than 20 million passengers each year. There are excellent rail connections to Tokyo via the Keisei Line and the Narita Line, as well as limousine bus service. Tokyo International Airport (q.v.), commonly called Haneda Airport, is the older airport, which opened in 1931. Located on the shore of Tokyo Bay in Ōta Ward, it handles the city's domestic air passenger traffic and some limited international flights. Connections to central Tokyo are by a monorail line that opened in 1964.

Tokyo's central rail station is called Tokyo Station (q.v.). It is the focus of a network of intercity rail lines operated by Japan Railways, and the terminus for three *shinkansen* or "bullet train" (q.v.) lines to other parts of Japan: the Tōkaidō Line, Tōhoku Line, and the Jōetsu Line. Several commuter rail lines and subways (q.v.) serve Tokyo Station as well. The central part of the city is served by twelve subway lines that carry approximately eight million passengers each day. Examples of important subway lines are the Ginza Line, the Hanzōmon Line, the Marunouchi Line, the Hibiya Line, and the Chiyoda Line. The city's subway system continues to expand and now totals at least 230.3 kilometers (143.1 miles) of track. The most heavily traveled commuter railway line is the Yamanote Line (q.v.), a rail loop around the heart of the city.

The city also has an extensive network of expressways and other highways to serve automobile, bus, and truck traffic. Traffic congestion is a major problem on most roads, and parking is very expensive. For many citizens, taxis are a convenient alternative. Construction is under way for new roads and bridges that are intended to alleviate traffic congestion in the center of Tokyo and provide alternative routes for vehicles traveling between opposite ends of the metropolis.

MAJOR DISTRICTS

The center of Tokyo is the grounds of the Imperial Palace (q.v.), the historic site of Edo Castle, where Japan's emperor resides with his family. It is a large forested tract hidden behind stone walls and old moats, and is closed to the public. It stands in stark contrast to the bustling office districts that press against it from all directions, most notably Marunouchi and Ōtemachi (qq.v.), corporate office areas that are just east of the Imperial Palace near major gates of the old castle. The government office districts of Nagatachō and Kusumigaseki are to the south of the Imperial Palace, the latter adjacent to Hibiya Park. A densely concentrated area of office buildings occupies most of the rest of central Tokyo (Chūō, Chiyoda, and Minato Wards), and is expanding to new islands that are being reclaimed from Tokyo Bay. The center also includes retailing districts such as Ginza and Nihombashi (qq.v.), the Kabutochō (q.v.) financial district, and such notable landmarks as Tokyo Tower, Tokyo Station (qq.v.), and the city's central Kabuki Theater. (see GINZA)

The lower reaches of the Sumida River are east of Tokyo's central business district. It is spanned by several historic bridges (see RYŌGOKU BRIDGE), as well as new ones that carry traffic on crowded elevated expressways and other roads. The neighborhoods on either bank of the river are mostly blue-collar districts with a mix of residences, small factories and workshops, warehouses, and other commercial land uses. There are also historic shrines and temples, gardens, parks, and other landmarks. The Asakusa (q.v.) district in Taitō Ward is a particularly lively temple district and commercial center with strong historical significance. Not far to the west from Asakusa is the commercial center of Ueno (q.v.). Ueno Park (q.v.) has many historic temples, popular museums, and other attractions. Many of the areas of Tokyo in the vicinity of the Sumida River are associated with historic *shitamachi* (q.v.) and its traditions.

Tokyo's *yamanote* (q.v.) neighborhoods are mostly to the south and west of the center. It is here in the southern and western portions of Minato Ward, in Shibuya and Shinjuku Wards and in Meguro Ward (as well as parts of Bunkyō Ward to the north), that we find many of the city's better residential neighborhoods, as well as most of its foreign embassies and other resident foreigners, the campuses of prestigious universities and private schools (see KEIŌ UNIVERSITY; TOKYO UNIVERSITY), and large international hotels surrounded by beautiful gardens. There are also large parks such as the Shinjuku Imperial Gardens (*Shinjuku Gyoen*), Yoyogi Park (q.v.), and the Meiji Shrine (q.v.) and its gardens. Roppongi (q.v.) is one of several districts in this general part of Tokyo, which is noted for fine specialty shops, popular restaurants and coffee shops, and a thriving nightlife. Yebisu Garden Place, located in Meguro and Shibuya Wards near Ebisu Station on the Yamanote Line, is a popular mixed-use development (commercial, recreational, residential) that reflects new trends in planning and urban design in Tokyo. It opened in 1994.

There are many other specialized districts within the 23 Wards area of Tokyo (see TOKYO METROPOLIS), many of them defined by the kind of shopping they offer. Collectively, they present a portrait of some of the routines of life in Tokyo and the considerable diversity of the city. Tsukiji (q.v.), at the waterfront in Chūō Ward, is known for its enormous wholesale market for fish and other seafood, and spirited early-morning auctions (see TSUKIJI MARKET). Ginza (mentioned above), also in Chūō Ward, is known for its many art galleries, fabulous department stores, and expensive clothing shops. Akihabara (q.v.), in the northeastern part of Chiyoda Ward, is world famous as an electronics emporium. Jimbōchō (also "Jinbōchō"), also in Chiyoda Ward and located near several college and university campuses, is well known for its many stores selling new and used books. Ueno (q.v.; also mentioned above), in Taitō Ward, has a shopping area along narrow alleys under railroad bridges that specializes in discount clothing and accessories. One narrow street beside the tracks, called Ameyayokochō, is a thriving marketplace for fresh seafood and other food items. The approach to Sensōji (q.v.), the great temple in Asakusa (q.v.; also in Taitō Ward), is also a busy retailing strip. Its shops offer souvenirs of Tokyo, specialty sweets and other snacks, and a variety of Japanese handicrafts. Nearby is Inarichō, which sells religious items for home use and for temples and shrines, while a little further is Kappabashi, a shopping district that specializes in kitchen equipment and supplies for restaurants and caterers.

On the other side of the central Tokyo is Shinjuku (q.v). Its own retailing areas include train-station-front department stores, two separate concentrations of camera and electronics stores, and Kabukichō, a brightly lit district of bars, restaurants, game arcades, and a great many sex shops of every kind. On the other hand, the commercial center of Shibuya (q.v.) specializes in shopping for young tastes and attracts hundreds of thousands of high school and college people on a single day to its stores, restaurants, and popular hang-outs. In Shibuya Ward as well, Harajuku (q.v.) is also known for crowds of young people buying clothing, accessories, CDs and music tapes, and many other items. The Aoyama district (q.v.), located between Harajuku and Shibuya in Shibuya

Ward, is known for its elegant boutiques, fine restaurants and coffee shops, and many foreign visitors. Yebisu Garden Plaza (q.v.) is a large new redevelopment complex on the site of an historic brewery at the boundary of Meguro and Shibuya Wards. It opened in 1994 and features a popular shopping mall, a major international hotel, several museums and movie theaters, office buildings, and new high-rise residential buildings with equally high rents.

Tokyo's largest residential districts stretch in all directions from these central areas. Tokyo Prefecture itself extends to the west and has many so-called bedroom towns along commuter rails such as the Chūō Line, the Keiō Line, the Odakyū Line, and the Seibu Shinjuku and Seibu Ikebukuro Lines. Housing consists of tightly packed detached dwellings, apartments and multistory condominium structures called *manshon* after the English word "mansion." In addition, there are planned bedroom communities such as the large new town in the Tama Area of Tokyo Prefecture named Tama New Town. There are busy shopping centers and other commercial developments at most commuter rail stations, particularly at interchange or terminal stations such as those at Kichijōji, Musashisakai, Machida, Chōfu, Tama Center, and Tachikawa. The residential belt of Tokyo Prefecture also includes many large industrial plants. Hachijōji, a fast growing city west of Tokyo Prefecture, is noted for having many college and university campuses as well as new industrial parks and office developments. Commuter-oriented residential developments, commercial centers, and industry extend as well into neighboring prefectures: Chiba Prefecture to the east of Tokyo, Saitama Prefecture to the north, and Kanagawa Prefecture mostly to the southwest.

To the south of Tokyo's central business district is Tokyo Bay. This has been an area of urban expansion since the early Edo Period (q.v.), as the shoreline has been extended into the water by way of reclamation projects in every period since the time of the first Tokugawa *shōguns* (1603–1868; see TOKU-GAWA IEYASU). There are also several large artificial islands that have been reclaimed from the bay, particularly in recent years. Islands that are closer in are older and are fully developed with urban land uses. For example, Tsukishima (or Tsukudajima) contains a mix of industry, harbor facilities and residences, including an historic fishing settlement with the same name as the island and a new complex of high-rise apartments and condominiums named River City 21. Harumi Island also has industry, wharfs, and apartment residences, as well as large exhibition spaces for trade fairs. Toyosu Island is mostly industrial. Further from shore, the newest islands, connected to Tokyo proper by Rainbow Bridge (1994) and a new monorail line, are being developed as Tokyo Teleport Town, a high-tech international business center and planned residential community. Tokyo's waterfront also has several new places for recreation such as the Odaiba Waterfront Park and the Kasai Seaside Park. The latter facility has a popular new aquarium and a freshly laid sand beach for sunbathing and swimming.

WARDS, CITIES, TOWNS, VILLAGES AND, ISLANDS OF TOKYO METROPOLIS

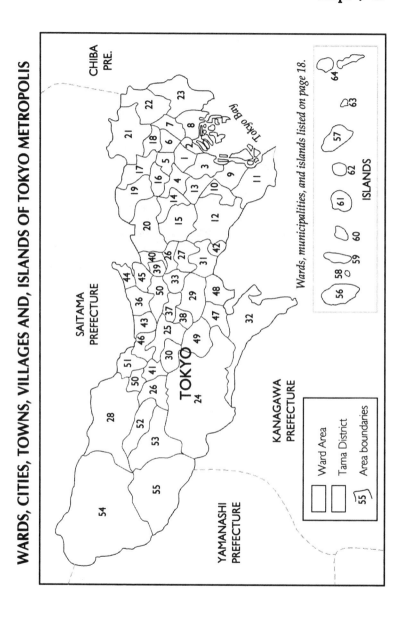

Wards, municipalities, and islands listed on page 18.

ISLANDS

CHIBA PRE.

Tokyo Bay

SAITAMA PREFECTURE

TOKYO

KANAGAWA PREFECTURE

YAMANASHI PREFECTURE

Ward Area

Tama District

Area boundaries

TOKYO METROPOLIS AND NEIGHBORING PREFECTURES

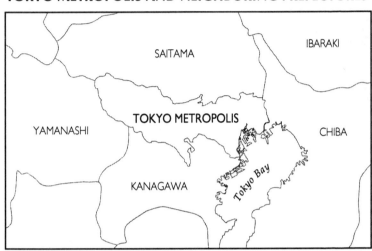

Wards
1. Chiyoda
2. Chūō
3. Minato
4. Shinjuku
5. Bunkyō
6. Taitō
7. Sumida
8. Kōtō
9. Shinagawa
10. Meguro
11. Ōta
12. Setagaya
13. Shibuya
14. Nakano
15. Suginami
16. Toshima
17. Kita
18. Arakawa
19. Itabashi
20. Nerima
21. Adachi
22. Katsushika
23. Edogawa

Municipalities
(Cities)
24. Hachiōji
25. Tachikawa
26. Musashino
27. Mitaka
28. Ōme
29. Fuchū
30. Akishima
31. Chōfu
32. Machida
33. Koganei
34. Kodaira
35. Hino
36. Higashi
     Murayama
37. Kokubunji
38. Kunitachi
39. Tanashi
40. Hōya
41. Fussa
42. Komae
43. Higashi Yamato
44. Kiyose
45. Higashi Kurume
46. Musashi
     Murayama

47. Tama
48. Inagi
49. Akikawa
(Towns)
50. Hamura
51. Mizuho
52. Hinode
53. Itsukaichi
54. Okutama
(Village)
55. Hinohara

Islands
(Towns)
56. Ōshima
57. Hachijō
(Villages)
58. Toshima
59. Niijima Honson
60. Kozushima
61. Miyake
62. Mikurajima
63. Aogashima
64. Ogasawara

TOKYO'S SETTING IN JAPAN

DICTIONARY

– A –

ADAMS, WILLIAM (1564–1620). A mariner born in Gillingham, England, who came to Japan in 1600 as a shipwrecked sailor. He then lived out the rest of his life in the country in the employ of Tokugawa Ieyasu (q.v.) and his successor as an adviser, informant, and translator. He was a captive of the *shōgun* (q.v.), who would not allow him to leave Japan, as well as his friend. Adams was given the rank of *samurai* (q.v.). The only foreigner ever to have this distinction, he was granted a fief on the Miura Peninsula, south of Yokohama. Even though he had a wife and children in England, he took a Japanese wife and fathered a son and daughter. He adopted the Japanese name Miura Anjin, meaning "Miura navigator." He maintained a residence in Edo (q.v.) near the bridge named Nihombashi (q.v.). He came to love the city and requested before dying that his grave marker be on a hilltop facing Edo so that he might keep watch over it forever. The Anjinchō district near Nihombashi is named for him. Adams's life in Japan is the subject of James Clavell's well-known novel *Shōgun* (1976).

AIR RAIDS OF 1945. The most damaging of the Allied bombing attacks against Tokyo during World War II, burning much of the city and causing more than 100,000 deaths. They were the culmination of attacks on the city that started on 18 April 1942, when 13 carrier-based U.S. B-25 bombers under the command of Lieutenant Colonel James A. Doolittle strafed the city or dropped bombs on its northern and southern edges. The next raids came on 24 November 1944 and continued through February

21

1945, with the heaviest attacks on 16 and 17 February. The planes came from the Marianas Islands and from aircraft carriers, and they dropped their bombs primarily on air bases and other military targets. The attacks continued through May. The planes came so often during the winter and spring of 1944–45 that residents came to refer to the planes in black humor as *okyakusama* ("honored guests"), "regular mail," and "Lord B." The total number of flights during this period exceeded 4,000.

The heaviest destruction took place on the night of 9–10 March 1945. The raid was carried out by 334 B-29 Superfortress bombers, and was aimed at Asakusa Ward and other crowded residential areas of central Tokyo. Some 700,000 incendiary bombs rained on the city that night over a three-hour period commencing about midnight, burning some two fifths of the city territory, destroying 276,000 buildings, killing approximately 77,000 civilians and injuring more than 110,000. These terrifying numbers put this raid on a par in terms of casualties with the atomic attacks against Hiroshima (6 August 1945) and Nagasaki (9 August 1945). Raids on April 13–15 were directed primarily against industrial districts in northern and western Tokyo and adjacent parts of Kanagawa Prefecture. On 25 May the main building of the Imperial Palace (q.v.) was destroyed in an air raid. Many other Tokyo landmarks, including Kabuki-za, the main buildings of Keiō University, and Zōjōji (qq.v.), were also destroyed or severely damaged on that day or during other May raids. Starting with the March 9–10 raids, casualty totals were especially high because the bombs were designed to spread fire, and because authorities had urged citizens to stay in the city rather than evacuate as they had done in response to earlier raids. (see EVACUATIONS OF TOKYO; FIRES)

AKASAKA. A district in the northern part of Minato Ward, central Tokyo, that is noted for its large international hotels, exclusive restaurants, and high-priced residences where many of Japan's political and business elites live. A number of its restaurants are of the *ryōtei* type, which feature entertainment for select customers by *geisha*. Because of its proximity to the bureaucratic center of Tokyo, Akasaka is said to be where businessmen and politicians come together over drinks and meals in *ryōtei* establishments to make their deals. In the Edo Period (q.v.), Akasaka was an area with many *daimyō* (q.v.) estates.

AKIHABARA. A district in Chiyoda Ward, Tokyo, that is noted for selling electronics goods and home appliances. The name of the place is traced to the Akiba Shrine ("autumn leaf shrine"), which was built there in 1870. The shrine was destroyed in one of the area's frequent fires, and the land was made into a firebreak, a cleared area called Akibagahara, or "Akiba field." The word "Akihabara" is a shortened form of Akibagahara. Later the field became the site of a freight depot. The district's role as a shopping area for electronics goes back to the time after World War II when the area near the rail tracks became one of the city's foremost centers for black market goods.

AMUSEMENT QUARTERS (See SAKARIBA)

ANSEI EDO EARTHQUAKE. Also called the Earthquake of 1855. A major earthquake disaster that occurred in Edo (q.v.) on 2 October 1855. The epicenter was directly beneath the estuary of the Ara River *(Arakawa)* in the eastern part of Edo. The vertical magnitude of the shake was an estimated 6.9 on the scale of the Japanese Meteorological Agency. It is estimated that about 6,000 people died. The greatest damage was in the *shitamachi* (q.v.) district of the city, where about 100,000 people lost their homes (about one fifth of the *shitamachi* population at that time). Approximately 4,000 of the 6,000 deaths occurred in *shitamachi*. There were many fires, but there was no major conflagration because winds were not strong. The earthquake is called the Ansei Edo Earthquake because it struck in the second year of the Ansei Era. (see EARTHQUAKES; NAMAZU-E)

AOSHIMA YUKIO (1932–). Thirteenth governor of Tokyo Metropolis (q.v.). He was elected on 9 April 1995 and assumed office on 24 April 1995.

Aoshima was born 17 July 1932. In March 1955 he was graduated from the department of commerce of Waseda University (q.v.). He undertook graduate study in sociology at Waseda University in 1957 but left the program before completing degree requirements and began a career as singer, actor, broadcast scriptwriter, lyricist, composer, and film director. The Japanese public came to know him especially well as a television comedian. His most famous role was on a TV show called *Ijiwaru bāsan* ("Nasty Granny") performing silly antics in an old woman's wig and kimono. At the same time, Aoshima developed a career in politics. He was elected to the House of Councilors in July 1968 and then reelected in July 1974, July 1980, July 1986, and July 1992. He held various committee posts during his terms, including posts dealing with communications, budgets and audits, science and technology, the electoral system, and decentralization and deregulation. He resigned from the House of Councilors in March 1995 to run for governor of Tokyo Metropolis.

Aoshima's election victory was considered an upset because he ran as an independent candidate against established political parties, campaigned very little, and spent little money on the election. His heavily favored principal opponent was Ishihara Nobuo, Japan's deputy chief cabinet secretary, who campaigned with the support of the powerful Liberal Democratic Party (LDP) and other major political parties. Aoshima's election is attributed to voter dissatisfaction with politicians in Japan and the condition of the economy, a lower than expected turnout of voters, and Aoshima's high name recognition and considerable personal charm. His most widely quoted campaign statement was a promise to close a proposed international exhibition referred to as "World City Expo '96" or "Tokyo Frontier" that was scheduled for 1996 because he saw it as a waste of taxpayers' money. He carried out this promise two days after assuming office with a formal announcement on 26 April 1995. (see SUZUKI SHUNICHI; WATERFRONT DEVELOPMENT)

AOYAMA. A fashionable district of central Tokyo in northern Minato Ward. It is noted for its exclusive shops and fashionable boutiques, trendy international atmosphere, and prestigious residential areas. Aoyama-dōri, which connects Shibuya and Akasaka (qq.v.), is the principal thoroughfare. Another landmark is Aoyama Cemetery, opened in 1872. In the Edo Period (q.v.), Aoyama was an area of estates, most notably that of the Aoyama family after which the area is named.

AOYAMA UNIVERSITY. A prestigious, private, coeducational university with nearly 20,000 students located in Shibuya Ward, Tokyo. It was founded in 1874 as a Christian school for girls and became a college in 1904. It was granted university status in 1948.

ARAGOTO. A style of acting in *kabuki* theater that is associated with the stage in Edo (q.v.) and Tokyo. It was pioneered by Ichikawa Danjūrō I (q.v.) and has been carried on by his descendants in the line of *kabuki* performers. The word *aragoto* is translated as "rough business" acting, and refers to a style in which brave, masculine heroes with superhuman powers fight off evil villains.

ASAHARA SHŌKŌ (1955–). Founder and leader of the religious cult Aum Shinrikyō (q.v.); accused of masterminding the 20 March 1995 sarin (a nerve gas) attack on the Tokyo subway system that killed at least ten people and sickened thousands more.

Asahara is a complex and secretive man. What little is known about his life is mostly from a 1991 book by journalist Egawa Shōko. Asahara was born in Kyushu to the family of a *tatami* (straw mat) maker. His birth name was Matsumoto Chizuo. He was born nearly blind in one eye and was sent to a special school for the blind in the larger city of Kumamoto (Kumamoto Prefecture). It is reported that at the school he was both a leader of fellow students and a bully, and that he was extraordinarily ambitious regarding his own future. He moved to Tokyo after graduation and practiced acupuncture. In 1978, after marrying Ishii Tomoko, he opened a traditional Chinese medicine shop. He was arrested in 1982 for quackery and was punished with 20 days of detention and a fine of 200,000 yen (approximately $800). This experience is said to have embittered him and made him more of a recluse. In 1984 Asahara opened a yoga school. He claimed to have experienced spiritual enlightenment and to have levitated, and began to see himself more and more as a religious leader. He founded Aum Shinrikyō in 1987. He has presented himself to followers and potential members as a messiah who can save Japan from the many evils he sees in modern society, from subversion by the United States, and from the imminent end of the world. In a 1995 booklet, Asahara predicted Armageddon in the form of a gas cloud released by the United States. It is alleged (but not yet proven in court) that under his direction, Aum Shinrikyō manufactured and stockpiled large quantities of sarin and other dangerous chemicals to be used as weapons of terrorism. Asahara was arrested on 15 May 1995 on charges of organizing the Tokyo sarin incident. At the time of this writing (early 1996) Asahara was awaiting trial.

ASAKUSA. Historic district of the city located in Taitō Ward on the west bank of the Sumida River (q.v.). It is known as a stronghold of distinctive *shitamachi* (q.v.) atmosphere. Various festivals and fairs are held there, several of which draw huge crowds each year. Its center is the temple named Sensōji (q.v.), also called Asakusa Kannon. The shopping streets leading to the temple are called Nakamise-dōri and Shin Nakamise-dōri. The principal gate to the temple, *Kaminarimon*, is a famous landmark. During the Edo Period (q.v.), Asakusa was a popular entertainment area with *kabuki* theater and pleasure quarters. It was also a gateway to the Yoshiwara (q.v.) pleasure quarter located nearby. From 1898 to 1923, the Asakusa Twelve Stories (q.v.) was a popular attraction in a subdistrict of Asakusa called Rokku. In the 20th century Asakusa declined somewhat when Tokyo residents shifted their attention to commercial centers on the west side of the city. The Hanayashiki Amusement Park in the northern part of Asakusa is a modern-day survivor of much larger entertainment functions that were in the area in earlier times.

ASAKUSA KANNON (See SENSŌJI)

ASAKUSA TWELVE STORIES. A twelve-story tower that stood in the entertainment quarter of Asakusa (q.v.) in Taitō Ward from 1890 to 1923. It was a popular attraction for visitors, and it is commonly regarded as the city's first high-rise building. The first ten floors were brick, while the top two stories were wood. The building was constructed under the direction of William K. Barton, an English engineer. It featured the first elevator in Japan, one imported from the United States. But it was considered unsafe and was ordered closed within a few months of the building's opening. The second to the eighth floors had shops that specialized in goods from around the world. The ninth floor was a gallery of paintings, while the eleventh floor had arc lights. There were observation levels on the tenth and twelfth floors, the latter equipped with a telescope. The official name of the building was *Ryōunkaku*, the "cloud-scraping pavilion,"after a nine-story building that had been built a year earlier in Osaka; however, it was more commonly called *Jūnikai*, meaning "the twelve-story." The building was destroyed in the Great Kantō Earthquake (q.v.) of 1923.

AUM SHINRIKYŌ. A religious sect founded in 1987 by Asahara Shōkō (q.v.); it is widely considered to be a cult. The sect is accused of masterminding and carrying out the 20 March 1995 sarin (a nerve gas) attack on the Tokyo subway system that killed at least ten commuters and subway workers and injured thousands of others. It is also suspected of a carrying out a gas attack in Matsumoto (Nagano Prefecture) on 21 June 1994 that killed seven individuals and injured approximately 200 more. Other murders, attempted murders, and disappearances are said to be linked to Aum Shinrikyō as well. Many of the leaders of Aum Shinrikyō, including Asahara himself, have been arrested since the Tokyo gassing incident. As a result, the movement seems to be in disarray.

Aum Shinrikyō grew out of a yoga school that had been founded by Asahara in Tokyo in 1984. Since then, the sect has expanded across Japan, where it claims a total of 10,000 members in 36 branches, and abroad. There are offices of Aum Shinrikyō in New York City, Moscow, Bonn, and Sri Lanka. The Russian membership is the largest outside Japan, and has been said to number between 10,000 and 40,000 individuals in six branches. Another estimate puts the total membership of Aum Shinrikyō worldwide at about 30,000. The sect has maintained a large compound in the town of Kamikuishiki (Yamanashi Prefecture) on the slopes of Mount Fuji. It is there that police raids after the Tokyo gassing incident uncovered stockpiles of toxic chemicals for making sarin.

Aum Shinrikyō is usually translated as "Supreme Truth." The group's practices are said to combine elements from Buddhist and Hindu theologies with yoga. Its success at recruiting members is attributed to Asahara's considerable charismatic powers, as well as his claims to have attained *satori*, the Japanese term for nirvana or perfect spiritual enlightenment, and self-levitation. Members show unusual and extreme devotion to Asahara. For example, Asahara always sits one level above his devotees and requires them to bow and kiss his toe. It is also reported that initiates to the group are held incommunicado while being forced to study Asahara's teachings, and that some members are held captive by Aum Shinrikyō against their wills. A central tenet of Aum Shinrikyō is that the end of the world is coming soon, perhaps as early as 1997. The group also claims that Japan is in great danger from poison gas attacks that would come from the United States, a country that Asahara has described as being in the control of Freemasons and Jews. Thus, there is an atmosphere of crisis and imposing doom within Aum Shinrikyō, and much of the sect's activity is devoted to rallying believers against alleged enemies of Japan and preparing them for some sort of final battle.

– B –

BAKUFU. A word that means shogunate, the type of government that existed in Japan under the rule of *shōguns*. (see TOKUGAWA SHOGUNATE)

BAKUHAN SYSTEM (*bakuhan taisei*). A term that refers to the structure of government and society in Japan during the Edo Period (q.v.). It comes from *baku*, referring to shogunate, and *han*, meaning domain or fief. (see TOKUGAWA SHOGUNATE)

BANNERMEN (See HATAMOTO)

BANK OF JAPAN BUILDING. The oldest building in a complex of buildings that houses the headquarters of the Bank of Japan *(Nippon Ginkō)*, the central bank of Japan. Located in the Nihombashi (q.v.) section of Chūō Ward in downtown Tokyo, the building was designed by Tatsuno Kingo (q.v.). Construction took place between 1890 and 1896. It is mostly of European Renaissance style. The building is one of the few surviving examples of the kind of Western style architecture that was popular in Tokyo during the Meiji Period (q.v.). It is the earliest example of a Western style building that was executed entirely by Japanese.

BANSHO SHIRABESHO. Translated as "Institute for the Investigation of Barbarian Books," this was an educational facility that the Tokugawa shogunate (q.v.) had set up in Edo (q.v.) in 1855 for the translation and study of books from Western countries. It was originally called Yōgakusho, the Institute for Western Learning. Its principal aim was to teach the Japanese about Western countries and to prepare them to serve the country as diplomats and negotiators. This was in the wake of the unexpected arrival of foreign ships commanded by Commodore Matthew C. Perry (q.v.) in Tokyo Bay (q.v.) in 1853 and the subsequent forced opening of Japan to foreign influences. In 1877, by which time the institute had been renamed *Tōkyō Kaisei Gakkō*, it merged with the Tokyo Medical School *(Tōkyō Igakkō)* to form Tokyo University (q.v.).

BATTLE OF SEKIGAHARA. Decisive battle that consolidated the power of Tokugawa Ieyasu (q.v.) and set the stage for his rise to the position of *shōgun* (q.v.). The battle took place on 20–21 October 1600 near the town of Sekigahara in what is now Gifu Prefecture and involved more than 100,000 troops on each side. It settled the rivalry that began after the death of warlord Toyotomi Hideyoshi in 1598 between *daimyō* from western Japan led by Ishida Mitsunari and those from the east led by Ieyasu.

BEARD, CHARLES AUSTIN (1874-1948). Well-known American historian and urban scholar from Columbia University who was an influential consultant to Tokyo's mayor Gotō Shimpei (q.v.) about improving city government and planning. While director of the Bureau of Municipal Research in New York, Beard advised Gotō on setting up both the Tokyo Institute for Municipal Research (q.v.) and the Training Institute for Municipal Service. The latter was an in-service training program for officials of Japan's largest cities, officials in the Home Ministry, and university professors in fields related to urban problems.

Beard's first visit to Japan began on 14 September 1922. He came at Gotō's invitation to advise him about more effective municipal government in Tokyo and other Japanese cities, as well as to give advice about such problems as taxation in cities, assessments, transportation, and civil service. Beard impressed Gotō and other officials by turning down all compensation for his work except for minimal living expenses. He stayed in Japan until March 1923. During the time that he was there, he gave more than 30 lectures in Tokyo and other cities about municipal administration and planning, as well as six special lectures at the Training Institute for Municipal Service. Lessons from the six lectures are summarized in Beard's booklet, *The Administration and Politics of Tokyo: A Survey and Opinions,* which was published in 1923 by Macmillan and is still highly regarded.

Shortly after his return to New York, Beard was

called back to Tokyo by Gotō (then Home Minister) in the wake of the Great Kantō Earthquake (q.v.). Before his arrival he cabled Gotō that he should rebuild the city as follows: "Lay out new streets, forbid building without street lines, unify railway stations." Gotō arrived in Tokyo on 6 October 1923, bringing with him plans that American cities had developed for reconstruction after disasters. He urged that Tokyo be modernized as it was being rebuilt, particularly transportation systems and housing, but insisted that it retain a distinctively Japanese flavor rather than copy architectural styles of the West. However, most of the plans that Beard and Gotō advocated for Tokyo were dismissed as being impractical and too costly (see BOARD OF RECONSTRUCTION OF THE CAPITAL CITY). In February 1948 Beard was invited to Tokyo for a third time, to help reconstruct the city following its devastation by the air raids of 1945 (q.v.). He declined the invitation because of poor health and died on September 1 of that year. The Tokyo Institute for Municipal Research is considered to be a memorial to Beard.

BOARD OF RECONSTRUCTION OF THE CAPITAL CITY. Established by imperial ordinance on 27 September 1923, its purpose was to oversee the reconstruction of Tokyo, Yokohama, and surrounding areas in the wake of damage caused by the Great Kantō Earthquake (q.v.). The director was Gotō Shimpei (q.v.), a national political figure who had not long before served as mayor of Tokyo. Gotō received advice about reconstruction from Charles Austin Beard (q.v.), an American scholar who had worked with him before on problems affecting Tokyo. Beard urged that the city be rebuilt at lower density with wide streets and a unified rail system. After a survey of the damage, Gotō proposed a budget of four billion yen for the reconstruction. This amount was slashed by the Finance Ministry to 700 million yen, and then further cut in December 1923 by the House of Representatives to 574,816,049 yen. Gotō was criticized for proposing a plan that was too extravagant, given the weak financial condition of both Tokyo and the national government at the time. The second cut in budget also removed 700,000 yen that had been earmarked for the operating expenses of the Board of Reconstruction. As a result, reconstruction was forced to proceed without a plan or much support from government. Consequently, Tokyo and the surrounding areas were rebuilt almost entirely along the old lines, with crooked narrow streets and crowded neighborhoods.

BONIN ISLANDS (See OGASAWARA ISLANDS)

BULLET TRAINS. High-speed intercity passenger trains in Japan operated by the Japan Railways system. The name comes from the shape and speed of the trains. In Japanese the trains are called *shinkansen,* "New Trunk Line." The first branch of the bullet train system was opened in 1964 just before the Tokyo Olympics (q.v.). It was called the Tōkaidō Shinkansen, and it connected Tokyo with Osaka. The line has since been extended west from Osaka to Hakata in Kyushu. It is known as the Tōkaidō-San'yō Shinkansen. The total length is 1,069 kilometers (664 miles), and the maximum speed is 270 kilometers (168 miles) per hour. Other bullet train lines are the Tōhoku Shinkansen connecting Tokyo with Morioka, 535.3 kilometers (332.6 miles) away in northern Japan, and the Jōetsu Shinkansen, connecting Tokyo with Niigata, 333.9 kilometers (207.5 miles) away on the Sea of Japan coast. Both the Tōhoku and Jōetsu lines were opened in 1982. Several other bullet trains lines are under construction or are planned in Japan. Tokyo is the focus of the system, and Tokyo Station (q.v.) is the main station.

BUNMEI KAIKAI (See MEIJI PERIOD)

BUSHI (See SAMURAI)

– C –

CHAMBERLAIN, BASIL HALL (1850–1903). An Englishman from a prominent family in Southampton who settled in Japan as a young man in 1873 and became one of the foremost Western experts on the culture of Japan. He taught at the imperial naval school in Tokyo from 1874 to 1882. In 1886 he began a position as professor of Japanese at Tokyo University (q.v.), where he taught language and literature. There he wrote several books about Japan and the Japanese language, as well as the first translation into English of the *Kojiki* (1906), Japan's chronicles of ancient times. These works were important sources of Western learning about Japan. In 1911 he retired from Tokyo University and resettled to Switzerland. (see also LAFCADIO HEARN)

CHŌNAIKAI (also called *chōkai*). Neighborhood associations in Tokyo and other Japanese cities. Members are the heads of every household in a given area, and leaders are chosen from the membership by popular consent. The associations are responsible for a wide variety of activities such as local festivals, relief activities, mediation between neighbors, funeral assistance, and various neighborhood improvement projects. They often represent the concerns of individuals or groups of neighbors to higher levels of government.

CHŌNIN. A word referring to the ordinary citizens of the city, especially during the Edo Period (q.v.), as opposed to high-ranking *samurai* and other officials. The literal meaning is "people of the *chō*" (a kind of urban administrative unit), but the word is generally translated as "townsmen" or "townspeople." In Edo itself (q.v.), *chōnin* described the shopkeepers, artisans, laborers, and peddlers who lived in the crowded, low-lying quarters of *shitamachi* (q.v.). A more restrictive definition is merchant and artisan property owners. While some *chōnin*, such as Kinokuniya Bunzaemon (q.v.), became exceedingly rich and enjoyed opulent lives, most were poor and had to struggle to afford necessities.

"CIVILIZATION AND ENLIGHTENMENT" (See MEIJI PERIOD)

COMMUTING. Because of Tokyo's large geographical area, as well as because of the geographical distribution of different housing costs (see LAND PRICES), many people in Tokyo live quite far from where they work or attend school and spend considerable time commuting. While people commute in every direction, and use many forms of transportation, the most common pattern of travel is from outlying residential areas to the center of Tokyo using trains and/or subways (q.v.). In 1990 some 3,617,000 commuters made daily journeys to the 23 Wards area of Tokyo Metropolis (q.v.) from the Tama Area (q.v.) or from one of the surrounding prefectures. Despite efforts by planners to redistribute land uses in the Tokyo area in a way that would reduce commuting to the center (see SUBCENTERS; WATERFRONT DEVELOPMENT), data show that the number of commuters to the 23 Wards area has been increasing with every survey of ridership that has been undertaken since the 1970s.

For many commuters the typical daily pattern is as follows. They begin their journeys to work or school by walking, riding a bicycle, or taking a public bus to a train station in their particular suburban community where they, along with many other riders, board a *nobori densha*, an inbound train. If they are lucky, their destination in the center of Tokyo is a short walk from one of the stations on the same rail line. Most commuters, however, have to change trains at an intermediate station and/or switch to a subway line at one of the many interchange stations in central Tokyo. Many commuters transfer at one of the stations along the Yamanote Line (q.v.). Once they arrive at the final station, there is often a walk of a few minutes to the destination building. For some riders this last part of the commuting trip has to be done by public bus or taxi. The journey home in the evenings is the reverse of the morning pattern.

According to a 1993 survey by Japan's Ministry of Construction, 23.4 percent of workers in the Tokyo metropolitan area (Tokyo Metropolis [q.v.] plus Chiba, Kanagawa, Saitama Prefectures) travel up 30 minutes each way in their daily commutes, while 26.7 percent travel between 30 and 60 minutes, and 18.4 percent travel between 60 and 90 minutes each way. Some 5.8 percent of commuters travel 90 to 120 minutes each way. The same survey showed that 10.9 percent of workers have no commutes to work, i.e., they work at home or walk. The total travel time was not known for the remaining 14.8 percent of respondents. The cost of travel increases with distance and is generally considered to be expensive. However, most employers pay commuting costs for their workers by reimbursing them for the costs of monthly passes. School students are allowed to purchase transportation passes between the stations nearest their homes and the stations closest to their schools at much reduced rates.

Crowding is a serious problem on many train and subway lines, particularly during peak travel times. Although the situation has improved since 1985, most trains and subways in the Tokyo metropolitan area are filled to at least double their capacity during the rush hour. Standing riders are pressed together so tightly that they find it almost impossible to move around. Many riders endure such conditions for an hour or more each way each day. The heaviest crowding occurs on passenger lines operated by the Japan Railways, particularly the Yamanote Line. The evening commute is somewhat less crowded than the morning one because the time when people return home is spread out over more hours.

In addition to trains and subways, Tokyoites use other forms of transportation to reach their destinations. People who live within walking or biking distance of their places of work generally consider themselves to be fortunate because of the time that they save from commuting. Automobile travel is fairly common, particularly in suburban areas. However, for most people it makes little sense to commute from the suburbs to the center of the city by car because of traffic congestion, steep tolls on some of the highways, and very high costs for parking in the city. Many residents of central Tokyo who own cars use them only on weekends because of these inconveniences. Nevertheless, rates of automobile ownership are high and are rising. In the suburbs many residents rely daily on automobiles.

CONDER, JOSIAH (1852–1920). British architect and city planner who came to Japan in 1877 and became the leading designer of Western style buildings in Meiji Tokyo. Between 1877 and 1888 he was a professor of architecture at Kōbu Daigakkō, later part of Tokyo University (q.v.), and an adviser to the Ministry of Engineering. He trained several Japanese architects who later became leaders in the profession. One of his students was Tatsuno Kingo (q.v.). After 1888 Conder left government employment and concentrated on contracts for buildings from private sources, as well as from the government. An inventory of his works between 1878 and 1907 counts more than 50 major Western style buildings in Tokyo. They include the Tokyo Imperial Museum (1881), the Rokumeikan (q.v.; 1883), a row of office buildings in the Marunouchi (q.v.) area called Mitsubishi Londontown (q.v.) constructed for the Iwasaki family (1884; see IWASAKI YATARŌ) and the Navy Ministry Building (1895). He also designed private residences for the Iwasaki family and other prominent residents of the city. An important surviving building is the Nikolai Cathedral (q.v.; 1891). Conder also published several books about Japan, including *Landscape Gardening in Japan* (1893). A statue of Conder stands on the campus of Tokyo University.

CRIME. Tokyo is widely regarded to be one of the world's safest cities. The many reasons for low crime rates include informal social control by institutions such as family, schools, employers, and the local community; the general absence in Tokyo (and Japan as a whole) of many of the internal social conflicts that characterize other societies; and the strong sense of group identity and common loyalty that most Japanese feel with respect to their fellow citizens. Low crime rates are also attributed to effective policing (see KŌBAN) and efficient criminal justice administration. Low rates of violent crime in comparison to large cities abroad such as New York City are also said to stem from the fact that guns and other lethal weapons are effectively controlled in Tokyo. Nevertheless, crime rates are rising in the city and are a source of increasing concern. In 1993 the number of criminal offenses reported in Tokyo rose by some 16,000 over the previous year to a total of approximately 257,000. This total translates to about 702 crimes each day, or one about every 123 seconds. Arrests were made in about 75 percent of all cases of murder, robbery, arson and other heinous crimes, and in about 70 percent of all burglaries. The number of murders in Tokyo averages about 100 per year. Many of the most serious crimes are blamed on gangsters *(yakuza)* and crime syndicates. Many crimes are also attributed to foreigners. In 1993, foreigners are said to have committed approximately 4,800 of the city's 257,000 reported crimes, an increase of approximately 1,100 over the previous year.

– D –

DAIMYŌ. Military lords who ruled over territorial domains in feudal Japan. Translated variously as "feudal lords," "military lords," or "territorial lords," the word comes from a combination of *dai*, which means large, and *myō*, which is from *myōden* and means "named land" or "private land." In the Edo Period (q.v.), *daimyō* were those military lords whose holdings produced at least 10,000 *koku* of rice each year (1 *koku* is about 180 liters or about 50 bushels). They were sworn vassals of the *shōgun*, and numbered 280–300, depending on the particular year. They gave absolute loyalty to the *shōgun*, providing him with military services and workers for construction projects on demand. In exchange, they were given considerable autonomy over their domains, including the right of taxation. The *fudai daimyō* ("allied lords") were those who were allied most closely with the Tokugawa family (q.v.), and who had been granted *daimyō* status by Tokugawa Ieyasu himself (q.v.) before the Battle of Sekigahara (q.v.) in 1600. They contrasted with the *tozama daimyō* ("outside lords"), who had achieved *daimyō* status independently.

Under the requirement of *sankin kōtai* (q.v.), *daimyō* were required to live in Edo (q.v.) in alternate years or half-years. The cost of maintaining two residences (one in Edo and one in the provincial domain), as well as the cost of the elaborate processions that were required between the two residences, was an onerous drain on the finances of *daimyō* (see HAIRYO YASHIKI). Near the end of the Tokugawa shogunate (q.v.), most *daimyō* were heavily in debt. Their domains were abolished after the Meiji Restoration (q.v.), and most *daimyō* became pensioners.

DANCHI. General term denoting large complexes of multi-story apartment buildings in Tokyo and other Japanese cities. Roughly comparable to what are known as "projects" in the United States and "government flats" in the U.K. Most *danchi* were constructed since about 1955 in response to severe housing shortages in crowded cities. The majority of them were constructed by the Housing and Urban Development Corporation (formerly the Japan Housing Corporation). Newer complexes have community shopping and recreation facilities, as well as attractive landscaping. However, the *danchi* that were built during the 1950s and early 1960s are bland in appearance and are generally thought of as minimum standard housing. (see DŌJUNKAI APARTMENTS; SHATAKU)

DEER CRY PAVILION (See ROKUMEIKAN)

DEN'ENCHŌFU. A prestigious residential area in Ōta Ward, Tokyo. It is a planned community, laid out in 1918, that was patterned after the "Garden Cities" concept that was espoused by British planner Ebenezer Howard (1850–1928). The area is known for a distinctive pattern of streets, which radiate like spokes on a wheel from the central train station (Den'enchōfu Station on the Tōkyū Rail Line), and a concentric series of semicircular streets that connect them. The houses along these streets are large by the standards of Tokyo, and there is a lot of greenery. The developer was Shibusawa Eichi (q.v.).

DEPARTMENT STORES (*depato*). Tokyo has many of these retailing establishments, including several stores that are among the largest in the world. As a whole, the stores are known for their extraordinarily high standards of service, wide varieties of merchandise of excellent quality, and attractive displays on sales floors and in store windows. Many of them are also noted for having exclusive sales departments with expensive goods, such as fine art or jewelry and choice fabrics. Some of the same stores also have art galleries with world-class exhibits. Other features are food floors (usually below ground) that sell dry goods, fresh produce, seafood, cakes and pastries, and breads, as well as a great variety of prepared foods that are ready to eat or can be taken home and reheated. In addition, most department stores have one or two floors of restaurants (usually the top floors) and rooftop gardens with attractions ranging from children's playgrounds and zoos to tennis courts and golf putting courses.

Department stores play an extremely important role in the daily routine of Tokyo citizens. Not only are the stores important as places to shop, they also serve as popular meeting places and cultural centers in which many Tokyoites visit with friends at in-store restaurants and coffee shops, or attend art exhibits or other attractions. The stores are especially crowded on Sundays and other days off from work and school. Other busy periods are the major gift-giving seasons in midsummer and at the New Year. Stores are also crowded at the end of the work day, as commuters jam the food floors and purchase food to take home for dinner. Many foreign visitors enjoy seeing department stores open in the morning (usually 10:00 A.M.) when uniformed sales personnel gather at the doorways to greet incoming customers with polite bows and words of welcome.

Most of the largest and best-known department stores are in downtown Tokyo, particularly in the Ginza and Nihombashi sections (qq.v.). The largest downtown stores include the Mitsukoshi, Tōkyū, and Takashimaya stores in Nihombashi, the Matsuya, Matsuzakaya, and Mitsukoshi (branch) stores in Ginza, the Hankyu and Seibu stores in Yurakuchō, and the Daimaru Department Store at the Yaesu entrance of Tokyo Station (q.v.). The Mitsukoshi store in Nihombashi was Japan's first department store. It was established in 1904 as an outgrowth of Echigoya, (q.v.), a dry goods store that had been established in 1673. Its early rival was Shirokiya (q.v.), located a short walk away across the bridge called Nihombashi (q.v.). It was the predecessor of the Tōkyū Department Store chain. Other major department stores or branches thereof are found at busy commercial centers such as Shinjuku, Shibuya, Ikebukuro, and Ueno (qq.v.), and at busy suburban commercial centers. The Shinjuku area, which has the flagship stores for the Isetan, Keiō, and Odakyū chains and a large branch of Mitsukoshi, is the first-ranking department store center in Tokyo. The largest individual store is the Seibu Department Store at Ikebukuro. Stores such as the Keiō and Odakyū stores in Shinjuku, the Seibu and Tōbu Department Stores in Ikebukuro, and the central Tōkyū store in Shibuya are built into the commuter rail stations at their respective commercial centers. The corporations that own these stores also operate rail lines to the suburbs and branch stores at major stations along those lines.

DIET BUILDING (See NATIONAL DIET BUILDING)

DŌJUNKAI APARTMENTS. Apartments that were built by the Dōjunkai, a nonprofit government agency that was set up in 1924 after the Great Kantō Earthquake (q.v.) for the purpose of building emergency shelter. These apartments were the first Western style public apartments in Japan. Between 1926 and 1933 some 2,501 ferroconcrete apartment units were constructed in 15 separate developments in Aoyama, Daikanyama, Toranomon, and other locations in Tokyo. These apartments were the first *danchi* (q.v.) in Japan. By 1941 the number of units constructed exceeded 12,000.

– E –

EARTHQUAKE OF 1923 (See GREAT KANTŌ EARTH-
QUAKE)

EARTHQUAKES. Tokyo is an earthquake-prone city. It sits
in one of the most geologically active zones in all of
Japan, a country that itself is one of the most earthquake-
prone in the world. There are about 20 or more percepti-
ble shakes in the city each year, while in some years the
total has exceeded 50. In addition, there are dozens of
lesser earthquakes that are felt only by detection equipment. Major earthquakes that cause property damage
and deaths are less frequent but have occurred many
times in history. A major earthquake could occur in
Tokyo at any time, which could completely destroy the
city. Therefore, a lot of attention is given to preventing
and reducing earthquake damage, as well as to arrang-
ing for aid and relief should a disaster take place.

The most recent major earthquake to strike Tokyo
was the Great Kantō Earthquake (q.v.) of 1923. It regis-
tered 7.9 on the scale used by the Japanese Meteorological Agency and affected a wide area of the Kantō Plain
(q.v.), including all of both Tokyo and Yokohama. The
total loss of life was in excess of 100,000, with about
60,000 of the deaths occurring in Tokyo. Before then the
most recent major shake was in 1855, the Ansei Edo
Earthquake (q.v.). It is estimated to have been about 6.9
on the Japanese scale. There were about 6,000 casualties.
Other major earthquakes took place in the city in 1771,
1703, 1649, 1647, and 1615. According to the late seismol-
ogist Kawasumi Hiroshi, the southern Kantō Plain (the
region with Tokyo at its center) has had an historical pattern of major shakes every 69 years. This observation has
caused many people to expect a big earthquake in Tokyo
in the 1990s. They believe that Tokyo is overdue for
another disaster because there has not been a major

earthquake in the city for more than 69 years. However, there is no scientific evidence to support Kawasumi's "sixty-nine year cycle theory," and it may be that the historical pattern of earthquake occurrence in the city is only coincidence.

Tokyo is at risk from earthquakes because it is located in a complex convergence zone of four tectonic plates. Offshore at the Japan Trench the Pacific Plate is moving under the Continental or Eurasian Plate (on which Japan is located) at a rate of several centimeters per year. At the same time, directly beneath the Kantō region the Pacific Plate is also rubbing against and sliding beneath the Philippine Sea Plate, while the Pacific Plate, in turn, is sliding under the Continental Plate at three to four centimeters per year near Tokyo at the Sagami Trough. A little more distant, and with less frequent direct impact on Tokyo, is interaction between the North American Plate and both the Continental and Pacific Plates. Analysis of the distribution of epicenters of earthquakes shows two main concentrations in the Tokyo area: (1) a band of epicenters that focuses on Tokyo Bay (q.v.) from Yokohama through Tokyo to Chiba and western Ibaraki Prefecture; and (2) a concentration south of Tokyo that runs along the Bōsō Peninsula into Sagami Bay. In addition to tectonic forces, Tokyo's vulnerability to earthquakes is exacerbated by soft soil conditions. This is particularly the case in areas that have been built up as land reclaimed from Tokyo Bay, a condition affecting virtually the entire shoreline of the city and almost all of its central business district.

Several aspects of Tokyo's disaster prevention efforts are related to earthquakes. First, architectural and engineering measures make the city more resistant to earthquake damage. These include strategic redevelopment of overcrowded urban districts, securing open spaces to serve as firebreaks and evacuation centers, and promoting fireproof building technology, as well as various improvements to roads, bridges, and other infrastructure. Second, there are efforts to minimize earthquake damage by reducing fire hazards, preventing objects from falling, safeguarding against the collapse of retaining walls and concrete block walls, and protecting against gas leaks and other chemical hazards. A third area of preparation concerns arrangements for relief and aid after an earthquake. This includes improvements to emergency communications systems, upgrading evacuation sites and routes, securing food and potable water, and improving medical care systems, rescue facilities, and other emergency systems. At the same time, efforts are made to improve citizens' disaster prevention skills. Finally, considerable attention has been given to research efforts that would result in increased public safety at the time of an earthquake, as well as to research efforts that deal with earthquake prediction.

ECHIGOYA. A dry goods store established by Mitsui Takatoshi (q.v.) in 1673 in the Nihombashi section of Edo (qq.v.). Originally a branch of a main store in Kyoto, it prospered enormously in Edo and became the foundation for the Mitsui financial conglomerate (q.v.). The store itself became the Mitsukoshi Department Store in 1928, now a large chain. The original store's success is attributed to high quality service, a fixed price system for all goods sold there, and cash sales. The store's motto was "cash payment and no discounts" (genkin, kakene nashi). This practice contrasted with an earlier pattern of arbitrary pricing and semiannual payment dates. Echigoya was also known for providing the kinds of goods that a broad public liked and could afford. In short, the store is an important milestone in the development of modern retailing in Japan, as well as in the emergence of Nihombashi as a principal department store section of Tokyo. (see DEPARTMENT STORES)

EDO. The historic name for the city of Tokyo. It was used from 1180 to 1868, when the name Tokyo (q.v.) replaced it after the Meiji Restoration. The word "Edo" also applies to the historic period (see EDO PERIOD) between 1603 and 1867, when Edo was the preeminent city of Japan; to Edo Castle (q.v.), which stood in the heart of the city; to the Edo River (q.v.), one of the city's major rivers, as well as to various art forms, folk crafts, foods, etc., that came to be associated with the historic city. The literal meaning of Edo is "rivergate," referring to the city's site where a river called the Hirakawa (since diverted and now part of the Nihombashi River) emptied into Edo Bay, now named Tokyo Bay (q.v.).

EDO CASTLE *(Edojō;* also called *Chiyodajō).* The castle that stood at the center of Edo and was the seat of power of the Tokugawa shogunate (q.v.) for more than 200 years

The original Edo Castle was constructed in 1457 by Ōta Dōkan (q.v.), a relatively minor feudal-era warlord. It later came under the control of the Hōjō clan, who ruled it from Odawara. In 1590 the castle was awarded by Toyotomi Hideyoshi, the warlord who unified Japan, to Tokugawa Ieyasu (q.v.) as a reward for his decisive role in the successful military campaign against Hōjō forces. By that time the castle was dilapidated and needed repairs. Nevertheless Ieyasu selected Edo to be his capital and the castle as his headquarters. In 1603, after becoming *shōgun,* he began to completely reconstruct Edo Castle. The work lasted until 1651 and was completed under the direction of the third *shōgun,* Iemitsu (q.v.). When it was finished, Edo Castle was the largest castle in the world (as measured by circumference), and was unrivaled in Japan as a symbol of authority. The walls and moats that defined the outer defensive perimeter *(gaikaku)* measured some 16 kilometers (10 miles), while those of the inner defensive perimeter *(naikaku)* measured 6.4 kilometers (four miles).

The grounds of Edo Castle measured 290,00 *tsubo,* or about 957,000 square meters. They were divided by walls and moats into various sections such as the main enclosure, called *honmaru,* and the second enclosure, *ninomaru.* In the main enclosure was the *shōgun's* residence *(nakaoku)* and residences for the compound's women, a complex of interconnected buildings called *ōoku.* There were 66 gates, counting the main gate named Ōtemon, and 36 watchtowers *(mitsuke).* The tallest structure was the main *donjon,* the central keep, which was about 45 meters (147.6 feet) in height. It was topped by a three-meter representation of a *shachihoko,* a mythical fish-dragon (or dolphinlike) creature.

Despite its size and fortifications, Edo Castle did not stand long. There were great fires (q.v.) that ravaged various sections even during the time of construction, but the greatest blaze of all was the Meireki Fire (q.v.) of 1657, which destroyed the interior enclosures, including the central keep. Many structures were rebuilt (but not the central keep), only to be lost to other fires in later years. A series of blazes in the 1860s was particularly destructive. As a result, except for the grounds themselves, various sections of wall and moat, and some guard towers and a few other buildings, little of Edo Castle remains today. The area of the central keep is little more than a stone foundation surrounded by a large empty space. The Edo Castle area as a whole is now called the Imperial Palace (q.v.) area, referring to the restoration of imperial rule in Japan after the fall of the shogunate and to the residence since then of the Japan's emperors, while the space where the innermost compounds once stood is a public park called the East Imperial Garden *(Higashi Gyoen).*

EDODANA. During the Edo Period (q.v.) these were branch stores in Edo of merchandisers whose principal stores were in Kyoto or Osaka.

EDOJŌ (See EDO CASTLE)

EDOKKO. Literally "child of Edo." The word refers to residents of Edo (q.v.) who were born in the *shitamachi* (q.v.) section of the city and could trace residence there for at least three generations. Such people were said to have developed a personal style and personality characteristics unique to Edo. The word *edokko* is still used sometimes by residents of Tokyo who are proud of their deep family roots in one of the city's traditional neighborhoods.

EDO PERIOD *(Edo jidai)*. The time period from about 1603 to 1867 when the Tokugawa shogunate (q.v.) ruled from Edo (q.v.), now Tokyo. The term is synonymous with Tokugawa Period. Sometimes the period is dated from 1600, the year of the decisive Battle of Sekigahara (q.v.), and is taken to 1868, the start of the Meiji Period (q.v.). The Edo Period is distinguished as a time of major social, political, and cultural transformation in Japanese life, and is identified with distinctive styles in arts, folk crafts, architecture, entertainment, social relations, and other aspects of daily existence. The Edo Period is also distinguished for being a time of relative peace in Japan, both domestic and foreign. Another defining characteristic is that for most of the period (1639–1854) a policy of national seclusion *(sakoku)* was in effect. During this time there were very few contacts of any kind between Japan and foreign countries.

EDO RIOTS (See RICE RIOTS)

EDO RIVER *(Edogawa)*. One of the larger rivers in the Tokyo area. It originates in Chiba Prefecture as a distributary of the Tonegawa, and flows south for approximately 60 kilometers (37 miles) to Tokyo Bay (q.v.). A part of its course forms the boundary between Tokyo and Chiba prefectures.

EDO-TOKYO MUSEUM. A large museum in the Ryōgoku (q.v.) section of the city (Sumida Ward) with displays about the history of Tokyo from the Edo Period (q.v.) to modern times (see LEISURE). It opened in March 1993 and is operated by Tokyo Metropolitan Government (q.v.). The architect was Kikutake Kiyonori.

EDOZU. Folding screens that were painted during the 1630s to illustrate the appearance of Edo.

EKŌIN (See RYŌGOKU)

ENVIRONMENTAL PROTECTION. The environmental degradation of Tokyo reached crisis proportions during the rush to rebuild the nation's economy in the 1960s, but recent decades have seen some improvement. Rivers such as the Sumida and Tama (qq.v.) are noticeably cleaner than before, as is Tokyo Bay (q.v.). The Tama River serves increasingly as a recreation resource for the Tokyo region (see LEISURE). Kasai Marine Park is an example of a new recreation area, complete with a sandy beach, that has been developed on Tokyo Bay (see WATERFRONT DEVELOPMENT). There are other new parks as well, including quite a few small ones that serve local communities. Trees and other greenery have been added to the sides of many streets. Many newly constructed office buildings and hotels have greenery as part of the landscaping around them. Air pollution problems have abated too, largely because of strict emission standards on automobiles and other motor vehicles, and because of the relocation of polluting industries from the center of the metropolitan area. Levels of sulfur oxide and carbon monoxide have been controlled to the point that they are now within allowable environmental standards. New laws also regulate noise in the city and require that attention be paid to the distribution of sunlight in the vicinity of high-rise construction.

Increasingly, the garbage of the city is being recycled or being used as either landfill in Tokyo Bay or fuel for generating electricity.

However, despite amelioration of the worst excesses, pollution is still a problem in Tokyo. There are concerns about eutrophication in Tokyo Bay because of reclamation efforts and inadequate sewerage, as well as about industrial pollution of the waters. Even though air quality has improved, photochemical smog still accumulates over the city on many days, causing breathing problems and reducing visibility. Other areas of environmental concern include storage facilities for dangerous chemicals in and around Tokyo, the city's reliance on nuclear power for generation of electricity, and ever larger quantities of solid wastes that are thrown out in the city. Many residents of the city also complain about increasing litter on the streets. Once an extremely clean city, Tokyo is growing dirtier, these residents say, as young people are less careful about where they put their trash. Streets in commercial centers such as Shinjuku (q.v.) are said to be much dirtier now than a generation ago.

EVACUATIONS OF TOKYO. Because of the increasing threat of air raids (q.v.) by U.S. forces against the city in the last stages of World War II, in summer 1944 Japanese government authorities evacuated the civilian population of Tokyo. These were the first planned evacuations of Tokyo during the war, and they were aimed especially at protecting the lives of children. The evacuations had become necessary because Tokyo had become vulnerable to air attacks as U.S. carriers came closer to the Japanese mainland, and as Allied forces advanced closer to the country by capturing territory that had previously been under Japanese control.

Within a two-month period in the middle of 1944, some 230,000 children were evacuated from the Tokyo area. They were moved in groups defined by their grade in school to the countryside where they stayed in camps at temples, youth hostels, and resorts. It is reported that many of the evacuated children suffered from loneliness and homesickness. Because of inadequate nutrition, the children's camps also had problems with dysentery and other illnesses. In addition to the planned evacuation of children, there were also spontaneous evacuations of Tokyo by citizens of all ages. By March 1945 some 1.7 million residents had departed the city, mostly in direct response to air raids against Tokyo or other Japanese cities. This number included approximately 20,000 people whose homes had been demolished to create fire-breaks. Most of the evacuees sought refuge in rural areas where they had family ties.

– F –

FEBRUARY 26 INCIDENT *(Niniroku Jiken)*. Also written as "2.26 Incident." The name given to an attempted coup d'état against the government of Japan that took place in Tokyo on 26 February 1936. The instigators were junior army officers who adhered to the "Imperial Way" *(kodoha)* and argued for unswerving devotion to the emperor rather than capitalism or socialism. They assassinated several political leaders and held control of the center of the city with about 1,400 members of the army's 1st Division until 29 February. The rebellion was suppressed by martial law, and the leaders, tried in secret, were executed or committed suicide. The incident was used by army generals to justify their rise to political power in Japan in the late 1930s.

FIRE BRIGADES (See FIRES)

FIRES. Fires were a chronic problem in Edo (q.v.) as well as a defining characteristic of the city's life and culture. They occurred often in the crowded neighborhoods and spread quickly amid the densely packed wooden houses, consuming large areas and taking many lives.

Records indicate that there were approximately 1,800 fires in the city during the Edo Period (1603–1867; q.v.). In addition there were many more that occurred during the Meiji and Taishō Periods (qq.v.), as well as later. By another measure, there were approximately 100 major conflagrations in the city during the Edo Period, and inhabitants of any one of the crowded townspeople's quarters (see CHŌNIN; SHITAMACHI) would consider it unusual if they were not chased by fire from their homes at least once in any two-year period. Edo Castle (q.v.) itself suffered at least eight large fires during the Edo Period.

The fire problem was most severe in the early part of the Edo Period (before the mid-17th century). Townspeople's quarters were densely built up at this time, and almost all houses were made of wood. Moreover, roofs were of straw. A further problem was that there was no organized system for fighting fires in the early years. Many of the worst fires occurred in winter and early spring, a dry and windy period when homes and shops were heated by charcoal or open flame.

According to American anthropologist William W. Kelly, fires were such a common sight in Edo that a distinctive vocabulary developed to refer to them. One of the most common terms for the fires was *Edo no hana*, the "flowers of Edo." The word *hanabi*, meaning "flower-fires," was also used. It is the modern Japanese word for fireworks. The city's fires were also referred to with the word *momiji*, comparing them to the bright colors of autumn maple leaves. Finally, fires were also called *shukuyū* and *kairoku*, words from ancient Chinese that came to be names for Japanese "fire gods."

Fire prevention and fire fighting were important concerns in Edo. One of the first attempts at fire prevention was introduced after a destructive blaze in 1602, when a decree was issued that houses should have roofs made of small strips of wood instead of straw. Fire prevention measures were stepped up after the Great Meireki Fire (1657). Citizens were encouraged to plaster their roofs or to cover them with tiles. Other directives included a ban on construction of three-story houses, the creation of strategic firebreaks *(hiyokechi)* that were supposed to be permanently vacant and fenced off, and construction of *hirokōji*, "widened streets." Furthermore, neighborhoods were instructed to keep large barrels *(taru)* of water on hand, as well as supplies of pails. Three bridges (the Ryōgoku Bridge [q.v.], Eitaibashi, and Shinohashi) were constructed after the Great Meireki Fire to reduce urban population densities by opening new land on the far side of the Sumida River (q.v.), as well as to provide an escape for citizens from the center of Edo in the event of fire. Other bridges came later, in part due to similar motivations. Still another measure for fireproofing the city was relocating temples and shrines to the outskirts of the city, as well as the Yoshiwara pleasure quarter (q.v.). They were thought to be especially dangerous fire hazards because of the huge crowds that they attracted, and because open flames were often used in ceremonies, for cooking, and for warmth.

At the beginning of the Edo Period there was no organized system for fighting fires. Instead, *daimyō* (q.v.) were responsible for protecting their own estates, *hatamoto* for protecting their residences, and the *chōnin* for protecting their quarters. The devastating losses in all sections of the city in the 1657 Meireki Fire showed this to be inadequate and led to reforms in the way fire brigades were organized. Fire fighting units known as *jōbikeshi* were expanded and made into permanent units commanded by high-ranking *hatamoto*. They were primarily responsible for protecting Edo Castle. The *daimyō hikeshi*, which had been established in 1629, were also enlarged and reorganized to enhance coverage of the *daimyō* areas. In 1718, *machi hikeshi* units were established to protect commercial districts from fire. Under the leadership of Ōoka Tadasuke (q.v.), a particularly influential city commissioner (see MACHI BUGYŌ), *machi hikeshi* were reorganized and expanded into 47 units and eventually into 48 units. These units were assisted by volunteers called *tobi* (q.v.) or *tobi ninsoku* who were particularly adept as roofers and carpenters. Their task was to create firebreaks by clearing structures from the path of fires. Before long, *tobi* came to regarded as rowdies who were more interested in fighting against rival units than against fires, and came to be thought of as something of a nuisance. For this reason they were confined to *chōnin* areas only for fire fighting.

The *jōbikeshi* and *daimyō hikeshi* were disbanded with the fall of the Tokugawa shogunate (q.v.). A new system of fire fighting companies called *shōbōgumi* was put in place after 1868. These companies were based on the earlier *machi hikeshi* and were put under the control of the Tokyo Metropolitan Police Office in 1881. Fire fighting responsibilities remained a part of the police force until 1948. The Tokyo Fire Department has more than 17,000 employees (mid-1990s), and is charged with providing rescue and ambulance services in addition to fire prevention and fire fighting.

FIVE-FAMILY GROUPS (See GONINGUMI)

FORTY-SEVEN RŌNIN INCIDENT *(Akō jiken)*. Famous incident that took place in Edo (q.v.) in January, 1703, in which a band of *rōnin* (masterless *samurai*) avenged the death of their former lord, Asano Naganori (1665–1701), the late lord of Akō province. The chronology is as follows. In 1701, while on a visit to pay respects to the *shōgun* in Edo Castle (qq.v.), Asano was slighted by Kira Yoshinaka, an official of the shogunate. He drew his sword and wounded Kira. Because drawing a sword in Edo Castle was illegal, Asano was made to commit suicide and his estate was confiscated. This cast adrift his *samurai*, who came to be *rōnin*, a word meaning "wave men." In January 1703, 46 of Asano's 47 warriors (one dropped out of the group shortly before the incident) raided Kira's mansion near Ryōgoku and killed him. They then marched to Sengakuji, a temple in what is now the Takanawa area of Minato Ward, and presented Kira's severed head to their master's grave. In March 1703, the 46 *samurai* were punished by being forced to commit suicide. Their graves are beside Asano's at Sengakuji. The incident is a celebrated story of unswerving loyalty to a master and *samurai* ethics, and has been retold often in books and films. Sengakuji is a popular visitors' attraction.

FUDAI DAIMYŌ (See DAIMYŌ)

FUDASASHI. A class of wealthy merchants in Edo (q.v.), who made their money dealing in rice and collecting interest on loans. Also called *kurayado*. They were distinguished by their opulent lifestyles and by the enormous power and influence that they attained. Late in the Edo Period (q.v.), various reform movements starting with the Kansei Reforms of 1787–1793 (q.v.) eroded their power, which then vanished completely by 1868 with the fall of the Tokugawa shogunate (q.v.).

FUKUZAWA YUKICHI (1835–1901). Preeminent educator and writer during the Meiji Period (q.v.), and leading propagator of Western learning in Japan. Generally regarded as one of the founders of modern Japan. His major works include a multivolume book called *Seiyō jijō (Conditions in the West)* that was published in 1866, 1868, and 1870. *Gakumon no susume* was published between 1872 and 1876 and later translated as *An*

Encouragement of Learning. Bummeiron no gairyaku was published in 1875 and later translated as *An Outline of a Theory of Civilization.* In 1873 he was one of a group of intellectuals who joined together to form an organization called *Meirokusha* that encouraged Western studies in Japan and published a journal called *Meiroku Zasshi.* In 1882 Fukuzawa founded the newspaper *Jijō shimpō.* In most of his works Fukuzawa was critical of traditional Japanese values, which he insisted held the country back in comparison to the West. He argued in favor of practical knowledge *(jitsugaku)* from the West, the learning of science, and a greater spirit of independence among Japanese. He also argued for improving the status of women in Japan. Fukuzawa's direct impact on Tokyo included a leading role in promoting that city as a clearinghouse for Western ideas in Japan, and the founding of Keiō Gijuku, which grew to become Keiō University (q.v.).

Fukuzawa was born in Osaka to a *samurai* family from Kyushu. He was introduced to Western studies in 1854 when he went to Nagasaki to study Dutch and Dutch learning. He also studied Dutch at a school in Osaka. He came to Edo (q.v.) in 1858 to start a school for the study of Dutch, but turned his attentions to mastering English when he learned that English was more important on the global scene and that it was the language spoken by most foreigners in Edo. In 1860 he traveled to the United States on the *Kanrin Maru* as part of Japan's first delegation to that country. In 1861 he left Japan for Europe on another official mission, visiting several of the major countries of western Europe as well as Russia. These landmark journeys and the many books that he brought back formed the basis of his knowledge about the West and its lessons for Japanese modernization.

FURISODE FIRE (See MEIREKI FIRE)

FUSHIN BUGYŌ. Commissioners of engineering works in Edo (q.v.). The title was used from the start of construction projects in Edo under Tokugawa Ieyasu (q.v.), and appointments were made on a regular basis after 1653. *Fushin bugyō* were responsible for overseeing land reclamation projects, excavation of moats and canals, the stone walls of Edo Castle (q.v.), widening of streets and creation of firebreaks, and other civil engineering projects.

– G –

GARBAGE (See ENVIRONMENTAL PROTECTION)

GENERAL HEADQUARTERS (GHQ) (See MACARTHUR, DOUGLAS; OCCUPATION)

GENROKU ERA *(Genroku jidai).* Also called the Genroku Period. The name of the imperial era *(nengō)* that is dated 1688–1704. The term is also used as a shorthand for the period from 1680 to 1709, the rule of the fifth *shōgun* of the Tokugawa family, Tokugawa Tsunayoshi (qq.v.). It was a time of growth and prosperity in Edo (q.v.) and other large cities of Japan, particularly Kyoto and Osaka. It is remembered mostly as a "renaissance period" that saw a flowering of arts and culture among townspeople (*chōnin*; q.v.) in these cities,along with a corresponding increase in *chōnin* consumer demands.

The Genroku Era is noted especially for the rise of theater as a popular form of entertainment for *chōnin* audiences, particularly *kabuki* theater and puppet theater *(ningyōgeki).* A distinctive acting style called *aragoto* (q.v.) that came to be identified with the city was pioneered in Edo during this period by the *kabuki* actor Ichikawa Danjūrō I (q.v.). Other advances in the arts came with improved woodblock techniques. The result was publication of small, simple books called *kana-*

zōshi, which were read widely by the general public, as well as *ukiyo-zōshi,* booklets of the floating world. The first generation of *ukiyo-e* (q.v.; woodblock prints) was also created during the Genroku Era. In the field of poetry, the era saw the development of the 17-syllable *haiku* poem. The works of the *haiku* poet Matsuo Bashō were especially popular.

GEOFRONT (also GEOFRONTIER). A term that is transliterated from Japanese usage by urban planners and construction company officials in Tokyo; it refers to construction of the urban facilities below ground. At one level the term applies to underground infrastructure already in place such as water lines, sewer lines, electrical cables, and gas pipes. It also refers to the city's extensive subway (q.v.) system, the several underground shopping arcades that have been developed at crowded commercial centers such as Shinjuku (q.v.), and the multiple basement levels (known as B1, B2, B3, etc.) in many new high-rise buildings in Tokyo that expand office and retailing space. At another level the term "geofront" refers to possible construction of large residential and commercial developments below ground. Many design proposals have been put forth for such construction by architects and construction companies as solutions to Tokyo's overcrowding and high land prices (q.v.; see "THE TOKYO PROBLEM").

GINZA. Commercial district in Chūō Ward, central Tokyo, noted especially for its department stores (q.v.) and other shops, and for its many restaurants and drinking establishments. Its first milestone in history was the opening of a silver mint by the Tokugawa shogunate in 1612. This accounts for the name "Ginza," which means "place where silver *(gin)* is minted." The mint remained there until 1800, when it was removed to Kakigarachō north of Nihombashi (q.v.). Until the 1840s Ginza was also noted for *kabuki* theater. However, for most of the Edo Period (q.v.) the district was a rather undistinguished area of artisans and small shops.

Ginza began the next phase of its history in 1872, when it started to take on more of a commercial character and developed a reputation for being cosmopolitan. In part, these changes were stimulated by the foreigners' settlement that had been established in 1867 at Tsukiji (q.v.). The changes were also encouraged by its nearness to the rail station that opened in 1872 in Shimbashi (q.v.), a station that connected the area with the international port of Yokohama (q.v.). An even bigger influence on Ginza's development were great fires (q.v.) that occurred there in 1869 and 1872 (before the rail station opened), and subsequent reconstruction. The latter fire, known as the Ginza Fire of 1872, was especially destructive. It originated at Wadakura Gate of Edo Castle (q.v.) and spread quickly to consume nearly all of Ginza and adjacent districts, such as Tsukiji. Redevelopment was in a Western style, and it produced a distinctive-looking district called Ginza Brick Town (q.v.), a place that soon became Tokyo's leading center of fashions from abroad. The main streets of the area attracted crowds of trend conscious young Japanese, generally referred to as *mo-bo* and *mo-ga* ("modern boys" and "modern girls"), who enjoyed *haikara* ("high-collar") fashions and the practice of *gin-bura*, "strolling in Ginza." The area was also famous for shops with imported consumer goods and Western style restaurants. The return of *kabuki* to the area and the opening of the *Kabuki-za* theater in 1889 added to the growing reputation of Ginza as an entertainment district.

Ginza was severely damaged in 1923 by the Great Kantō Earthquake and then again by the air raids of 1945 (qq.v.). Both times it was rebuilt. It was one of the first places in Tokyo to show the return of prosperity in the post-World War II period. Its many fine shops earned

Ginza the nickname "Fifth Avenue of Tokyo" in the 1950s and 1960s. The area continues to be a fashionable commercial district, although now it is thought of as a fairly conservative place with high prices. The area is also known for its many fine art galleries. With more than 300 such establishments in a few square blocks, Ginza is probably the largest concentration of art galleries in the world. The *Kabuki-za* theater continues to be a popular attraction.

GINZA BRICK TOWN (also GINZA BRICKTOWN; *Ginza renga-gai*). The name of a reconstructed section of the Ginza district (q.v.) after the Ginza Fire of 1872. It was designed by the English architect Thomas Waters (q.v.) and was made of red brick. The goal was to replace the city's traditional wood construction with a fireproof building material and to add a modern, Western style look to the city. The area covered several blocks and featured two-story brick structures with colonnades and balconies as well as sidewalks, gaslights, and trees lining the streets. It became a leading symbol of modernization and Western influence in Japan during the Meiji Period (q.v.). Reviews about the practical success of the architecture were mixed, as many of the first occupants complained about dampness and poor air circulation. Most of the brick buildings were destroyed in the 1923 by the Great Kantō Earthquake (q.v.), while most of those that survived were destroyed by the air raids of 1945 (q.v.).

GINZA LINE (See SUBWAYS)

GOKAIDŌ. The five highways that crossed central Japan and converged on Nihombashi (the bridge; q.v.) in Edo (q.v.) during the Edo Period (q.v.). Their names were the Tōkaidō (q.v.), Nakasendō, Kōshū Kaidō, Nikkō Kaidō, and Ōshū Kaidō. They were under control of the shogunate, which was able to monitor communications and troop movements along the roads, as well as the frequent processions of territorial lords *(daimyō)* that were required under the *sankin kōtai* (q.v.) system. There was a system of post-station towns *(shukuba machi)* along these highways to provide services for travelers. The highways and the post-station towns are credited with enhancing the integration of Japanese territory by facilitating safe and speedy travel.

GOKENIN. Generally translated as "housemen." These were lower-ranking retainers of the *shōgun* (q.v.). Unlike *hatamoto* (q.v.), they did not have the privilege of personal audiences with the *shōgun*, and they received smaller stipends. During the Edo Period (q.v.) there were approximately 20,000 *gokenin*, many of them in Edo (q.v.) itself.

GONINGUMI. Translated as "five-family groups," these were groups of homeowners and landlords who were organized in the early Edo Period (q.v.) as communal associations in the residential quarters of Edo (q.v.). They answered to the neighborhood chiefs (see NANUSHI) and were responsible for day-to-day management of many neighborhood activities. They collected a local tax called the *machi nyūyō* or the *machi iriyō*, which was then applied to costs of fire fighting (see FIRES), maintaining fire towers and guardhouses, local festivals, and other uses. A single quarter might have several *goningumi* who answered to the same *nanushi*.

GOTŌ SHIMPEI (1857–1929). Important politician and administrator in the national government during the Meiji and Taishō Periods (qq.v.), holding numerous prominent positions both in Japan and in Japanese colonies abroad during a distinguished career. He was mayor of Tokyo from 1920 to 1923. As home minister starting in 1923, he was in charge of the reconstruction effort after the city was devastated by the Great Kantō Earthquake (q.v.).

Gotō was born in what is now Iwate Prefecture to a *samurai* family. He left home as a young man to study medicine at the Sukagawa Medical School (Sukagawa Igakkō) in Fukushima Prefecture, and graduated in 1876. He also studied at the Nagoya Medical School. In 1881 he became director of the Aichi Hospital in Nagoya. He joined the Home Ministry in 1883. In 1892, after a break to continue studies in Germany, Gotō was put in charge of the Home Ministry's Health Bureau. He was particularly occupied with improving public health in Japan through better sanitation and with establishing a quarantine system to protect Japanese troops during the Sino-Japanese War, which started in 1894. In 1898 he was sent to Taiwan, which had become a Japanese possession, and was charged with its civil administration. He established a reputation there for getting things done, for which he was rewarded with increasingly higher government positions, first in Manchuria, another Japanese possession, and then at home in Japan. He became the first president of the South Manchuria Railway Company in 1906. From 1908 to 1912 he was Minister of Communications in the second and third Katsura Tarō cabinets. During that time he also directed the National Railways Bureau *(Tetsudōin)* and the Colonization Bureau *(Takushokukyoku)*. In 1916 he was appointed to his first term as Home Minister in the cabinet of Terauchi Masatake. In 1918 he was made Minister of Foreign Affairs. While holding that position, he promoted policies for Japanese expansion in China and Siberia, advocating the deployment of Japanese troops to take possession of Siberia during the time that Russia was preoccupied with revolution.

In December 1920 Gotō agreed to serve as mayor of Tokyo. He was coaxed out of a brief retirement to take the job because of an urgent need to reform the municipal government following a bribery and corruption scandal among city officials. As mayor, Gotō proposed ambitious plans for improving the city and carried out numerous projects, including widening and paving major streets, constructing sewer systems, improving the public education system, and making various innovations in social welfare. In 1922 he founded the Tokyo Institute on Municipal Research (q.v.) as a vehicle for improving government and applying "scientific methods" to urban problems. Because of such progressive endeavors, as well as the research-based approach that Gotō applied to earlier work in public health and colonial administration, his biographers have referred to him as "Japan's statesman of research."

Gotō resigned as mayor on 25 April 1923 and turned his attentions to Japan's relations with Soviet Russia. However, he returned to his work in Tokyo immediately after the Great Kantō Earthquake of 1 September 1923. He oversaw rescue work right after the disaster and within two days began to make large-scale plans for rebuilding the city. On 27 September he was put in charge of the Board of Reconstruction of the Capital City (q.v.). He saw the damage from the earthquake as an opportunity to completely modernize Tokyo, and with his adviser, the American historian Charles Austin Beard (q.v.), proposed plans that called for wide and straight streets, new parks, and improved housing. The plans were criticized for being grandiose and too expensive, and were largely ignored as the city was rebuilt on predisaster foundations. After Tokyo was reconstructed, Gotō finished his public service by representing Japan in negotiations to normalize diplomatic and commercial relations with Russia.

GREAT KANTŌ EARTHQUAKE (*Kantō daishinsai*; also called TOKYO EARTHQUAKE OF 1923). Powerful earthquake with epicenter in Sagami Bay that struck at 11:58 A.M. on 1 September 1923. It caused great damage and loss of life in Tokyo and surrounding prefectures, particularly in Yokohama (q.v.) in Kanagawa Prefecture, which was closer to the epicenter. The quake has been assigned a magnitude of 7.9 on the Japanese scale. There was also a second strong temblor the next day, and hundreds of aftershocks.

The Great Kantō Earthquake is considered to be one of the most destructive earthquakes in modern times. More than 100,000 people lost their lives, 60,000 of them in Tokyo. Property damage totaled billions of dollars. It included almost all of the center of Tokyo and 63.2 percent of its homes. In Yokohama 72.4 percent of the homes were lost. Most of the casualties were attributed to fires rather than the temblor itself. Many of the fires were started when the quake and winds scattered hot coals from people's noon meals. Firestorm conditions and cyclones developed over much of the city, adding greatly to the destructiveness. One cyclone killed more than 38,000 people who had gathered to seek safety in an open space at the Military Clothing Depot in Honjo (now in Sumida Ward). It was especially difficult to fight the fires because water mains and fire hydrants had been damaged by the quake, and because streets were impassable with debris. There was also a breakdown of social order, requiring imposition of martial law and the introduction of some 35,000 troops into the disaster area. In the days immediately after the earthquake, several thousand Korean residents of Tokyo, as well as many Chinese and Japanese, were killed by riotous mobs. The killings were in response to false rumors that Koreans and other foreigners had started the fires and were poisoning wells. A related tragedy was the Kameido Incident (q.v.) of 4 September 1923, in which ten leftist labor union activists were killed by military police after they were arrested while on patrol against neighborhood vigilante groups. (see BOARD OF RECONSTRUCTION OF THE CAPITAL CITY; EARTHQUAKES)

GREAT MEIREKI FIRE (See MEIREKI FIRE)

– H –

HACHIKŌ (1923–1935). An Akita dog whose bronze statue is a well-known landmark and popular waiting area outside the commuter rail station at Shibuya (q.v.). He was the pet of Ueno Eisaburō, a professor of agriculture at Tokyo University who used to commute to work from Shibuya Station. Each day the dog would accompany his master on walks to the station, scamper home, and then return to the station in time for the professor's return. When the professor died at his office in May, 1925, the dog waited at the station for almost ten years until his own death. Even when he was taken to a new home on the other side of Tokyo, the dog would wander back to Shibuya to resume his wait. Tokyo residents learned about this story from newspaper articles and came to admire Hachikō for single-minded devotion. Many people left food for him during his years of waiting. The bronze statue was originally cast in 1934, but was melted down during the period before World War II. It was recast shortly after the war and placed on a pedestal at the entry of Shibuya Station, a few feet from where it stands now. The real dog was stuffed and is on display at the Tokyo Museum of Art.

HAIRYŌ YASHIKI. Mansions and estates belonging to feudal lords in Edo (q.v.). (see DAIMYŌ; SANKIN KŌTAI)

HANEDA AIRPORT (See TOKYO INTERNATIONAL AIRPORT)

HARAJUKU. Commercial and residential district on the west side of Tokyo in Shibuya Ward. It is best known for exclusive fashion boutiques, as well as many cheaper clothing and accessory shops that appeal to large crowds of young people. There are also quite a few popular restaurants and snack shops. The area attracts especially large crowds on Sundays for strolling and shopping along streets such as Omote Sandō and Takeshita-dōri, and for visits to nearby Yoyogi Park and the Meiji Shrine (qq.v.). Many foreign residents of Tokyo and tourists gather in this area as well.

HARRIS, TOWNSEND (1804–1878). American merchant and diplomat who laid the groundwork for the opening of foreign trade and diplomatic relations between the United States and Japan. He was born in Sandy Hill, N.Y., and worked in the importing business in New York City in the early part of his career. In 1847 he traveled to Southeast Asia to engage in trade, and in 1854 he was appointed U. S. consul in Ningpo, China. Soon thereafter he sought and received the first U.S. consular post in Japan. He arrived in Japan in 1856 and was based in the small port of Shimoda on the Izu Peninsula. For more than one year he negotiated a commercial treaty with the Tokugawa Shogunate (q.v.). The United States-Japan Treaty of Amity and Commerce (*Nichibei shūkō tsūshō jōyaku*; "Harris Treaty") was signed on 29 July 1858, providing for the exchange of diplomats between the two countries and the opening of several ports. Harris remained in Japan as a diplomat until 1861, when he returned to New York and retired from public life except for philanthropy.

HATAMOTO. Generally translated as "bannermen." *Hatamoto* were direct retainers of the *shōgun* (q.v.). Their positions that were similar to those of officers in a standing army or government bureaucrats. Many of them had positions in Edo (q.v.), where they maintained fine houses. There were approximately 5,000 *hatamoto* at any one time during the Tokugawa Shogunate (q.v.). The positions were hereditary, but could be revoked. Most of the positions originated from within the ranks of warriors who had supported Tokugawa Ieyasu (q.v.) during his rise to power. *Hatamoto* were given annual stipends of at least 100 *koku* of rice (one *koku* is about 180 liters or about 50 bushels) or small fiefs *(chigyō)*. They were the lowest ranking of the military orders that had direct access to the *shōgun*.

HEARN, LAFCADIO (1850–1904). Western writer and educator who resided in Japan from 1890 until his death in 1904. He was born in Greece to an Anglo-Irish father and Greek mother and was raised in Ireland. He lived for a while in the United States, where he was employed as a newspaper reporter. In Japan, he became a Buddhist, took a Japanese wife, and changed his name to Koizumi Yakumo. In 1894, while teaching at a government college, he completed the book *Glimpses of an Unfamiliar Japan*. Shortly after he a position with the English-language newspaper *Kobe Chronicle,* his friend Basil Hall Chamberlain (q.v.) arranged for Hearn to be offered a position teaching English literature at Tokyo University (q.v.). He worked there until 1903, during which time he wrote several books about Japan and a collection of lectures that was published in 1904 under the title *Japan: An Attempt at Interpretation*. His works are noted for their emphasis on the exotic aspects of Japanese culture, presenting them to Western readers as curiosities. Along with Chamberlain, Hearn was an important early source for Western learning about Japan.

HIBIYA INCENDIARY INCIDENT (*Hibiya yakiuchi jiken*). A riot that took place in Tokyo on 5 September 1905 after a large rally in Hibiya Park (q.v.) protesting terms of the treaty that ended the Russo-Japanese War (1904–5). Marchers clashed with police at the Imperial Palace (q.v.) and destroyed more than 300 buildings in central Tokyo, including the offices of a progovernment newspaper, the residence of the home minister, and many police boxes. Martial law was declared the next day, and the disturbances were soon quelled. There were hundreds of injuries among both police and civilians, and a total of 17 deaths.

HIBIYA PARK. Located in Chiyoda Ward, Tokyo, next to the Imperial Palace (q.v.). It opened in 1903 as the first Western style park in the city. It measures 16 hectares (40 acres), and includes a central fountain and flower garden, an open-air bandstand, the Hibiya Library, Hibiya Public Hall, Shinji Pond and garden, and a children's playground (see LEISURE). Originally the land was the site of mansions of feudal lords. In 1871 it served as a parade ground for the Imperial Army.

HIE SHRINE (*Hie Jinja*; also called *Sannō-sama*). Located in the Nagatachō district (q.v.) of Chiyoda Ward, it is the site of the Sannō Festival (q.v.), one of the three major festivals that are held in Tokyo. It is dedicated to Ōyamakui-no-kami, the deity of Mount Hiei near Kyoto, whose role in this instance was to provide divine protection for Edo Castle (q.v.) and its occupants. The original shrine was constructed within the castle compound, but the shrine was moved outside the walls in 1607 by Tokugawa Ieyasu (q.v.). This was to give protection to the castle against evil spirits that would approach the castle from the southwest. After being destroyed in the Meireki Fire in 1657 (q.v.), the shrine was rebuilt on its present hilltop site, also southwest of the castle. The present shrine building, completed in 1967, replaces a historic structure that was destroyed in the air raids of 1945 (q.v.).

HIKESHI (See FIRES)

HIRAGA GENNAI (1728–1780). Naturalist, technician, and writer during the Edo Period (q.v.); one of the leading intellectuals of his time. He was a specialist in herbal medicine and an expert on the practical uses of plants and minerals. He and Tamura Ransui (1718–1776) put together three exhibitions about useful plants, animals, and minerals at Yushima in Edo (q.v.). In 1763 he assembled a large encyclopedia on this topic called *Butsurui hishitsu* ("Classification of Various Materials"). As a technician, he produced a heat-resistant asbestos cloth called *kakampu*, initiated gold and iron mining in Japan's central mountains, and learned to copy Dutch technology for items such as pottery, thermometers, and electric generators. He also learned Western oil painting. In addition, Gennai was an accomplished writer of a type of comic literature known as *kokkeibon*, producing works called *Nenashigusa* ("Rootless Weeds") and *Fūryū Shidōken den* ("Gallant History of Shidōken") in 1763. In 1777 he published a satire titled *Hōhiron* ("Breaking Wind"). In later life he developed psychological illnesses. He died in prison in 1780, where he had been sentenced for murdering one of his followers.

HIRATSUKA RAICHŌ (1886–1971). Feminist leader, involved for nearly half a century in many Tokyo-based efforts to improve the status of women in Japan. By the middle of the 20th century she had achieved global prominence as a leader in women's movements.

Hiratsuka was born in Tokyo and graduated from Japan Women's University. In 1911 she and other feminists founded a women's organization named *Seitōsha* (q.v.; "Bluestocking Society"). For several years it published a literary magazine, *Seitō*. In 1920 Hiratsuka helped found *Shin fujin kyōkai*, the "New Woman's Association," which campaigned for expanding women's rights, welfare, and higher education. In 1922 the group was able to influenced a change in laws that allowed women to participate more freely in Japan's politics. In the 1930s Hiratsuka became involved in the peace movement and was a vocal critic of Japan's militarization. In 1953 she became the first president of *Nihon fujin daitai rengōkai*, the Federation of Japanese Women's Societies.

HIROKŌJI (See FIRES)

HITOGAESHI. A word that means "returning the people." It refers to generally unsuccessful policies that were enacted during the Edo Period (q.v.) to encourage people who had migrated to cities, particularly Edo (q.v.), to return to the countryside from whence they came. The policies were enacted in 1790 and 1843, especially in connection with the Kansei Reforms (q.v.) and Tempō Reforms, respectively. They were aimed at peasants who had come to Edo to escape food shortages, low wages, and heavy taxation. All in all, the *hitogaeshi* policies had little effect, as the city remained a powerful magnet for poor people from the countryside.

HIYOKECHI (See FIRES)

HOEHN, H. F. (1839–1892). One of the many foreigners who came to Japan during the Meiji Period (q.v.) to advise on modernization. He was born in Prussia and became a police official in Berlin, rising to the rank of captain. He stands out for his contributions to improving the police system in Tokyo and other Japanese cities during his stay in the country from 1885 to 1890. He was an instructor at the Training School for Police Duties that the Home Ministry had established in Tokyo's Akasaka section, where he taught hundreds of graduates and advised local police forces in all parts of Japan. He is credited with introducing the idea of dispersing police personnel around a city into small substations. (see KŌBAN)

HOTERUKAN. A large hotel that was built in 1868 in what is now Chūō Ward, Tokyo, to serve the settlement of foreigners in the Tsukiji district (q.v.). Its name comes from *hoteru*, a newer Japanese term for hotel, and *kan*, an older word with the same meaning. The design of the building also combined western and Japanese elements. It was a popular landmark in the early Meiji Period (q.v.), but had a short life, as it was destroyed in the great fire of 1872 and never rebuilt (see FIRES). The builder was Shimizu Kisuke, the founder of the Shimizu Corporation, one of the country's largest construction firms.

– I –

ICHIKAWA DANJŪRŌ. The name of the most famous of the family lines of actors in *kabuki* theater; identified with the stage in Edo (q.v.) and Tokyo specifically. The first actor in this line was Ichikawa Danjūrō I (1660–1704), who made his debut on the stage of the Nakamura Theater in Edo in 1673. He created the *aragoto* (q.v.) style of *kabuki* acting. His son Danjūrō II (1688–1758) was also extremely successful and popular as an actor, and is credited with firmly establishing the prestige of the family line. Several other descendants were also particularly illustrious for the roles they played and innovations they made on stage. The present Ichikawa Danjūrō is Danjūrō XII, the son of Ichikawa Danjūrō XI. His real name is Horikoshi Natsuo; he assumed the acting name in 1985.

IKEBUKURO. An important commercial center west of downtown Tokyo in Toshima Ward. It is centered on Ikebukuro Station, the terminus for crowded commuter rail lines to northern and western suburbs, as well as a key stop on the Yamanote Line (q.v.), the busy rail loop that serves central Tokyo. Ikebukuro Station is also an important subway stop (see COMMUTING; SUBCEN-

TERS; SUBWAYS). The commercial center is a large concentration of department stores (q.v.) and other shops, offices, hotels, restaurants, bars, amusement arcades, and movie theaters. The large commercial development called Sunshine City (q.v.) is an important landmark.

IKI. A word that refers to the distinctive style or aesthetic standards that prevailed among the citizens of Edo (q.v.), particularly the *chōnin* (q.v.), during the late 18th and early 19th centuries (middle Edo Period; q.v.) Some of the key characteristics included just the right display of wealth, a keen wit, a critic's appreciation of theater and other arts of the city, and full enjoyment of good food, drink, and sexual pleasures in Yoshiwara (q.v.) or other amusement quarters, but not to excess. The word *iki* is often used in combination with the word *sui* (i.e., "*iki* and *sui*" or "*iki to sui*"), a related but slightly different aesthetic ideal that developed in Osaka in the late 17th and early 18th centuries to refer to the sense of style that characterized big-city life in Japan during the height of the Edo Period.

IMPERIAL HOTEL. Large luxury hotel in central Tokyo across from Hibiya Park (q.v.). Its former building was especially noteworthy. Designed by American architect Frank Lloyd Wright, it was completed in 1922 after six years of construction and was one of the few major buildings of the city to survive the Great Kantō Earthquake (q.v.) of 1923. The original building stood until 1967, when it was replaced by the present structure. The lobby of Wright's building has been reconstructed and is on display at the Meiji open-air museum in Inuyama, Aichi Prefecture.

IMPERIAL PALACE *(kōkyo)*. The official residence of Japan's emperors. It is now located in Chiyoda Ward, central Tokyo, on the grounds where Edo Castle (q.v.) once stood. The emperors have lived at this location since 1868, when the Meiji Emperor (q.v.) moved his residence from Kyoto. He settled in a remaining part of Edo Castle, but that structure was destroyed in 1873 by fire. A new palace was built in 1888, which stood until being destroyed by the air raids of 1945 (q.v.). The present Imperial Palace was completed in 1968. It is a sprawling complex of interconnected buildings called the *Kyūden*, and is built in a traditional style with gently sloping roofs. The grounds cover 1.15 square kilometers (0.44 square miles). The Imperial Palace is a very private place that is hidden from view in Tokyo by the old walls of the castle and by vegetation. The public is allowed on the grounds only on two days each year, New Year's Day and the birthday of the Emperor.

INOUE KAORU (1836–1915). Powerful political leader who held several important positions in the national government during the Meiji Period (q.v.). Before the Meiji Restoration of 1868, he was a leading proponent of the *sonnō jōi* movement, which advocated restoration of power to the emperor and the expulsion of foreigners from Japan, but after a trip to England in 1863 he became aware of the impracticality of isolating Japan from other countries. Consequently, he stressed the need for Japan to learn as much as possible from abroad, especially the West. His official positions in the Meiji government included appointments as Vice-minister of Finance in 1871, Minister of Public Works in 1878, Minister of Foreign Affairs in 1879, Minister of Agriculture and Commerce in 1888, and Minister of Home Affairs in 1892. In 1898 he became Minister of Finance. In 1876, 1884, and 1894 he was sent as an envoy to Korea on special diplomatic missions. He was also a key adviser to the imperial household and various ministries. In 1901 Inoue began serving the government as an elder statesman *(genrō)*, specializing in finance and foreign affairs. A major goal of his career was the revision of the so-called Unequal

Treaties that Japan had negotiated with foreign powers in the 1850s and 1860s.

In terms of direct impact on Tokyo, Inoue can be credited with policies that promoted industry and helped to change the city into a modern commercial-industrial center. During a brief hiatus from government service in the 1870s, Inoue helped to found the Senshū Kaisha trading company, a predecessor of the powerful Tokyo-based Mitsui & Co., Ltd. (see MITSUI). He was also instrumental in putting a Western face on Tokyo during the Meiji Period as part of a calculated strategy to strengthen Japan's negotiating position with Western powers. In this regard, Inoue was a chief political advocate for construction of the Rokumeikan (q.v.), a prominent Western style building in the Hibiya section of Tokyo that became a popular meeting place for Japanese and foreigners.

ITCHŌ RONDON (See LONDON BLOCK)

ITŌ NOE (See SEITŌSHA)

IWASAKI YANOSUKE (See IWASAKI YATARŌ)

IWASAKI YATARŌ (1834–1885). Business leader of the Meiji Period (q.v.); founder of the Mitsubishi business empire (q.v.; also see ZAIBATSU). He was born in the Tosa domain (now Kōchi Prefecture) in Shikoku, the son of a farmer. At age 20 he purchased *samurai* (q.v.) status for himself so that he could work in government service. In 1865 he took a position with the Industry Promotion Office *(Kaiseikan)* of Kōchi Prefecture, for which he worked in both Nagasaki and Osaka. Two years later he was put in charge of accounting for Tosa Shōji, a firm that had been set up to promote trade with Korea. In 1870 Iwasaki took personal control of Tosa Shōji and reorganized it as the Tsukumo Company, a shipping company. Its principal assets were eleven trading ships.

The firm became a private enterprise in 1871 when domains were abolished. In 1873 the firm was reorganized again, this time under the control of a partnership between Iwasaki and his younger brother Yanosuke (1851–1908). It was renamed Mitsubishi Shōkai and headquarters were relocated to Osaka.

The company flourished as exclusive transporter of Japan's troops and provisions to Taiwan during a military expedition in 1874. It then acquired other ships and trading routes, including those to China, and soon came to be the dominant force in Japan's ocean shipping. By 1877 Iwasaki owned 80 percent of all the ships in the country. The headquarters of the company were moved to Tokyo, where it diversified into copper and coal mining, money lending, warehousing, and other fields. Iwasaki also acquired considerable real estate in the city, mostly by buying up neglected *daimyō* (q.v.) mansions and gardens. The main Iwasaki family mansion was built by architect Josiah Conder (q.v.) on such land in the Hongō section of Tokyo, while land that was acquired by Iwasaki near the Imperial Palace (q.v.) was developed after his death by Iwasaki Yanosuke into the principal office district for Mitsubishi concerns. (see LONDON BLOCK; MARUNOUCHI)

IZU ISLANDS. A chain of volcanic islands in the Pacific Ocean south of Tokyo that are administered by Tokyo Metropolitan Government (q.v.). They extend for approximately 540 kilometers (335 miles) and include Ōshima, Toshima, Niijima, Kōzushima, Miyakejima, Mikurajima, Hachijōjima, Shikinejima, and Udonejima.

– J –

JIMAWARIMONO. A word meaning "local goods" that refers to products for the Edo (q.v.) market that were produced in the area near the city. It referred especially to firewood, charcoal, and food items from the Kantō Plain. The contrasting term is *kudarimono* (q.v.), which refers to goods for the Edo market that were "brought down" (imported) from the Kyoto and Osaka areas.

JINDAIJI. Major Buddhist temple of the Tendai sect located in Chōfu City, Tokyo. Its full name is *Fugakusan-Shoraku-in Jindaiji*. It was built in 733 as a Hossō Sect temple and became affiliated with the Tendai Sect about 100 years later, when the Tendai priest Eryo established a seminary there. Jindaiji was a popular temple during the Edo Period (q.v.) and was patronized by the Tokugawa family (q.v.). It continues as a popular place for worshipers and visitors. The Daruma Fair held each year on March 3–4 is especially well attended. Jindaiji is one of the finest examples of Edo Period architecture remaining in Tokyo.

JINRIKSHA (See RICKSHAW)

JŪHACHI DAITSŪ. Translated as "The 18 Connoisseurs," this was a loosely organized group of wealthy merchants and high-ranking *samurai* (q.v.) in Edo (q.v.) who served as unofficial arbiters of fashion and good taste for the city during most of the 18th century (i.e., the middle of the Edo Period; q.v.). They set standards and defined the spirit of *iki* (q.v.) that characterized the life of Edo in the late 18th and early 19th centuries. Their number was not always limited to 18.

– K –

KABUKI-ZA (See GINZA)

KABUKICHŌ. Nightlife and entertainment district in Shinjuku (q.v.; Shinjuku Ward). Named for a *kabuki* theater that investors had hoped to build in the area during reconstruction from bombing in World War II (see AIR RAIDS OF 1945), it became instead a center of movie theaters, bars, and restaurants, and sex clubs. During the 1960s the area was noted for foreign films, coffee shops, as well as artists, writers, and other intellectuals who came there. Although there is a great variety of establishments now, the reputation of Kabukichō is linked mostly to prostitution, hostess clubs, pornography, and live sex shows. It is also thought of as a place that is dangerous relative to other areas of Tokyo—the domain of gangsters who control many of the businesses. Kabukichō's clients include many male office workers (salarymen; *sarariman*) who are employed nearby or who pass through Shinjuku Station on their commutes.

KABUTOCHŌ. Commercial district in Chūō Ward, downtown Tokyo, noted for the offices of securities companies and the Tokyo Stock Exchange (q.v.).

KAMEIDO INCIDENT *(Kameido jiken)*. On the night of 4 September 1923, in the wake of mass confusion and martial law following the Great Kantō Earthquake (q.v.), military police arrested more than 700 residents of Korean ancestry and leftists in the Kameido district of Tokyo in what is now Kōtō Ward, and detained them in the local police station. Ten of the arrested labor union members and four other men, who were arrested for being part of a group that patrolled their neighborhood against anti-Korean mobs, were killed by police while being detained. News about these deaths was not made public until 10 October. The resulting demonstrations were led by the Japan Federation of Labor *(Nihon rōdō sōdōmei)*. The incident reflects the breakdown in public order that followed the earthquake.

KAMINARIMON (See ASAKUSA)

KANDA. A prominent district of Chiyoda Ward, central Tokyo. It has a mixture of commercial, institutional, and residential land uses, including an important concentration of colleges and universities in the Surugadai section, and a cluster of bookstores, publishing houses, and printers in the Jimbochō section. Many traditional restaurants and shops have thrived in this area for many years. It was one of the most important residential and commercial districts of the city during the Edo Period (q.v.), and a center of many crafts and specialized industries. (see EDO; SHITAMACHI)

KANDA CANAL *(Kanda jōsui)*. Also called the Kanda Aqueduct. One of the three main systems for supplying drinking water to Edo (q.v.) during the time of the Tokugawa Shogunate (q.v.). It was constructed during the 1660s. It took fresh water from Inokashira Pond in what is now Mitaka city in Tokyo Prefecture (q.v.) and brought it eastward to supply the Kanda and Nihombashi (qq.v.) districts of the city. The length of the system was approximately 17 kilometers (11 miles). The Kanda Canal was used until about 1900.

KANDA FESTIVAL *(Kanda matsuri)*. One of the three major festivals in Tokyo; held every other year on 15 May at Kanda Shrine (q.v.) and nearby streets. It is one of the most colorful of Tokyo's traditional events, and attracts enormous crowds. The highlight is a parade of floats *(dashi)* and portable shrines *(mikoshi)* through the streets of central Tokyo.

KANDA MYŌJIN (See KANDA SHRINE)

KANDA SHRINE. Also called Kanda Jinja and Kanda Myōjin. Located in Chiyoda Ward, central Tokyo, it is one of the most important of Tokyo's historic shrines. It dates back to approximately 730, when it was founded in the village of Shibasaki (q.v.), a precursor of Edo (q.v.). It was dedicated to the deities Ōnamuchi-no-Mikoto and Sukunahikona-no-Mikoto. Later it became strongly connected with the spirit of Taira-no-Masakado (q.v.), who was killed in 940 after leading a revolt against the emperor in Kyoto and declaring himself to be emperor. The shrine was moved to its present site in 1616. It was one of the city's most popular shrines through the Edo Period (q.v.), in part because many citizens of the city had a special fondness for the story of the rebellious Taira-no-Masakado. The buildings on the site now were completed in 1934, replacing earlier structures that were lost in 1923 to the fires that followed the Great Kantō Earthquake (q.v.). On 15 May every other year, Kanda Shrine hosts the Kanda Festival (q.v.), one of the most colorful and most popular religious festivals in Japan.

KAN'EIJI. Historic Buddhist temple affiliated with the Tendai sect in the Ueno (q.v.) district in Tokyo, Taitō Ward. It was established in 1625 as a guardian temple against evil spirits from the northeast, thought in old Chinese tradition to be the most unlucky direction. Kan'eiji was a favorite temple of the Tokugawa family (q.v.). By the end of the 17th century it had grown to encompass a splendid main hall that imitated the great Kiyomizu temple in Kyoto, 36 subsidiary buildings, and 36 subsidiary temples on its site of 119 hectares. Six Tokugawa *shōguns* are interred on the grounds. In 1868 the temple was the site of a fierce battle between a force loyal to the deposed *shōgun* and imperial troops (see SHŌGITAI), and was burned in the process. The main building that stands in Ueno now was reconstructed in 1879 from a temple that had stood in what is now Kawagoe, Saitama Prefecture.

KANŌ TAN'YU (1602–1674). Influential painter of the early Edo Period (q.v.); the painter-in-attendance *(goyō eshi)* for the Tokugawa Shogunate (q.v.). He was born in Kyoto into a family of professional artists known as the Kanō school *(Kanōha)*. His father was Kanō Takanobu (1571–1618), the son of Kanō Eitoku (1543–1590). His real name was Kanō Morinobu. He came to Edo (q.v.) at a young age at the behest of the shogunate and established a painting school at a house that was given to him near Kajibashi. His commissions included art for Edo Castle (q.v.), other important castles, and the Tōshōgū shrine in Nikkō. In 1639–1640 he completed *Tōshōgū engi*, five scrolls that depicted the life of Tokugawa Ieyasu (q.v.).

KANSEI REFORMS *(Kansei no kaikaku)*. A series of reform programs that were undertaken by the Tokugawa Shogunate (q.v.) between 1787 and 1793. They were the second of three reform programs, the earlier one being the Kyōhō Reforms of 1716–1745, and the other one being the Tempō Reforms of 1841–1843. The Kansei Reforms emphasized efficiencies in the central bureaucracy and improvements in the countryside, such as tax reform and increasing the amount of rice reserved for bad years. The reforms also addressed the needs of Edo (q.v.) itself: they called for peasants who had migrated to the overcrowded city during famines to return to their lands (see HITOGAESHI), and they called for economic development of the area surrounding the city. The principal author of the Kansei Reforms was Matsudaira Sadanobu (q.v.), chief senior councilor for the Tokugawa Shogunate (q.v.) between 1787 and 1793.

KANTŌ PLAIN. The relatively flat area on the Pacific coast of central Honshū in which the Tokyo metropolitan area is situated. It is composed of thick layers of volcanic ash called Kantō loam and alluvial deposits associated with the rivers Arakawa, Tamagawa, and Tonegawa.

KASUMIGASEKI. A district in Chiyoda Ward of central Tokyo that, along with the neighboring Nagatachō district (q.v.), is the location of many offices and institutions of Japan's central government, including the Ministry of Finance, the Ministry of Foreign Affairs, the Ministry of International Trade and Industry, and the Ministry of Justice. The area also houses the headquarters of the Tokyo Metropolitan Police Department and the Tokyo High Court. A landmark of a different sort is the Kasumigaseki Building (q.v.). The area's role as headquarters for government bureaucracies dates back to the early Meiji Period (q.v.) when new government institutions were established in Japan. In the Edo Period (q.v.), Kasumigaseki was the location of many mansions of feudal lords (*daimyō*; q.v.).

KASUMIGASEKI BUILDING. A 36-story office building in the Kasumigaseki (q.v.) district of central Tokyo that is generally considered to be the city's first skyscraper. It was designed by Yamashita Architects and was completed in 1968 after six years of construction. The top floor has an observation facility.

KEIŌ UNIVERSITY. Major private university in the Mita area of Tokyo (Minato Ward). It was founded in 1858 as a school for Western studies by Fukuzawa Yukichi (q.v.). In 1868 it was named Keiō Gijiku (Keiō private school). It expanded quickly during the Meiji Period (q.v.) and in 1904 was renamed Keiō Gijiku University. In 1920 it was formally accredited as a university. The school has a reputation for independence from government, as well as for academic excellence. Many of its graduates have become important leaders in business. Enrollment is more than 20,000.

KINOKUNIYA BUNZAEMON (1665–1734). Also known as Senzan. Lumber merchant in Edo (q.v.) who was known for his great wealth and lavish lifestyle. He was born in Kii Province (now Wakayama Prefecture) and inherited his father's successful timber business in the Hatchōbori district of Edo. The business grew tremendously after 1703 when Kinokuniya was able to supply the lumber for reconstruction of Edo after a great fire (see FIRES). He became the official supplier of lumber for the Tokugawa Shogunate (q.v.), in particular for large construction projects such as the Kan'eiji (q.v.) temple in the Ueno (q.v.) district.

Kinokuniya Bunzaemon was apparently an exceedingly colorful character. He was known as a generous host and entertainer for officials of the shogunate, as well as a frequent patron of the theater and brothel quarters. At one point he was able to ransom Miuraya-no-Kichō, the most famous courtesan of the time. He spent money almost as fast as it came in. After an unlucky investment in coin minting in 1709 his fortune declined, and he lived out the rest of his life as a pauper.

KŌBAN. A word generally translated as "police box" that refers to small neighborhood police stations located in various parts of Tokyo. In comparison to the 99 larger police stations in the city in March, 1994, there were 1,232 *kōban* in Tokyo. Many *kōban* are located at train and subway stations through which many people enter various neighborhoods. Therefore, one function of these facilities is to provide directions to people who are new to the area. Most *kōban* are staffed around the clock by police officers who alternate duty behind a desk in the *kōban* itself with daily patrols of the neighborhood, usually on bicycle. Thus, police are in daily contact with residents and shopkeepers in the neighborhood, and are able to distinguish strangers from those who "belong" in the area. This is said to be an effective method of policing that helps keep Tokyo's neighborhoods relatively free from crime (q.v.) and related problems. (see HOEHN, H. F.)

KOISHIKAWA YŌJŌSHO. The name of a charitable hospital that was established in the Koishikawa section of Edo (q.v.) in 1722. It was established in response to a suggestion by a local physician, Ogawa Shōsen (1672–1760), that was left in a suggestion box (*meyasubako*; q.v.) for the *shōgun* Tokugawa Yoshimune (qq.v.). The hospital was administered by Edo city commissioners (*machi bugyō*; q.v.) and accepted only patients who had no means of support. It eventually became incorporated into the medical school of Tokyo University (q.v.).

KOKUGIKAN. The *sumō* wrestling stadium in Tokyo. The present structure was built in 1985 in the Ryōgoku (q.v.) section of the city. There is a *sumō* museum on its ground floor. The Kokugikan that was used before was built in 1954 across the Sumida River (q.v.) from Ryōgoku in the Kuramae district, while the original Kokugikan, built in 1909, was in Ryōgoku. (see LEISURE)

KŌSATSU. Signboards that were used during the Tokugawa Shogunate (q.v.) for official notices and pronouncements.

KUDARIMONO. A word that means literally "wares that have come down." It refers to the many items such as textiles, clothing, manufactured articles, and food products that were exported from the Kamigata region of Japan (the Kyoto and Osaka areas) as supplies for Edo (q.v.). As the city grew it began to produce more and more goods of its own and to draw increasingly on the towns and countryside of the surrounding Kantō Plain (q.v.) as a source for its needs (see JIMAWARIMONO). In this way Edo changed from a city of consumption in the early Edo Period (q.v.) to a city of both consumption and production by the early 19th century (late Edo Period).

KUMOTORI (MOUNTAIN) (*Kumotoriyama*). With an elevation of 2,018 meters (6,619 feet), this is the highest point in Tokyo Metropolis (q.v.). The mountain is located at the westernmost part of Tokyo, where it borders both Yamanashi Prefecture and Saitama Prefecture. The local mountain area is called Oku-Tama, "Deep Tama."

– L –

LAND PRICES. Tokyo has some of the highest land prices in the world. Detailed comparisons with other cities are difficult because comparable data are generally not available, so round-number estimates are often used. For example, a study in 1989 by the Japanese Association of Real Estate Appraisal estimated that, on the average, a square meter (10.764 square feet) of land in Tokyo cost one million yen ($7,200 at the time). This amount is said to have been 99 times more than a similar parcel in Los Angeles and 30 times more than one in London or Frankfurt. It has also been estimated that the total value of all real estate in Tokyo, $7.7 trillion in the late 1980s, was worth more than double all of the land in the entire United States. Prime land in Tokyo, such as commercial land in the Ginza and Marunouchi (qq.v.) districts, sold in the late 1980s for as much as 30 million yen ($215,000) per square meter. (The figures quoted here are from the analysis of the Tokyo land market by Michael Wegener, which is cited in the bibliography.) Prices have dropped somewhat since the late 1980s, when a speculators' frenzy peaked, and are reported to have leveled off by the mid-1990s, albeit at a level that is still extraordinarily high in comparison to other cities in the world.

High land prices make the cost of living in Tokyo extremely expensive. Not only is the cost of housing and office space high, the costs of other consumer purchases, ranging from food to durable goods to the price of a movie ticket, are high as well because retailers pass on their land costs to customers. Other effects of high land prices include replacing lower buildings with taller ones, and developing unusually narrow buildings on tiny slivers of land that might have remained vacant under less crowded conditions. More subtle effects of high land prices include crowding tables and chairs (and rather small ones at that) in many restaurants in order to maximize the number of customers who could fit inside.

With respect to housing, it is often observed that because of the expense of land, most people in Tokyo live in rather small units regardless of whether that housing is near the center of the city or in outlying districts. Furthermore, detached dwellings are fast disappearing from most parts of the city and are being replaced by multistory residences or commercial land uses. Increasingly, housing consumers in Tokyo are being pushed by high land prices to distant fringes of the metropolitan area, where they become long-distance commuters (see "THE TOKYO PROBLEM"). It is in large part because of high land costs that many people in Tokyo have argued recently for relocating the capital of Japan.

LEISURE. While Tokyo is known primarily as a hard-at-work economic center, it is also a city in which residents and visitors engage in leisure activities of all kinds. There are several well-known parks in the city that draw large numbers of people, including families with small children, young couples, and groups, to enjoy nature and engage in sports activities, picnics, and other relaxation. Some of the most popular such places are Hibiya Park, Ueno Park, and Yoyogi Park (qq.v.), as well as the many recreation areas that are provided along city rivers such as the Tama River (q.v.). The parks are particularly crowded on Sundays and other holidays when schools and most workplaces are closed. Tokyoites also enjoy visiting historical landmarks such as the Imperial Palace (q.v.); popular religious shrines such as Jindaiji, the Kanda Shrine, the Meiji Shrine, Sensōji, and Zōjōji, (qq.v.), particularly at festival times; the city's many museums (see EDO-TOKYO MUSEUM; UENO PARK); and amusement parks such as Tokyo Disneyland (q.v.). Tourist attractions such as Tokyo Tower (q.v.) and the observation levels atop the city's tallest buildings are also popular (see SUNSHINE CITY; TOKYO METROPOLI-TAN GOVERNMENT). Shopping (or simply strolling in shopping districts) is also a common leisure activity in places such as Aoyama, Ginza, Ikebukuro, Shinjuku and Ueno (qq.v.; See DEPARTMENT STORES; YEBISU GAR-DEN PLACE). Young people (e.g., junior high school, high school, and college students) are drawn in especially big numbers to the shopping streets of Harajuku and Shibuya (qq.v.), as well as to movie theaters, game arcades, and fast-food restaurants in these areas. After dark, many Tokyoites enjoy themselves in the bars, restaurants, and nightclubs of districts such as Kabukichō in Shinjuku (qq.v.), and in Akasaka, Roppongi (qq.v.), and other night spots. (see SAKARIBA)

There is a full range of sports activities, including team sports such as baseball, rugby, and volleyball, as well as individual challenges such as golf, tennis, and swimming. Golf has been especially popular in the 1980s and 1990s. There are many practice driving ranges in various parts of the city, some having golfers stacked one atop the other at multilevel driving facilities. The rooftops of some department stores have practice greens for putting. Golf courses themselves are in the Tama Area of Tokyo Metropolis (qq.v.) and in neighboring prefectures. The mountains near Tokyo attract many hikers, mountain climbers, and nature photographers. Fishing is popular as well. Many young people enjoy surfing or wind sailing in the ocean near Tokyo. Baseball and *sumō* are the most popular spectator sports (see

KOKUGIKAN; TOKYO DOME). In addition to all of the above, Tokyoites enjoy travel to other places. New Tokyo International Airport (q.v.) is always busiest during holiday periods, when many Tokyoites and other Japanese go abroad for relaxation.

LONDON BLOCK. Also called Londontown, Mitsubishi Londontown, and *Itchō Rondon*, this is the name given to the office district that was developed in the 1890s by the Mitsubishi (q.v.) conglomerate in the area of downtown Tokyo that today is called Marunouchi (q.v.). The principal architect was Josiah Conder (q.v.), but other architects were involved as well. The district stood out because of brick construction and an appearance reminiscent of commercial streets in London. No trace remains today; the last of the original buildings were cleared after World War II to make room for new office buildings.

LONG-SLEEVES FIRE (See MEIREKI FIRE)

– M –

MACARTHUR, DOUGLAS (1880–1964). American general who commanded Allied forces in the Far East during World War II and was Supreme Commander of the Allied Powers (see SCAP) during the Occupation (q.v.) of Japan after the war.

MacArthur was born on a military reservation near Little Rock, Arkansas, where his father was a prominent army officer. In 1899 he entered the U.S. Military Academy at West Point and began his lifelong career with the armed forces. He graduated first in his class in 1903 and was assigned as an engineer to the Philippines. Other notable posts included work in the Army Engineer Office in San Francisco, assignment to East Asia in 1905 as an observer of the Russo-Japanese War, and distinguished command of the 42nd Infantry Division in France during World War I. From 1919 to 1922 he was superintendent of West Point. In 1925 he was promoted to major general and in 1930 was appointed chief of staff of the U.S. Army. He divided his time between the United States and the Philippines, which he regarded as a second home. He retired from the military in 1937 but stayed in the Philippines as a military adviser. With the threat of war against Japan, he was recalled to active duty on 26 July 1941 and was named commander of the U.S. Army in the Far East. Forced from the Philippines by Japanese advances, he issued his famed "I shall return" proclamation, and then began his counteroffensive from Australia. After a campaign from island to island in the southwest Pacific against Japanese forces, MacArthur fulfilled his promise and returned to the Philippines in October 1944 by wading ashore on Leyte Island. On 2 September 1945 MacArthur received Japan's formal surrender aboard the battleship *Missouri* in Tokyo Bay (q.v.). After overseeing the Occupation of Japan, MacArthur commanded forces in Korea during the Korean War (1950–1953). On 11 April 1951 he was dismissed from command after a public disagreement with President Harry Truman. In both 1948 and 1952 he was mentioned prominently as a possible Republican Party candidate for President of the United States.

As commander of the Allied forces in Japan during the Occupation, MacArthur worked from an office in the Daiichi Insurance Company Building in downtown Tokyo. He selected this building as his general headquarters (GHQ) because of its imposing form and location directly across from the Imperial Palace (q.v.). He lived a short walk away in the Imperial Hotel (q.v.). MacArthur was responsible for the demilitarization of Japan, remodeling its government and instituting a new constitution, land reform, and major changes in the structure of the economy, including the breakup of the

A part of the Imperial Palace complex, formerly Edo Castle, in the center of Tokyo.

Statue of Ōta Dōkan (1432–1486), founder of Tokyo.

Kaminarimon, the main gate to Sensōji, a historic temple in Tokyo's Asakusa district.

Historic Nezu Shrine.

Giant archway *(torii)* at the entry to the Meiji Shrine.

The Marunouchi side of Tokyo Station.

Yasuda Hall, Tokyo University.

National Diet Building.

Tokyo National Museum in Ueno Park.

The historic bridge, Nihombashi, and an expressway bridge above.

Statue of noted business leader Shibusawa Eiichi (1840–1931) in downtown Tokyo.

The industrial waterfront at Tokyo Bay and Tokyo Tower in the background.

Edo-Tokyo Museum.

Tokyo Metropolitan Government headquarters in Shinjuku, the tallest building in the city.

Rainbow Bridge connecting central Tokyo with new islands reclaimed from Tokyo Bay.

Tokyo's new waterfront at Odaiba, featuring high-quality residences, shopping centers and entertainment, and a freshly laid sandy beach on a newly made island in Tokyo Bay.

zaibatsu (q.v.). He endeared himself to many Japanese people as he guided their country from the devastation of war to the beginnings of prosperity.

MACHI BUGYŌ. Generally translated as "city magistrate" or "city commissioner." In Edo during the Edo Period (qq.v.) these were high-ranking city administrators charged with overseeing the city's residential quarters and the affairs of their inhabitants. They were drawn from the ranks of *hatamoto* (q.v.). For most of the Edo Period, there were two *machi bugyō* at any one time, alternating service from month to month. They reported to the *shōgun* through the *rōjū* (q.v.), the senior councilors.

MACHIDOSHIYORI. Generally translated as "city elders." These were high-ranking city officials during the Edo Period (q.v.) charged with assisting the *machi bugyō* (q.v.). In Edo (q.v.) their duties included transmitting laws and decrees issued by the shogunate to residential quarters, collecting various taxes, investigating issues related to petitions submitted by commoners, and laying out new residential areas on land reclaimed from Tokyo Bay (see WATERFRONT DEVELOPMENT). *Machidoshiyori* were not salaried, but received grants of land from the *shōgun*, which they were free to rent out. They also received grants and loans. The position of *machidoshiyori* was hereditary. After the 1610s, there were three city elder positions in Edo claimed by the Naraya, Taruya, and Kitamura, families.

MACHI KAISHO. This was the city savings association in Edo (q.v.). It was established by the shogunate in 1792 after a series of riots in the 1780s by the city's commoners (see RICE RIOTS), and became the city's principal source of charity. It provided grants to individuals and families who had suffered losses due to fire, earthquake, or disasters such as epidemics and famines, as well as loans to individuals owning property that could be pledged as collateral. It also helped to stabilize rice prices by buying and selling large quantities of rice on the market. The funds came mostly from levies on the residential quarters of merchants and artisans, with wealthier neighborhoods paying proportionately more than poorer ones. There were also endowments for the fund from the shogunate in 1793 and 1800. The fund was managed by a board comprised of five neighborhood chiefs (see NANUSHI) who were appointed for this task.

MARU BIRU (See Marunouchi Building)

MARUNOUCHI. An important commercial district in Chiyoda Ward, downtown Tokyo. During the Edo Period (q.v.) the site housed residences of wealthy feudal lords. In the 1890s it was developed into an office district for the Mitsubishi (q.v.) commercial empire founded by Iwasaki Yatarō (q.v.). One part of this district had a distinctive European appearance, as was typical of many buildings in Tokyo during the Meiji Period (q.v.), and was called Mitsubishi Londontown (q.v.). None of these older buildings survive. Today, Marunouchi is headquarters for many large Japanese corporations, most notably companies in the Mitsubishi industrial conglomerate.

MARUNOUCHI BUILDING. Also called *Maru Biru*. An eight-story office building in the Marunouchi district (q.v.) of central Tokyo. It was designed by Sakurai Kotaro and constructed in 1926 by the Fuller Construction Company of New York. Until completion of the Kasumigaseki Building (q.v.) in 1968, it was the city's largest office building. It was often used in colloquial Japanese as a standard for describing large volumes (e.g., so many "Maru-birus" of oil, beer, etc.). It was one of the first buildings in Japan to employ *biru*, the loan-word from English for building. Because of a rounded corner on the building, the name *Maru* is a play on the Japanese word for circle *(maru)*, as well as a reference to the toponym Marunouchi. The building still stands. In 1951 a companion building with a similar appearance, the New Marunouchi Building *(Shin Marunouchi Biru)*, was built across the street.

MATSUDAIRA SADANOBU (1758–1829). Important political leader and reformer during the middle part of the Edo Period (q.v.). He was born in Edo (q.v.) to one of the three junior collateral houses of the Tokugawa family (q.v.), but because of political intrigue was adopted in 1774 by Matsudaira Sadakuni, the *daimyō* (q.v.) of the Shirakawa domain (now part of Fukushima Prefecture). In 1783 he succeeded his father as *daimyō* and embarked on a series of improvements to the domain such as reforestation, enhanced agricultural productivity, and increased education. Because of improvements in the storage and transportation of rice and other foodstuffs that Sadanobu had directed in advance, the Shirakawa domain was able to avoid the Temmei Famine (1782–1787), which took as many as one million lives in other parts of Japan.

In 1787 Sadanobu was appointed chief senior councilor (*rōjū shuseki*; see RŌJŪ) and turned his attention to national affairs, as well as those of Edo. He was the principal architect of the Kansei Reforms (q.v.; 1787–1793), which brought government reform, tax reform, and agricultural improvements to a wide area of Japan. The reforms also built up rice reserves and enhanced employment opportunities in the countryside for peasants who had migrated to the cities (see HITO-GAESHI). In Edo specifically, Sadanobu worked to combat political corruption, enforce sumptuary laws, strengthen the city's coastal defenses, diversify the economy, and improve farming in the surrounding countryside. His most controversial action was the so-called Ban on Heterodoxy *(Kansei igaku no kin)*, a policy that promoted a specific school of Neo-Confucianism and required the adherence of all government officials. Because of this and other controversies, he was dismissed from his position in 1793 and returned to his domain in Shirakawa where he established a school of Confucian studies called the Rikkyōkan and wrote poetry and scholarly essays.

MEIJI EMPEROR. Term used to designate Mutsuhito (born 1852), the 122d emperor of Japan who reigned from 1867 until his death in 1912. His reign was called "Meiji," meaning "enlightened rule," and he came to be referred to as the Meiji Emperor after he died. He succeeded his father, the Emperor Kōmei, at the age of 14. During his rule Japan embarked on a crash program of modernization and transformed itself from a semifeudal, agrarian state to an industrial and imperialist power. (see MEIJI PERIOD; MEIJI RESTORATION)

MEIJI PERIOD *(Meiji jidai)*. The period from 1868 to 1912 when the Emperor Meiji (q.v.) reigned. The Meiji Period followed the Edo Period (1603–1867; sometimes identified as 1600–1868) and was succeeded by the Taishō Period (1912–1926) (qq.v.).

The Meiji Period was a time of rapid and profound transformation of the social, political, and economic structure of Japan. The first great changes were the restoration of imperial authority on 3 January 1868 (see MEIJI RESTORATION) and the designation of Edo (q.v.) as the national capital with the new name "Tokyo" (q.v.). During this period, the country was transformed from a feudalistic system to a modern industrial nation; its policy of national isolationism which had been enforced by the *shōgun's* authority changed to one of aggressive contacts of all kinds with nations around the globe. This period witnessed a particularly strong push for modernization so that the country could catch up in technology and military power with Western nations, and so that unfavorable treaties that had been forced on Japan by Western powers could be revised. Consequently, one of the defining characteristics of the Meiji Period was a crash program of learning from the West. Many Japanese traveled abroad to study during this period, often in service to the government, and a great many foreign experts of all kinds were invited into Japan to serve as teachers and advisers. (see YATOI)

Another important characteristic of the Meiji Period was the rise of Japan as a major power in East Asia. In the latter half of the Meiji Period, Japan won decisive victories in the Sino-Japanese War of 1894–1895 and in the Russo-Japanese War of 1904–1905. It gained control of territory in China (Manchuria), Korea, and southern Sakhalin (Karafuto). The new colonies were exploited for their resources and for the advancement of Japanese industry. Thus, the Meiji Period is defined by rising militarism in Japan, as well as by rapid modernization as summarized by two slogans that were commonly used by political leaders in the early part of the Meiji Period: *fukoku kyōhei*, which means "rich country and strong military;" and *bunmei kaika*, which is most often translated as "civilization and enlightenment."

MEIJI RESTORATION *(Meiji ishin)*. The historic transfer of power in 1868 from the Tokugawa Shogunate (q.v.) to the emperor of Japan. There was a palace coup on 3 January 1868 in which antishogunate forces from the southern domains *(han)* of Satsuma, Tosa, and Chōsū declared that the shogunate was abolished and that authority in Japan was being restored to the emperor after eight centuries of military rule. This was followed by a brief civil

war (the Boshin War), which was won by the antishogunate forces. The Meiji Emperor (q.v.) then moved the
imperial capital from Kyoto to Edo (q.v.), which was
designated the national capital and renamed "Tokyo".
(see MEIJI PERIOD)

MEIJI SHRINE. Shintō shrine consecrated to the Meiji
Emperor (1852–1912) and his consort, the Empress
Dowager Shōken (1850–1914). It is located in the Yoyogi
area of Shibuya Ward, Tokyo, adjacent to Yoyogi Park
(q.v.). Construction of the shrine was started soon after
the Meiji Emperor's death, and the project was completed in 1920. It was reconstructed in 1958 after being
destroyed in the air raids of 1945 (q.v.). It is an extremely
popular shrine that attracts many thousands of visitors
on most Sundays and holidays. The entrances to the
Meiji Shrine are marked by giant *torii* (Shintō arches)
made of cypress wood more than 1,700 years old. On the
first day of a new year, more than two million visitors
come to the Meiji Shrine for *hatsumōde*, their first shrine
visit of the year.

MEIJI UNIVERSITY. A large private, coeducational university located in the Sarugakuchō section of Chiyoda
Ward, Tokyo. It has a diversified curriculum in the sciences, social sciences, and humanities, and enrolls more
than 32,000 students. The university was founded in
1881 as the Meiji Law School *(Meiji hōritsu gakkō)*. It
was reorganized and named Meiji University in 1903.

MEIREKI FIRE *(Meireki no taika)*. One of the largest of the
many great fires that burned in Edo during the Edo
Period (qq.v.; see FIRES). It occurred in early 1657 and
destroyed about 60 percent of the city, including most of
Edo Castle (q.v.) and its central tower, 930 mansions of
the elite class, 350 temples, 60 bridges, and countless
thousands of shops and dwellings belonging to com-

moners. An estimated 100,000 lives were lost. The initial blaze broke out in a temple in the Hongō area of the city. It is said to have started when flames from a girl's *kimono* that was being burned in a religious ritual blazed out of control. As a result, the fire is sometimes called the "Furisode (*kimono* or Long Sleeves) Fire." The next day additional blazes started in a *daimyō* (q.v.) residence in the Koishikawa area and spread to Edo Castle and the Kōjimachi area.

A number of important fire prevention measures were adopted in the reconstruction of Edo. Firebreaks were created at strategic points in the city, streets were widened, and a height limitation of two stories was put on the residences of commoners. In addition, citizens were encouraged to apply plaster to their roofs in place of straw. Other changes included relocating temples and shrines (now thought to be fire hazards) to the outskirts of the city, as well as the Yoshiwara (q.v.) pleasure quarter. Furthermore, the Ryōgoku Bridge was constructed across the Sumida River (qq.v.), in large part to provide citizens with an escape from the most crowded quarters of the city in case of fire. It is commonly observed that historic Edo vanished as a result of the Meireki Fire and that the city created in the reconstruction was markedly different in appearance from the original city.

MEYASUBAKO. A box that was put up in 1721 at the gates of Edo Castle (q.v.) by *shōgun* Tokugawa Yoshinobu (qq.v.) to collect suggestions from the citizens of Edo (q.v.; see CHŌNIN) and to register their complaints. Yoshimune kept the key to the box and is reported to have spent hours by himself working through the letters that came in. Most complaints were about delays in judicial matters. Many other letters were suggestions for improving fire prevention (see FIRES). A charitable hospital, the *Koishikawa yōjōsho* (q.v.), was establihed in Edo in 1722 as a result of a suggestion left by a local physician, Ogawa Shōsen. Other *meyasubako* were put up in Kyoto and Osaka.

MINOBE RYŌKICHI (1904–1984). Educator and politician, three-term governor of Tokyo Prefecture (q.v.). Born in Tokyo, son of Minobe Tatsukichi, a noted scholar of constitutional law and member of the House of Peers. After graduating from Tokyo University (q.v.), he taught economics at Hōsei University. He lost that job in 1938 when he was arrested in the so-called Popular Front Incident, a government repression of suspected leftist scholars and antiwar activists. After World War II he resumed his teaching at Tokyo University of Education (now Tsukuba University). He was an outspoken critic of what he saw to be Japan's overemphasis on rapid economic growth at the expense of improved housing, roads, and sanitary facilities. In 1957 he campaigned for governor of Tokyo Prefecture on a reform platform with a strong environmental message that called for a city with "blue skies and fireflies." He won the election with support from the Socialist and Communist Parties, and was reelected in 1971 and 1975. His terms in office were noted for an emphasis on social welfare and environmental improvement, as well as for growing fiscal problems in Tokyo. In 1980 Minobe was elected to Japan's House of Councilors.

MITAKA INCIDENT *(Mitaka jiken).* A terrorist act that took place on 15 July 1949 in Mitaka city in the Tama Area (q.v.) of Tokyo Prefecture (q.v.). An unmanned train that had been set to continue moving forward derailed at Mitaka Station and killed six people. The act is thought to have been a protest against the economic policies of the American Occupation (q.v.) of Japan, as well as a strike against the Occupation's strong antileftist stance. Ten members of Japan's National Railway Workers' Union (NRWU), nine of whom were also members of the

Japan Communist Party (JCP), were charged with the crime. Nine were found innocent, while the tenth was sentenced to death. However, he died in prison of natural causes in 1967. The incident was one of two other violent acts that took place in 1959 with allegedly similar motivations. One is called the Matsukawa Incident, another act of train sabotage that took place in Matsukawa, Fukushima Prefecture; the other is known as the Shimoyama Incident (q.v.).

MITSUBISHI. The name of one of Japan's most powerful commercial empires. Before World War II it was one of the four leading *zaibatsu* (q.v.) in Japan, along with those of Mitsui, Sumitomo, and Yasuda (qq.v.). It controlled 209 companies. It was broken up during the U. S. Occupation (q.v.) of Japan and then reorganized as an enterprise grouping *(keiretsu)*. Its major concerns are headquartered in Tokyo (see MARUNOUCHI) and include banking, automobile manufacturing, real estate, heavy machinery, chemicals, synthetic fibers, plastics, papers, electronic equipment, and warehousing. The Mitsubishi name is attached to almost all of the affiliated companies.

The Mitsubishi empire was established in the early 1870s by Iwasaki Yatarō (q.v.) as a trading and shipping firm named the Tsukumo Company. The name was changed to Mitsubishi Shōkai (Mitsubishi Commercial Company) in 1873 and then to Mitsubishi Kisen Kaisha (Mitsubishi Steamship Company) in 1875. In 1874 the company prospered from exclusive government contracts to transport troops and provisions for a military expedition to Taiwan. It later gained control of numerous other shipping routes, including those to China, and greatly enlarged its number of ships. After the 1885 merger of Mitsubishi shipping concerns with those of a rival firm controlled by the Mitsui Company (q.v.), Iwasaki family interests gained control of some 80 percent of all ships in Japan. The shipping firm that resulted from the merger was called Nippon Yūsen Kaisha (NYK; "Japan Shipping Company"). Diversification first came in 1873 with acquisition of the Yoshioka Copper Mine. In 1881 the company acquired the Takashima Coal Mine. Other early ventures included money lending, warehousing, and real estate. After the death of Iwasaki Yatarō, the firm was led in its growth by Iwasaki Yanosuke (1851–1908), Yatarō's younger brother, and then by Iwasaki Koyata (1879–1945). In 1920s and 1930s the firm expanded into heavy industry, including the manufacture of ships and aircraft for Japan's military build-up before World War II. In 1937 Mitsubishi Ltd. was reorganized as a joint-stock company.

The name "Mitsubishi" means "three diamond shapes." It is taken from the design of the Iwasaki family crest.

MITSUBISHI LONDONTOWN (See LONDON BLOCK)

MITSUKOSHI DEPARTMENT STORES (See DEPARTMENT STORES; ECHIGOYA)

MITSUI. The name of one of the oldest and largest commercial empires in Japan. It began in 1673 as a chain of dry goods stores in Kyoto and Edo (q.v.) founded by Mitsui Takatoshi (q.v.). In Edo the chain was called Echigoya (q.v.), the predecessor of the Mitsukoshi department stores chain (see DEPARTMENT STORES). The firm soon branched into money lending and currency exchange. In 1691 it became the official transmitter of tax collections for the Tokugawa Shogunate (q.v.). It maintained close ties to government during the Meiji Period (q.v.) and grew to become the largest of Japan's powerful *zaibatsu* (q.v.). Its foundations were in banking, trading, and mining. In 1892 the Mitsui enterprises were reorganized as a limited partnership that was separated from Mitsui family affairs and then reorganized again in the early 20th century as joint-stock companies. At the end of World War II, the Mitsui *zaibatsu* controlled 273 companies. This arrangement was broken up during the Occupation (q.v.) of Japan after the war. It was later reconstituted as an enterprise grouping *(keiretsu)*. Its major concerns are headquartered in Tokyo and include banking (Sakura Bank), construction, mining, shipping and shipbuilding, insurance, trading, and retailing.

MITSUI TAKATOSHI (1622–1694). Extremely successful merchant of the Edo Period (q.v.) and founder of the Mitsui (q.v.) commercial empire. He was born in Ise Province (now Mie Prefecture), where his father, also named Mitsui Takatoshi (but with different Chinese characters for the given name), was a *sake* merchant and pawnbroker. The son's initial fortune came from lending money and selling rice. In 1673 he opened dry goods stores named Echigoya (q.v.) in Kyoto and Edo (q.v.). The stores prospered because of innovative sales practices. Mitsui then entered banking, currency exchange and other financial fields. The businesses that Mitsui set up were divided among many sons. They evolved into the Mitsui commercial empire, one of the largest and most powerful of Japan's *zaibatsu* (q.v.).

MORI, TAIKICHIRŌ (1904–1993). Major land developer and office building magnate in Tokyo. He began his career in academics rising to the rank of professor and dean of the faculty of commerce at Yokohama City University. In 1959 he turned to the real estate business and established the Mori Building Company to develop land in the Tora-nomon section of Tokyo (Minato Ward), where his family had owned farmland. By the time of his death his empire had grown to 80 office buildings in downtown Tokyo, many of them named *Mori Biru* (Mori Building) and numbered in sequence of construction. These holdings also included the Ark Hills complex in Roppongi (q.v.; Minato Ward). The U.S. business magazine *Forbes* named him the world's richest person in 1991 and 1992.

MORSE, EDWARD SYLVESTER (See ŌMORI SHELL MOUNDS)

MUKŌJIMA. Meaning the "island on the other side," Mukōjima is the name for the district of Edo (q.v.) that was on the far side (east bank) of the Sumida River (q.v.) from the main part of the city. It is a district of Sumida Ward today.

During the early Edo Period (q.v.) Mukōjima was an area of rice paddies and vegetable gardens. It was also a falconry area favored by the *shōguns (q.v.)*. Tokugawa Yoshimune (q.v.), the eighth *shōgun* (ruling from 1716 to 1745) had cherry trees planted along the river bank. This helped to make Mukōjima a popular place for outings among the citizens of Edo. Many visitors came by ferry and combined trips to Mukōjima with outings to Asakusa (q.v.), directly across the river, or to the Yoshiwara (q.v.) pleasure quarter. In the late Edo Period (e.g., the start of the 19th century), Mukōjima became a haunt for the city's writers, artists, and other intellectuals who gathered in the teahouses and temples of the area. It is from their activities that a pilgrimage circuit dedicated to the Seven Deities of Good Fortune *(shichifukujin)* was put together in Mukōjima. The circuit connects seven temples and shrines in the area. It continues as a popular activity today, particularly during the first week of a new year. In the Meiji Period (q.v.), Mukōjima became a manufacturing area. Its leading industry was textiles. The district was badly damaged by the Great Kantō Earthquake (q.v.) of 1923 and the air raids of 1945 (q.v.).

MULTICORE METROPOLIS (See SUBCENTERS)

MUSASHI PROVINCE. Historic province established in 646

as part of a broad administrative reform known as the Taika Reform. It was one of 15 provinces that were established at that time in central Japan, covering what is now Tokyo, Saitama, and eastern Kanagawa provinces. From the 12th century until 1590 it was ruled successively by various families: the Minamoto family, the Hōjō family, the Uesugi family, and the "Later Hōjō" family. In 1603 the territory came under the authority of Edo (q.v.).

– N –

NAGAI KAFŪ (1879–1959). Writer of numerous novels, stories, and essays, noted mostly for his descriptions of 19th-century Tokyo and nostalgia for the styles and traditions of Edo (q.v.) that were fast disappearing with modernization. His major work is the novel *Bokutō kidan,* written in 1937 and translated in 1958 as *A Strange Tale from East of the River.* It is the story of Ōe Tadasu, an aging writer who enjoys escaping the modern city by immersing himself in one of Tokyo's traditional pleasure districts. Other titles include *Udekurabe* (1916–17), *Okamezasa* (1918), *Ame shōshō* (1922), and *Tsuyu no atosaki* (1931). Early in his career he traveled to the United States and France and published collections of stories from both countries, *America monogatari* (1908) and *Furansu monogatari* (1909), respectively.

Nagai Kafū was born in Tokyo as the eldest son of an important bureaucrat. His real name was Nagai Sōkichi. He studied for a short time in the Chinese language department of the Tokyo School of Foreign Languages, as well as in the United States at Kalamazoo College. From 1910 he was a professor of literature at Keiō Gijuku, the forerunner of Keiō University (q.v.), where he edited a literary magazine called *Mita Bungaku.* He enjoyed immense popularity during his career, and he received the Order of Culture in 1952.

NAGATACHŌ. A district of Chiyoda Ward, central Tokyo, that is known for its many offices and institutions related to Japan's central government (see KASUMI-GASEKI). Among other important structures, it houses the National Diet Building (q.v.), the Office of the Prime Minister, and the Prime Minister's Official Residence. It also has the offices of members of the Diet, headquarters buildings of Japan's major political parties, and the Hie Shrine (q.v.). In the Edo Period (q.v.), the area had mansions of feudal lords (*daimyō*; q.v.).

NAGAYA. A type of residential building that was common in Edo (q.v.) and other Japanese cities during the Edo Period (q.v.). It was a one-story, woodframe row house with, as the word *nagaya* indicates, a long roof line. Individual *nagaya* housed up to ten families in separate apartment units, each with its own doorway. The apartments were small. Units usually had a small kitchen with an earthen floor and one other room that was floored with *tatami* (straw mats). Water and toilet facilities were outdoors and were shared. *Omote nagaya* were *nagaya* that faced larger streets, while *ura nagaya* were buildings of this type that were along back alleys. Most *nagaya* from the Edo Period have long since disappeared from Tokyo, having been destroyed in the city's many fires (q.v.) and other disasters, or cleared away in connection with urban renewal efforts. However, some neighborhoods in Tokyo still have some newer *nagaya*-type structures that were erected as temporary housing during the housing shortage after World War II.

NAKAMURA KANZABURŌ. The professional name used by one of the leading families of *kabuki* actors in Edo (q.v.) and Tokyo. The family line was started by Kanzaburō I (1598–1658), who established an acting troupe and theater called the Nakamura-za. The name Kanzaburō is held by successive leaders of the acting troupe. Kanzaburō XVII

(1909–1988) was designated a Living National Treasure in 1975 and received the Order of Culture in 1980.

NAKASENDŌ (See GOKAIDŌ)

NAMAZU-E. A particular kind of woodblock print that appeared in Edo (q.v.) in 1855 after the Ansei Edo Earthquake (q.v.). It sold well among the city's townspeople (see CHŌNIN). The prints depicted catfish *(namazu)*, which were believed to live beneath the earth and to cause earthquakes through their movements. Some prints faulted the catfish for having brought destruction to the city, while others treated the catfish as a blessing that brought restoration work to carpenters, plasterers, and other artisans. (see UKIYO-E)

NANUSHI. Generally translated as "neighborhood chief." The word also means village chief, particularly in the Kantō Plain during the Edo Period (qq.v.). (The word for village chief in the Kansai region was *shōya*, while in northern Japan the preferred term was *kimoiri*.) In the early 17th century there were *nanushi* in only a few neighborhoods of Edo (q.v.), but because of rapid population growth and attendant conflicts between neighbors, their number increased to over 250 by the early 18th century. The position became a hereditary one. Because Edo had well over 1,000 distinct residential quarters, relatively few *nanushi* had responsibilities for only one neighborhood. Instead, it was common for one person to be chief of several places at once. The duties of a *nanushi* typically included mediating neighborhood disputes, maintaining a twice annual census for each quarter, supervising festivals, investigating the causes of fires and supervision of fire fighting squads, and verifying details about various petitions, property transactions, and other official matters involving individuals within the area of jurisdiction.

NARITA AIRPORT (See NEW TOKYO INTERNATIONAL AIRPORT)

NATIONAL DIET BUILDING *(kokkai-gijido)*. The building that houses Japan's parliament (Diet). It is a Western style building modeled after statehouses in Europe and the U. S. that is located in the Nagatachō (q.v.) district of Chiyoda Ward in central Tokyo. It is one of the main landmarks of Tokyo. There are separate wings for the House of Councilors *(Sangiin)* and the House of Representatives *(Shūgiin)* on either side of a central tower made of gray granite. Construction began in 1920 and lasted until 1937. The architects were Ōkuma Yoshikuni and Yabashi Kenkichi.

NEW SHIMABARA. The name of a licensed quarter (regulated pleasure district) that was opened in 1869 by the new government of Japan in the Tsukiji (q.v.) area of Tokyo (see MEIJI RESTORATION). It was near the Hoterukan (q.v.) and was intended for the pleasure of Tokyo's recently arrived foreign residents. However, few foreigners actually used it, and the place was closed after a little more than one year of operation. The name "New Shimabara" was taken from the famous Shimabara pleasure quarter of Kyoto.

NEW SHINJUKU CITY CENTER *(Shin Toshin Shinjuku)*. A large redevelopment project on the west side of Shinjuku Station in the Shinjuku (q.v.) commercial district, Shinjuku Ward; part of the largest designated subcenter (q.v.) in the Tokyo metropolitan area. It was built on the site of an outmoded water filtration plant (the Yodobashi Waterworks) and some adjacent blocks, and is distinguished as the largest concentration of high-rise office and hotel buildings in Tokyo. Several of the city's tallest buildings are in this district, including the headquarters building of Tokyo Metropolitan Government (q.v.), the city's tallest building. It opened in 1991. The redevelopment project was first announced in June 1960. The first high-rise building was the Keiō Plaza Hotel, completed in 1971. Other noteworthy buildings are the Shinjuku Sumitomo Building, the Shinjuku Mitsui Building, the Yasuda Fire and Marine Insurance Company head office, the Shinjuku Nomura Building, the Shinjuku Center Building, and the Hilton, Century-Hyatt and Washington Hotels, all opened in the 1970s and 1980s. The Shinjuku Park Tower Building opened in 1994 (see TANGE KENZO). The skyline of New Shinjuku City Center is widely recognized in Japan and serves a principal symbol of Tokyo.

NEW TOKYO INTERNATIONAL AIRPORT *(Shin Tōkyō kokusai kūkō).* Tokyo's major international airport. It is located about 66 kilometers (41 miles) east of Tokyo in Narita, Chiba Prefecture, and is also known as Narita Airport. It opened in May 1978 and replaced Tokyo International Airport (q.v.), which had become too small. Access to Tokyo is by the Keisei and Narita rail lines, as well as by limousine bus service and taxi. More than 20 million passengers pass through New Tokyo International Airport each year.

The airport has been a source of controversy ever since it opened. Passengers complain that it is too far from the center of Tokyo and that travel there is both costly and time-consuming. There are also complaints about crowding at the airport itself, poor design, and inadequate facilities. Specific problems include cramped, uncomfortable waiting lounges, an insufficient variety of shops and restaurants, and expensive parking. Many foreign travelers dislike Narita Airport because of long lines at immigration check points. The airport has also been criticized for having high landing fees. In addition, the airport has been plagued by a long-standing conflict with farmers in the surrounding area who argue that the facility should never have been built without their approval and that land for the airport was taken unfairly from previous owners. Some farmers and their political supporters have waged a small war against the airport since construction began in the 1970s, with occasional bombing attacks and other guerilla tactics. As a result, the airport is heavily fortified, and all passengers must pass through strict security procedures. Opinion polls of frequent air travelers consistently rank New Tokyo International Airport near the bottom among the world's major airports.

NEZU. Historic district in the western part of Bunkyō Ward, Tokyo. It is noted for its many narrow streets lined with old wooden houses and small shops, and for a strong, community-based historic preservation movement. The area mostly survived the damage from the Great Kantō Earthquake of 1923 and the air raids of 1945 (qq.v.), with the result that it is one of the few places in the city that gives an authentic glimpse into the landscape of old Tokyo. Nezu is commonly thought of as a leftover bit of *shitamachi* (q.v.) because of the strong sense of neighborhood and history, although much of the area is actually on a slope and would be more properly identified with *yamanote* (q.v.). The Nezu Shrine is a famous landmark in the area.

NIHOMBASHI (BRIDGE). The word means "Japan Bridge." It refers to an historic wooden bridge that was first built in 1603 across one of the main canals of Edo (q.v.), now called the Nihombashi River. The bridge was the focus of early commerce in the city, and the starting point for highways leading from Edo to the provinces (see GOKAIDŌ; TŌKAIDŌ). A copper plaque on the bridge marked the point from which distances were measured along Japan's roads. The current bridge was built in 1911. It is a European Renaissance style structure with cast-iron lampposts, bronze Chinese lions, and other decorative touches. It is an important landmark in the city. An elevated expressway was constructed overhead in 1962 in preparation for the Tokyo Olympics (q.v.).

NIHOMBASHI (DISTRICT). Important commercial district in Chūō Ward, downtown Tokyo. It is named after an historic bridge that was built in 1603 (see NIHOMBASHI [Bridge]), and is considered to be the city's earliest commercial district. It began with a fish market that was opened at the foot of the bridge in 1603 to serve Edo Castle (q.v.), and soon expanded to include the shops of artisans and craftsmen and the offices of money changers. Today the district is noted for its several large department stores, offices of banks, securities firms, and other financial companies, and various other commercial and institutional uses. The Tokyo Stock Exchange (q.v.) is in the Kabutochō (q.v.) section of Nihombashi.

NIHON UNIVERSITY. A large private, coeducational university with main offices and a campus in Chiyoda Ward, Tokyo, and other campuses in many parts of Japan. Total enrollment exceeds 60,000 students. There are many academic departments in various branches of the sciences, social sciences, arts, humanities, medicine, law, engineering, agriculture, and other fields, as well as several prestigious research institutes. The university was founded in 1889 as *Nihon Hōritsu Gakkō* (Japan Law School) by Yamada Akiyoshi (1844–1892). It took its present name in 1903, receiving university status in 1920.

NIKOLAI CATHEDRAL. Cathedral of the Russian Orthodox Church in Japan and prominent landmark from the Meiji Period (q.v.) in the Kanda (q.v.) area of Chiyoda Ward, Tokyo. It was designed by Josiah Conder (q.v.) after designs by a Russian artist, and was constructed in 1884–1891. The formal name is *Tokyo Fukkatsu Dai*

Seidō; it is also called *Nikoraidō*. The cathedral is associated with Nikolai (Ioann Dmitrievich Kasatkin), a Russian Orthodox missionary who came to northern Japan in 1861, and then to Tokyo in 1872, to undertake missionary work. The building was badly damaged in the earthquake of 1923. It was restored under the direction of architect Okada Shin'ichirō, but on a smaller scale and with less ornamentation than the original.

NIKORAIDŌ (See NIKOLAI CATHEDRAL)

– O –

OCCUPATION (OCCUPATION OF JAPAN). The time after World War II when the United States and its allies controlled Japan and directed its affairs from a base in Tokyo. The Occupation lasted from 14 August 1945, the date of Japan's acceptance of the Potsdam Declaration, to 28 April 1952, the date of the San Francisco Peace Treaty. The supreme authority in Japan during this time was the Supreme Commander for the Allied Powers (see SCAP). From the start of the Occupation until April 1951 this person was General Douglas MacArthur (q.v.); after April 1951 the acronym SCAP referred to MacArthur's successor, General Matthew Ridgway, as well as to the supporting bureaucracy. General Headquarters of the Occupation (GHQ) was in the requisitioned Daiichi Insurance Company Building across the moats from the Imperial Palace (q.v.).

The objectives of the Occupation can be summarized under two headings. First was the demilitarization of Japan to prevent the country from waging war in the future. Among other measures, this involved demobilization of Japanese troops, destruction of military supplies and bases, and the banning of ultranationalist organizations. The second objective was democratization of Japan. To this end the Occupation called for the rise of competing political parties, the establishment of workers' movements and labor unions, changes in the form and content of education, land reform, and the dissolution of the *zaibatsu* (q.v.) economic empires. In 1947 a new constitution was formulated for Japan. After 1948 a major objective of the Occupation was to rebuild Japan as an Asian ally of the United States to counter the Soviet Union's increasing influence in China. At this time there was also a repression of left-wing political and labor movements in Japan.

OGASAWARA ISLANDS *(Ogasawara shoto).* Also known as the Bonin Islands. A group of volcanic islands approximately 1,000 kilometers (620 miles) south of Tokyo. They were occupied by the United States after World War II (see OCCUPATION) and were returned to Japan in 1968. Since then they have been administered by the Tokyo Metropolitan Government (q.v.). The population of approximately 2,300 lives mostly by farming.

OHTA ENZŌ (1881–1926). A civil engineer who was appointed director of the Civil Engineering Bureau by Gotō Shimpei (q.v.) after the Great Kantō Earthquake (q.v.) of 1923 and charged with overseeing the reconstruction of Tokyo after that disaster.

Ohta was born in Itō, Shizuoka Prefecture, and was educated in the engineering department at the Imperial University of Tokyo (see TOKYO UNIVERSITY). From 1910 to 1912 he studied in Europe and the United States. At the time of his appointment to the Civil Engineering Bureau, he was chief of civil engineering at the Construction Bureau of the Ministry of Railways. In reconstructing Tokyo, Ohta emphasized roads, bridges, parks, and other public facilities. He was especially interested in constructing fireproof bridges across the city's rivers and providing them with a pleasing design. Biographer

Shōji Sumie quotes Ohta as saying, "I can't die until I witness the completion of the bridges of the Sumida" (see SUMIDA RIVER). Ohta committed suicide in 1926. He left behind no note, but it is believed that he had been distressed by having too much work and by budget cuts and political maneuvering that interfered with his reconstruction targets.

ŌKUMA SHIGENOBU (1838–1922). One of the foremost statesmen of the Meiji Period (q.v.). He held a number of posts in national government during his long career, including overlapping appointments as Finance Minister, Home Minister, and Foreign Minister and Prime Minister (1898 and again in 1914). His direct impact on Tokyo included leadership in the construction of the Tokyo-Yokohama railway (Japan's first; see YOKOHAMA) and establishment of a mint in the city. In 1882 he founded *Tokyo Semmon Gakkō* (Tokyo College), the forerunner of Waseda University (q.v.).

OLYMPIC GAMES (See TOKYO OLYMPICS)

ŌMETSUKE. Translated as "inspectors general," these were officials in the bureaucracy of the Tokugawa Shogunate (q.v.) who were responsible for conducting investigations and recommending solutions to a wide variety of difficult matters that concerned the government. They also undertook surveillance of individuals and institutions that were thought to be possible threats to the shogunate. These included Christians and certain *daimyō* (q.v.). The position was established in 1632 by the third *shōgun*, Tokugawa Iemitsu (qq.v.), as part of his campaign to consolidate the power of the shogunate. He designated four *ōmetsuke* from the membership of *hatamoto* (q.v.) of relatively high rank. These individuals worked independently and made recommendations to *rōjū* (q.v.), the "senior councilors" to whom they reported.

ŌMORI SHELL MOUNDS. An important archaeological site in Ōta and Shinagawa Wards, near the original waterfront of Tokyo. It was excavated in 1877 by Edward Sylvester Morse (1838–1925), an American zoologist who became a professor at Tokyo University (q.v.). The digs included pottery, stone tools, bone articles, and skeletal remains from the late Jōmon period (ca 2000 BC–ca 1000 BC), an early hunting and gathering civilization in Japan.

ŌMURA HIKOTARŌ (See SHIROKIYA)

ŌOKA TADASUKE (1677–1751). Also known by the title Ōoka Echizen-no-Kami, he was a powerful city magistrate or city commissioner (*machi bungyō*; q.v.) in Edo (q.v.) for 45 years starting in 1717. He was appointed to the position by Tokugawa Yoshimune (q.v.), the eighth *shōgun*. Yoshimune became impressed with Ōoka when he observed his skills as a young commissioner in Yamada, a town in Yoshimune's fief in Kii province, now Wakayama Prefecture. Ōoka became the principal architect of the Kyōhō economic reforms (1716–1736), as well as the major force behind reorganization of the system of fire fighting in Edo (see FIRES). As Edo magistrate, Ōoka developed an outstanding reputation for just decisions. The book *Ōoka seidan* is supposedly a record of his decisions, but it has been shown to contain many fabrications and other misinformation.

ŌSAKI NEW CITY (See SUBCENTERS)

ŌTA DŌKAN (1432–1486). A feudal warrior and vassal of the Ōgigayatsu branch of the Uesugi family who built a castle at Edo (q.v.; now Tokyo) in 1457. This act is commonly regarded as the beginning of Tokyo's history; Dōkan is considered to be the city's founder. The castle was not especially impressive and was somewhat run-down by 1590, when Tokugawa Ieyasu (q.v.) arrived on the scene and began to greatly expand the structure (see EDO CASTLE). During an armed conflict between two branches of the Uesugi family, Dōkan was falsely accused of being disloyal to his lord and was killed.

ŌTA NAMPO (1749–1823). Popular poet and fiction writer during the Edo Period (q.v.), known especially for his humorous satires of the society of Edo (q.v.). Much of his writing was in the form of *kyōka*, meaning "mad verse," a comic poetry style, and *kyōshi*, "wild Chinese-style poetry," which he wrote under his real name, Ōta Tan. His best-known collection of *kyōka* was *Manzai kyōkashū*, published in 1783. A second collection of *kyōka* called *Shokusan hyakushu* was published in 1818. His first *kyōshi* collection was *Neboske sensei bunshū* ("Literary Works of Master Groggy"), a humorous critique of Edo society published in 1767. Nampo is also known for the collection of essays called *Ichiwa ichigen* published between 1775 and 1820.

ŌTEMACHI. A major commercial district in Chiyoda Ward in downtown Tokyo. It is home to many large corporations, particularly newspapers and communications companies, and to government agencies. The name of the district is from Ōtemon, a gate to the nearby Imperial Palace (q.v.).

ŌTSUKI GENTAKU (1757–1827). A physician and leading intellectual figure in Edo (q.v.) during the middle Edo Period (q.v.). He is especially known as a scholar of *rangaku* or Dutch learning, in which he brought knowledge about medicine, world geography, and other sciences to Japan from the western world. His major work is *Rangaku kaitei*, "A Ladder to Dutch Learning," published in 1788. Other publications include a work on anatomy and dissection and an atlas of the world.

OZAKI YUKIO (1858–1954). Major figure in Japanese politics from early in the Meiji Period (q.v.) until after World War II. He was elected to the House of Representatives 25 consecutive times beginning in 1890. While Ozaki was a supporter of Japan's expansionism during the Sino-Japanese War (1894–1895), he also advocated democratic domestic policies such as constitutional government and universal suffrage. During the 1930s he spoke up against the rise of military power in Japan.

From 1903–1912 Ozaki served as mayor of Tokyo. During his administration many improvements were made to physical infrastructure in Tokyo and to living conditions in some of the worst neighborhoods. He is also remembered for sending 3,000 cherry tree seedlings to Washington, D.C.

– P –

PERRY, MATTHEW CALBRAITH (1794–1858). Distinguished American naval officer who "opened" Japan to world trade in 1854. He was born in Newport, Rhode Island, and at age 15 enlisted as a midshipman on a vessel commanded by his brother, William Hazard Perry. He served in the War of 1812 and was an officer on a ship that help found Liberia as an African refuge for freed slaves from the United States. His first command was the *Concord*, which he took to Russia in 1830 to deliver the U.S. envoy. Other assignments included directorship of the first school of naval gunnery aboard the steamship *Fulton II*, command of the African Squadron in 1843 to eliminate the slave trade, command of the *Mississippi* on the gulf coast of Mexico during the Mexican War (1846–1848), and supervision of the construction of mail ships in the New York navy yard from 1848 to 1852.

In 1852 Perry was selected to command the U.S.

naval mission to Japan. His charge was to arrange for a treaty that would open trade between the United States and Japan, provide for the purchase of coal for U.S. steamships, and assure the safety in Japan of ship-wrecked American sailors. He arrived in Edo Bay (now Tokyo Bay; q.v.) on 8 July 1853 with a squadron of four ships, referred to now as the "black ships" *(kuroi fune)*, and presented his own credentials and a letter from U.S. President Millard Fillmore. He then departed for China, where he waited until his return in February 1854 for an answer from Japan. On both voyages his vessels made an impressive show of force and technology. This enabled Perry to secure the favorable terms of the Kanagawa Treaty on 31 March 1854. Among other provisions, the treaty granted trading rights in Japan to the United States and access to ports in Hakodate and Shimoda. In 1856 Perry published a record of his expedition, *Narrative of the Expedition of an American Squadron to the China Seas and Japan.*

POLLUTION (See ENVIRONMENTAL PROTECTION)

POST-STATION TOWNS (*shukuba machi*; sometimes *shukueki*). Officially regulated settlements that catered to travelers along the larger roadways of historic Japan. The earliest post-station towns date back to the Nara Period (710–794). Those in the Tokyo area were founded during the Edo Period (q.v.) along the Gokaidō (q.v.), the five highways that radiated from Edo to the provinces. The towns served *daimyō* (q.v.) and their entourages as they traveled to fulfill *sankin kōtai* (q.v.) obligations, providing them with food, lodging, and entertainment. Examples of Tokyo districts that developed initially as post-station towns include Shinjuku (q.v.) on the Kōshu Kaidō, Senju (q.v.) on the Nikkō Kaidō, and Shinagawa (q.v.) on the Tōkaidō (q.v.).

– R –

RECREATION (See LEISURE)

RELOCATION OF THE CAPITAL. Tokyo has been capital of Japan since 1868 (see TOKYO). However, there has been much public discussion about the possibility of moving the national capital functions from the city, either completely or in part, since 1964, when the city began entering a new phase of its growth and development after reconstruction following World War II. This is because Tokyo is widely regarded to be too big and overcrowded, because land prices (q.v.) are excessively high, and because of the city's vulnerability to earthquakes (q.v.; see "THE TOKYO PROBLEM"). The need to promote economic development in parts of Japan that are lagging is also a reason why many people, especially residents of these poorer regions, favor relocation of the capital.

A special panel of 32 members, including academics, representatives of the business community, and members of the Diet, was established by the Prime Minister's office in late March 1993 to study capital relocation. The panel is chaired by Osamu Uno, former chairman of the Kansai Economic Federation. One of the panel's major reports has recommended that a "legislative city" be constructed somewhere in Japan outside Tokyo to house the Diet and various ministries that would be relocated from their present headquarters. This new city would have a population of about 100,000 and be surrounded by satellite cities, also new, that would have a total of as many as 500,000 additional residents. Representatives from various locations in Japan, ranging from the northern part of the Kantō Plain (q.v.) near Tokyo to remote regions in Tōhoku, northeast of Honshū Island, have proposed possible locations for the new capital. However, some observers of the debate doubt that the capital will ever leave Tokyo. They point out that relocation of the capital has been discussed for more than 30 years, but little has happened except for talk and the production of thick reports. Tokyo has continued to grow during this period, increasing rather than decreasing its hold on the economy and political life of the nation.

RICE RIOTS. Three times during the Edo Period (q.v.) and once early in the 20th century the population of Edo (q.v.) or Tokyo rioted over shortages of rice, the staple food, and high prices. All four episodes had counterparts in other cities and in the countryside of Japan, and reflected widespread dissatisfaction with the lot of peasants and urban commoners in times of economic hardship and crop failure.

The first riot occurred in 1733 in conjunction with failures of the rice crop that began in 1732. It was directed specifically at the shop of one particular merchant, Takama Denbei, who was accused of hoarding rice. The riot was small in scale and erupted at Denbei's shop in the heart of the city after negotiations about the price of rice broke down between neighborhood chiefs (see NANUSHI) representing Edo citizens and city magistrates. The next riot, in mid-1787, also came at a time of crop failure. It lasted for about one month until rice was brought to the city and distributed free to hungry citizens. The rioting erupted in the various sections of Edo where the poor lived: Asakusa (q.v.), Honjo, and Fukagawa, and spread quickly to the center of the city and other districts. Again the targets of the rioting were rice merchants who were accused of hoarding grain. In contrast to 1733, there were thousands of rioters and many shops that were smashed (see UCHIKOWASHI). Only merchants who who gave away rice to the rioters escaped destruction. Although there were no deaths, the damage to property was enormous. In seeking an explanation for what transpired, rioters and officials alike blamed supernatural forces such as *tengu*, a half-man, half-bird creature. One result of this rioting was the establishment in 1792 of the first institutions in Edo to assist the poor in times of financial hardship. (see MACHI KAISHO)

The third Edo riot took place in 1866. It too was triggered by high commodity prices. It originated in Fukagawa and soon spread to nearby districts and then to other areas of the city. The rioters' targets included not only shops and rice warehouses, but also shops that handled imported goods of all kinds. There was one instance of stone-throwing at the American consul to Japan. This combination of targets reflected the fact that poor citizens linked their inability to afford rice to the presence in the city of increasing numbers of foreigners. The 20th-century rice riot occurred in mid-August 1918. It had spread to the city from the Sea of Japan coast, and appeared first as a disorderly rally in Hibiya Park (q.v.) on the night of 13 August. In the next days, rioting occurred in various commercial districts in the center of Tokyo, Asakusa, Ueno (qq.v.), and other districts. There were more than 1,000 arrests.

RICKSHAW *(jinriksha)*. Also ricksha, jinriksha, and jinricksha. The word comes from *jinri,* meaning manpower, and *sha,* meaning vehicle. It was a form of transportation in Tokyo and other Japanese cities that was common during the Meiji Period (q.v.). It was a small two-wheeled passenger carriage that was pulled by a man. It replaced the palanquin *(kago),* a boxlike enclosure on poles that was carried by two or more men. The rickshaw is said to have been invented in 1869 in Tokyo by three Japanese men who were inspired by the horse-drawn carriages that foreigners had introduced to the country. In the 1870s as many as 50,000 rickshaws were working the streets of Tokyo. Initially these vehicles were for two passengers, but after 1887 the one-passenger vehicle became more common. Most rickshaws had a folding cover that could shelter passengers from rain. Rickshaws were replaced by the automobile after the Great Kantō Earthquake (q.v.) of 1923. They are no longer used.

RIKKYŌ UNIVERSITY. A large university located in Toshima Ward, Tokyo. It was founded in 1874 in the Tsukiji district (q.v.) by Channing Moore Willams, an Episcopal missionary, and was called St. Paul's School. It relocated to its present site in 1918. In 1922 it was given university status.

RIOT OF 1918 (See RICE RIOTS)

RIVER CITY 21 (See WATERFRONT DEVELOPMENT)

RŌJŪ. Generally translated as "senior councilor." These were top-level officials in the bureaucracy of the shogunate, with wide authority for policy making, legislation, and supervision of all lands, cities, and towns in the domain of the *shōgun*. They were specifically responsible for all religious establishments, the imperial court, and the other officials, including the *machi bugyō* of Edo (qq.v.) and other cities. There were usually four or five *rōjū* at one time, usually chosen from within the ranks of *fudai daimyō* (q.v.). They alternated routine duties from month to month, but met together as a council to deliberate difficult matters.

ROKUMEIKAN. A two-story brick building built between 1881 and 1883 in the Hibiya section of Tokyo that was a major stage for westernization in the early Meiji Period (q.v.). It was the site of many balls and various social events attended by prominent Japanese and foreigners, and the place where many Western fashions were introduced to Japan. The architect was Josiah Conder (q.v.). The building was of Italianate style, and included a ballroom, billiard room, music room, reading room, and Western style guest suites. Its political purpose, inspired by Inoue Kaoru (q.v.), was to protest the so-called Unequal Treaties by demonstrating that Japanese could mix on an equal basis with foreigners. When this strategy ended in failure, and when some of the novelty of its activities wore off, the Rokumeikan was converted into the Peers' Hall *(Kazoku Kaikan)* in 1890, and later the offices of an insurance company. It was torn down in 1941. The word "Rokumeikan" has been translated as "Deer Cry Pavilion" or "House of the Cry of the Stag."

ROPPONGI. A district in Minato Ward, Tokyo, that is noted for its nightlife and cosmopolitan atmosphere. It was an elite residential area during the Meiji Period (q.v.) as well as a base of the Imperial Japanese Army. During the Occupation (q.v.) of Japan, the area housed a U.S. Army base. Roppongi's role as a hub of bars and nightclubs is traced to this foreign military presence. The area continues to attract many foreigners because it is close to the offices of many foreign businesses, embassies, and foreign residential enclaves. In addition to its nightlife, Roppongi is noted for having many fine restaurants and cafes, art galleries, boutiques and other shops.

RYŌGOKU. Historic district of Tokyo on the east bank of the Sumida River (q.v.). Much of its development is tied to construction of the Ryōgoku Bridge (q.v.) after the Meireki Fire (q.v.) in 1657 to connect the central wards of Edo (q.v.) with this less developed area, as well as to the construction of Ekōin, a temple near the Ryōgoku end of the bridge where corpses from the fire were taken. To help generate revenue, the temple was allowed to hold *sumō* wrestling events on its grounds. Ryōgoku continues as a *sumō* district to this day. The neighborhood is home to the Kokugikan (q.v.), the city's *sumō* wrestling stadium, as well as a *sumō* museum, several *sumō* stables and training facilities, and a thriving tourist business based on *sumō*. The area is also the site of the Edo-Tokyo Museum (q.v.). The word "Ryōgoku" means "two countries," i.e., the feudal provinces of Musashi (q.v.) and Shimōsa, which the bridge connected.

RYŌGOKU BRIDGE *(Ryōgokubashi)*. Historic span across the Sumida River built in 1657 after the Meireki Fire (q.v.). Its purpose was to connect the crowded wards of Edo (q.v.) with less developed land on the other side of the river so that the city could expand, as well as to provide an escape from the central city in case of fire (see FIRES). A firebreak at the west end of the bridge developed as *Ryōgoku Hirokōji*, an extremely popular amusement quarter *(sakariba;* q.v.) for the citizens of Edo (q.v.). The present Ryōgoku Bridge was built in 1922. (see RYŌGOKU)

RYŌUNKAKU (See ASAKUSA TWELVE STORIES)

– S –

SAKAI TOSHIHIKO (1871–1933). Journalist and one of the pioneers in socialist movements in Japan. He was born in Fukuoka Prefecture. From 1899 to 1903 he was a writer with the Tokyo-based newspaper *Yorozu chōhō,* where he distinguished himself for feature articles about politics and social problems. He left the newspaper to protest the editor's support for the Russo-Japanese War (1904–1905) and founded an antiwar, socialist organization named *Heiminsha* ("Society of Commoners") and its newspaper, *Heimin shimbun.* In 1906 he was one of the founders of the Japan Socialist party *(Nihon shakaitō).* In 1922 he was one of the founders of the Japan Communist Party *(Nihon kyōsantō).* In 1931 Sakai joined the National Labor-Farmer Masses Party

(Zenkoku rōnō taishūtō).

Sakai involved himself in city as well as national politics. In 1929 he was elected to the Tokyo Metropolitan Assembly. In the campaign for that office and afterwards, he championed social causes on behalf of the city's poor residents and workers. In particular, he advocated policies such as progressive taxes and taxes on increased land value, and projects such as low-cost hospitals and day-care centers. He was especially critical of what he regarded as "backroom" politics in Tokyo, urging that political decision making in the city be brought out into the open. To this end on 10 June 1929 he started the newspaper *Proletarian Citizen* to keep citizens informed about the daily activities of the Metropolitan Assembly. Another of Sakai's notable campaigns was to control the rise in gas rates in the city, which had become burdensome for many households and small businesses.

SAKARIBA. Often translated as "amusement quarters," "entertainment districts," or "popular spots," these were areas in Edo (q.v.) where large numbers of people of all social ranks gathered to eat, drink and be entertained. The entertainment included at various times and places storytellers, children's theater, musicians, jugglers, women's *sumō,* and other attractions. There were quite a few *sakariba* in Edo, the largest ones being Ryōgoku Hirokōji near the Ryōgoku Bridge (q.v.) and Okuyama in Asakusa (q.v.). Most other large *sakariba* were also located at bridges, at open spaces created as firebreaks, and at temple grounds. The word *sakariba* is used to today to refer to popular night-spots in Tokyo such as Kabukichō in Shinjuku, Akasaka, and Roppongi (qq.v.).

SAMURAI. The hereditary class of elite feudal warriors. The word means "one who serves" and refers to the loyalty that these warriors gave to their lords. Also called *bushi,* or "military gentry." The origins of *samurai* date back before the 10th century. They became particularly influential after 1192 when Minamoto-no-Yoritomo, the victor in a five-year war between the Minamoto and Taira clans and founder of the Kamakura shogunate (1192–1333), established a military government under his direction as *shōgun (q.v.)*. The *samurai* class was less active during the peace of the Tokugawa Shogunate (1603–1867; q.v.), but maintained a high status. It was then that the *samurai* code of conduct, *bushidō,* or the "way of the warrior," was articulated as a vehicle for maintaining loyalty to their masters and preparedness for battle. A great many *samurai* resided in Edo (q.v.) because of requirements imposed by *sankin kōtai* (q.v.). *Samurai* lost their positions with fall of the Tokugawa Shogunate. Dissolution of the class occurred in 1873 and 1876 in conjunction with transformations that took place in the structure of both the military and the government in Japan. However, the descendants of *samurai* enjoyed distinction as a hereditary class called *shizoku* until 1947 when the practice was abolished during the Occupation of Japan (q.v.).

SANJA FESTIVAL *(Sanja matsuri).* A major annual festival held on the third weekend in May at Asakusa Shrine (see SENSŌJI) and the streets of the Asakusa (q.v.) district. Among the highlights is the parading of more than 100 portable shrines *(mikoshi).* (see KANDA FESTIVAL; SANNŌ FESTIVAL)

SANKIN KŌTAI. A policy of the Tokugawa Shogunate (q.v.) that required territorial lords *(daimyō;* q.v.) to reside in alternate years or half-years in Edo (q.v.) and attend the *shōgun (q.v.).* The policy was made compulsory between 1635 and 1642 under the third *shōgun,* Tokugawa Iemitsu (q.v.). It stayed in force until 1862. The *shōguns* used this policy to exert control over the more than 260 *daimyō* under their rule. The *daimyō* were required to maintain residential estates called *hairyō yashiki* (q.v.) in Edo, where their wives and children lived permanently, and to make annual or biannual journeys between these estates and their domains. The journeys were made on the main highways under control of the shogunate (see GOKAIDŌ), and they required long processions of vassals and servants. The entourage of major *daimyō* often numbered in the thousands. The combination of estates in Edo and the costs of the processions typically consumed between 70 and 80 percent of a *daimyō's* income. One practical effect of *sankin kōtai* was to help swell the population of Edo and to increase demand in the city for housing and other commodities.

SANNŌ FESTIVAL *(Sannō matsuri)*. One of the three major festivals in Tokyo, the others being the Kanda Festival and the Sanja Festival (qq.v.). It is held at the Hie Shrine (q.v.) every other year in the second week of June, alternating with the Kanda Festival. Highlights include a parade through downtown Tokyo (Ginza; q.v.) that includes a sacred palanquin pulled by an ox, followed by a procession of portable shrines *(mikoshi)* and shrine parishioners dressed in traditional costumes.

SANYA. Neighborhood at the boundary of Taitō and Arakawa Wards that is sometimes described as Tokyo's closest equivalent to a slum. It is noted for the many day laborers, mostly middle-aged and older men, who live there in rooming houses, cheap hotels, and on the streets. Alcoholism is a major problem.

SCAP. Acronym for Supreme Commander for the Allied Powers *(Rengōkoku saikō shireikan)*, the chief executive of the Occupation (q.v.) of Japan by the Allied Powers (principally the United States) from 14 August 1945 to 28 April 1952. General Douglas MacArthur (q.v.) held the position from the start of the Occupation until he was relieved of command on 11 April 1951. His successor was General Matthew B. Ridgway. Both generals also served as Commanders in Chief of the U.S. Far East Command at the same time that they held the SCAP title. SCAP also referred to the general headquarters (GHQ) of the chief executive. Thus, an order that was said to have come from SCAP was both from the general in charge and from the bureaucracy that he commanded. During most of the Occupation, the headquarters building of SCAP was the Daiichi Insurance Building, located in downtown Tokyo directly across from the Imperial Palace (q.v.).

SEITŌSHA ("BLUESTOCKING SOCIETY"). Pioneering feminist organization based in Tokyo. It was founded in 1911 by Hiratsuka Raichō (q.v.) and others. It was dedicated to improving the condition of women in Japanese society. The organization was particularly effective in helping women enter professions such as education, nursing, the arts, and office work that until then had been open to men only. In September of 1911 the organization began publishing a magazine called *Seito* ("Bluestocking"). The publication had a goal of "developing women's talent," and featured literary works by and for women. The principal editor was Hiratsuka Raichō, but in January 1915 she turned the magazine over to Itō Noe (1895–1923). Itō published *Seito* until its last issue in February 1916. *Seitōsha* also disbanded in 1916.

SEKIGAHARA (See BATTLE OF SEKIGAHARA)

SENJU. An historic area of Tokyo at a crossing of the Sumida River (q.v.) in what is now Adachi Ward (Kita Senju) and Arakawa Ward (Minami Senju). The area developed as the first post-station town (q.v.) on the Ōshū Kaidō, one of the major early roads (see GOKAIDŌ) from Edo (q.v.). Its nucleus was Ōhasi, a "Great Bridge" that was built over the Sumida in 1594 under orders of Tokugawa

Ieyasu (q.v.). The bridge was so well constructed that it withstood many of Edo's floods and fires (q.v.). A flood finally swept it away in 1886. Senju was noted for many inns and brothels that served travelers. Today the area is mostly residential and light industrial, and the site of a large wholesale market. There are many historical markers as well.

SENJU WOOLEN MILL *(Senju seijūsho).* The first woolen mill in Japan. It was set up by the Meiji government in 1879 in the Senju district (q.v.) of Tokyo as a model factory for industrialization in Japan (see MEIJI PERIOD). The machinery and technical advisers were imported from Germany (see YATOI). Woolen cloth and military uniforms were the principal products. The mill produced wool until early in the 20th century.

SENSŌJI. Historic Buddhist temple in the Asakusa (q.v.) district of Taitō Ward. It is also called Asakusa Kannon; its formal name is Kinryūzan Sensōji. It is believed to be one of the two oldest temples in the Tokyo area, the other being Jindaiji (q.v.), west of the city proper. The original temple dates back to 628. It was opened to enshrine a small gilt statue of the *bodhisattva* Kannon, goddess of mercy, that two siblings, Hinokuma Hamanari and Hinokuma Takenari, are said to have found in their nets while fishing in the Sumida River. Over the centuries a succession of temples and other buildings has occupied the site, some of them constructed to replace structures that were destroyed by fire. One of the grandest rebuilding projects was ordered by Tokugawa Ieyasu (q.v.) in the first decade of the 17th century. The present main building of the temple was completed in 1958, erected to replace a structure that had been destroyed in the air raids of 1945 (q.v.). The statue of Kannon is said to be still on the site, buried deep beneath the temple.

In addition to the main hall of Sensōji, there are several other notable structures on the temple grounds. Asakusa Shrine (*Asakusa Jinja*) honors the memory of the two fishermen who found the statue and their lord, Haji-no-Nakamoto, who converted his house into the first temple, and is popularly known as the Shrine of the Three (*Sanja-sama*). Its original structure dates back to 1649, when it was ordered built by the third *shōgun*, Tokugawa Iemitsu (q.v.). Asakusa Shrine is the focus of the annual Sanja Festival (q.v.). Other important structures at Sensōji are a five-story pagoda, a temple named Awashima Myōjin that is dedicated to women's health, and two massive gates known for their sculptures and other ornamentation, Kaminarimon and Hōzōmon. The principal approach to the main hall is Nakamise-dōri, a narrow pedestrian lane that is lined on both sides with many small shops. In addition to the Sanja Festival, Sensōji and its grounds attract large crowds at the start of every new calendar year for *hatsumode* (New Year's temple visits), and an annual fair every 10 July, called *hōzuki ichi*, during which Chinese lantern plants are sold. Sensōji also attracts many tourists, both domestic and foreign.

SHATAKU. Apartment complexes that are built by individual companies for their workers. (see DANCHI)

SHIBASAKI. The name of a small fishing village that was a precursor of Edo (q.v.). It stood at the mouth of a river called the Hirakawa (since diverted to become part of the Nihombashi River), which emptied into Hibiya Inlet, once a part of Tokyo Bay. It probably dates before the 8th century. The site is now Ōtemachi (q.v.) in central Tokyo.

SHIBUSAWA EIICHI (1840–1931). Noted business leader and entrepreneur; a major figure in the establishment of modern industry in Japan after the Meiji Restoration (q.v.). He was born in the village of Chiaraijima in what is now Saitama Prefecture to a family of farmers. He left

home in 1863 to become a *samurai* attached to the Hitot-
subashi branch of the Tokugawa family (q.v.). In 1867–68
he traveled to France with a group headed by the
shōgun's younger brother, Tokugawa Akitake, as part of
Japan's delegation to the Paris International Exposition.
There he was impressed by Western business practices
and technology, and was determined to apply what he
learned to Japan. In 1869 he joined the Ministry of
Finance and played a key role in founding the Shōhō
Kaisho, one of the country's first joint-stock companies,
and in establishing the government-run Tomioka Silk-
Reeling Mill.

After resigning from the Ministry of Finance in 1873,
Shibusawa devoted himself to private business. He
became president of the forerunner of Dai-Ichi Kangyō
Bank and the Ōji Paper Company, and in 1882 organized
the Osaka Spinning Mill. He also advised on the organization of many other banks, both private and national, as
well as many industrial corporations. During his life-
time, he had a hand in founding more than 300 commercial enterprises in Tokyo and other cities, most of them
organized as corporations. He also contributed
immensely to enhancing the social respectability of business as a profession in Japan by showing that successful
businesses strengthened the country. For 38 years he
headed the Tokyo Chamber of Commerce.

In 1909 Shibusawa retired from direct involvement
with business and turned to philanthropy. He founded
schools and homes for the aged, and was involved in
various efforts to improve international relations
between Japan and the United States. He continued in
the role of adviser to Japanese commercial enterprises
until his death. A statue of Shibusawa Eiichi stands in
downtown Tokyo, amid the office towers and bank
headquarters in the Ōtemachi district (q.v.; see
DEN'ENCHŌFU).

SHIBUYA. Major commercial center on the west side of central Tokyo in Shibuya Ward. Also the name of one of the 23 Wards of the city. The commercial center emphasizes department stores, clothing and accessory stores, sporting goods, movie theaters, restaurants, and a variety of amusement arcades. It is especially popular among young people. (see SUBCENTERS)

SHIMBASHI (also *Shinbashi*). Commercial district near downtown Tokyo in Minato Ward. It is now primarily an area of office buildings with many small restaurants and drinking places that cater to a clientele of salarymen. In 1872 it was the terminus of the first passenger rail line in Tokyo. The area was also the site of a thriving *geisha* quarter through much of the Meiji and Taishō Periods (qq.v.).

SHIMOYAMA INCIDENT *(Shimoyama jiken)*. The term that refers to the violent death on 6 July 1949 of Shimoyama Sadanori (1900–1949), the president of the Japanese National Railways (JNR). His dismembered body was found along rail tracks in Adachi Ward (northern Tokyo) after it had been run over by a train. It has never been proven whether the death was murder or suicide. Shimoyama had been ordered by government and U.S. Occupation (q.v.) officials to fire 97,000 railroad workers as part of the postwar economic reform, and he had sent termination notices to 37,000 of those workers just two days before his death. The many people who suspect that Shimoyama was murdered believe that his death was revenge for the firings by members of the communist-oriented National Railway Workers' Union (NRWU).

The Shimoyama Incident was the first of three widely publicized incidents of violence related to the JNR in 1949. The second incident is known as the Mitaka Incident (q.v.), after the city in Tokyo Metropolis (q.v.) where it occurred. The third one took place in Matsukawa, Fukushima Prefecture, and is known as the Matsukawa Incident.

SHINAGAWA. Commercial district in Tokyo built around Shinagawa Station, southwest of the downtown in Minato Ward. Also the name of one of the 23 wards of Tokyo, located just south of Shinagawa Station. In the Edo Period the original Shinagawa (in today's Shinagawa Ward) was a post-station town on the Tōkaidō (qq.v.), the main highway connecting Edo (q.v.) with Kyoto. In the late 19th century the area became heavily industrialized, eventually specializing in the manufacture of electronics goods and machinery. Shinagawa Station is a major transportation node and a gateway to central Tokyo from the southwest.

SHINBASHI (See SHIMBASHI)

SHINJUKU. Major retailing and office center in Shinjuku Ward on the west side of Tokyo. Also the name of the principal commuter rail station that serves this center, and the name of one of the 23 wards of the city. The retailing center is one of the largest in Tokyo and features several prominent department stores, clothing and accessory stores, cameras and electronics, and various other goods. There are also many restaurants and drinking places, movie theaters, and other attractions. One part of Shinjuku, Kabukichō (q.v.), is well known for sex-related businesses. The west side of Shinjuku is an area of highrise office buildings and international hotels, including the offices of Tokyo Metropolitan Government (q.v.), which opened in 1991 (see NEW SHINJUKU CITY CENTER). Shinjuku's rise as a commercial center is traced to growth that took place there after the Great Kantō Earthquake (q.v.) of 1923, and to black markets that thrived in the area after World War II. (see DEPARTMENT STORES; SUBCENTERS)

SHINKANSEN (See BULLET TRAINS)

SHIN TOSHIN SHINJUKU (See NEW SHINJUKU CITY CENTER)

SHIROKIYA. The name of a famous shop in Edo (q.v.) that was the predecessor of the Tōkyū Department Store at what is today the main intersection in the Nihombashi (q.v.) section of Tokyo (see DEPARTMENT STORES). The word means "white tree house." The shop was founded on the main street in Nihombashi in 1662 by Ōmura Hikotarō, a merchant from Ōmi province who had earlier opened a lumber business in Kyoto. Initially Shirokiya sold personal accessories from Kyoto, but the business expanded to emphasize sale of high-quality silks and other textiles (see KUDARIMONO). In the Meiji Era (q.v.) Shirokiya was the first shop in Tokyo to have shop windows in the European style and the first to have a department selling European clothes.

SHITAMACHI. Historic district of Tokyo along the lower reaches of the Sumida River and along Tokyo Bay (qq.v.) near the mouth of the Sumida River. Much of it was reclaimed from marshes (see WATERFRONT DEVELOPMENT). The area dates back to early the Edo Period (q.v.). It is the district where the *chōnin* (q.v.) or "townspeople" resided in crowded quarters outside the perimeter of Edo Castle (q.v.) and kept their shops. As is suggested by the word *shitamachi* itself, which means "low city" or "downtown," the area is low-lying and flat. This is in contrast to the other "side" of historic Tokyo (or Edo), which was higher ground called *yamanote* (q.v.) and was associated with the mansions of feudal lords. There were no set boundaries for *shitamachi*, but the area is generally thought of as having comprised large parts (or all) of what today are Chūō, Taitō, Sumida, and Kōtō Wards. Kyoto and Osaka, as well as some other historic castle towns in Japan, had their own areas called *shitamachi.*

The *shitamachi* area of Tokyo played an enormously important role in the historical development of the city. It was where the city's first major commercial districts such as Nihombashi and Ginza (qq.v.) emerged, as well as the incubator for many of the city's early industrial enterprises. It was also the locus of the famous Asakusa and Yoshiwara pleasure quarters (qq.v.). In these areas especially, the district was the center of cultural life such as *kabuki* theater, *bunraku* puppet theater, *rakugo* story-telling, and the *ukiyo-e* (q.v.) woodblock print. Distinctive styles of dress, speech, and personal habits were associated with *shitamachi*. Even though there has been considerable change in *shitamachi* in modern times (i.e., since the end of the Edo Period), and almost none of the old buildings or streetscapes remain, the area is still thought of as Tokyo's principal historic district and the keeper of the city's old traditions. Many Tokyoites today enjoy exploring the *shitamachi* area, looking for vestiges of the past amid the modern city and attending neighborhood festivals and other celebrations that are linked to the history of Edo (q.v.).

SHŌGITAI. Loyal supporters of the deposed Tokugawa *shōgun* Yoshinobu (qq.v.) who banded together in March 1868 to resist imperial forces who were coming to Edo (q.v.) to take over the city. They numbered about 2,000 and held out at Kan'eiji temple in the Ueno district (qq.v.) even after the city surrendered in May 1868. On 4 July 1868 they were defeated in a bloody battle against the emperor's troops called the Battle of Ueno or the Ueno War *(Ueno Sensō).*

SHŌGUN. Term used to refer to the military dictators who ruled Japan for most of Japanese history between 1192 and 1867. The word is an abbreviation for *seii tai* *shōgun,* which is usually translated as "barbarian-subduing generalissimo." The regimes of *shōguns* were called *bakufu* (q.v.), or "tent governments," a word that is generally translated as "shogunate." There were three shogunates: in Kamakura between 1192 and 1333; in the Muromachi district of Kyoto between 1338 and 1573; and the Tokugawa Shogunate (q.v.) in Edo (q.v.) between 1603 and 1867.

SHŌHEIKŌ (See YUSHIMA SEIDŌ)

SHŌHEIZAKA INSTITUTE OF LEARNING (See YUSHIMA SEIDŌ)

SHŌRIKI MATSUTARŌ (1885–1969). Civic and business leader in Tokyo during much of the Shōwa Period (q.v.). He was born in Toyama Prefecture and came to Tokyo as a young man to study at Tokyo University (q.v.), from which he graduated. His career began in the bureaucracy of the Tokyo Metropolitan Police Department, but he resigned in 1924 after taking responsibility for the so-called Toranomon Incident, the attempted assassination on 27 December 1923 of the prince regent Hirohito. The same year he became president of the *Yomiuri Shimbun.* Under his leadership many innovations were added to this newspaper, and it grew to have the largest circulation in Japan. He founded the Yomiuri Giants baseball team (see TOKYO DOME) in 1934 and the first professional baseball league in Japan in 1936. Shōriki was also an early proponent of the expansion of television programming in Japan; in 1951 he founded the Nippon Television Network Corporation (NTV) and became its first president.

SHŌWA PERIOD *(Shōwa jidai).* The term that refers to the period when the Emperor Shōwa (Hirohito) reigned (1926–1989). The Shōwa Period followed the Taishō

Period (1912–1926; q.v.) and has been succeeded by the present imperial era, the Heisei Period (1989–). It was the longest reign of any emperor in Japanese history. The period began with an economic depression that was followed by the rise of Japanese militarism. Japan's defeat in World War II, the subsequent Occupation (q.v.) by Allied troops (1945–1952), and remarkable rebuilding from defeat also took place during the Shōwa Period. By the end of the Shōwa era, Japan was a major economic power in the world and an exceedingly wealthy nation. Tokyo grew to enormous size during the Shōwa Period and became one of the world's most influential cities.

SHUKUBA MACHI (See POST-STATION TOWNS)

SOPHIA UNIVERSITY. A private Roman Catholic coeducational university operated by the Jesuit order. It was founded in 1911 and has some 10,000 students. The main campus is located in the Yotsuya district of Chiyoda Ward. It is especially well known for its international division and many foreign students. The university is known as *Jochi daigaku* in Japanese.

SPORTS (See LEISURE)

STOCK EXCHANGE (See TOKYO STOCK EXCHANGE)

SUBCENTERS. A translation of the Japanese term *fukutoshin* ("secondary city center") that Tokyo Metropolitan Government (q.v.) has adopted for use in its publications in English about urban planning in Tokyo. It refers to busy commercial areas that are being developed at key commuter rail interchanges (see COMMUTING) in Tokyo Metropolis (q.v.) and neighboring Chiba, Kanagawa, and Saitama Prefectures to relieve crowding and reduce land prices (q.v.) in downtown Tokyo (see AKASAKA; GINZA; KABUTOCHŌ; KASUMIGASEKI;

MARUNOUCHI; NAGATACHŌ; NIHOMBASHI; ŌTEMACHI; TOKYO STATION). They are part of a master plan for the Tokyo area that has been developed by Tokyo Metropolitan Government planners under the administration of governor Suzuki Shunichi (q.v.) to transform the metropolis from a "unipolar structure" to a "multicore structure." Most subcenters are existing commercial districts in which expansion is being encouraged, while others are new and are being developed for the first time. Each subcenter has a central train and subway station surrounded by many commercial land uses. These include department stores (q.v.) and other shops, restaurants, movie theaters and other amusements, office buildings, hotels, and other businesses.

The innermost subcenters are located on or near the Yamanote Line (q.v.), the crowded rail loop that circumscribes much of Tokyo's downtown. The biggest subcenter is the commercial district of Shinjuku (q.v.). In order of decreasing size (as measured by numbers of passengers at the rail stations), the other subcenters on the Yamanote Line are Shibuya, Ikebukuro, and Ueno (qq.v.), followed by a new subcenter that has been built at Ōsaki Station on the Yamanote Line called Ōsaki New City. Other subcenters within Tokyo Metropolis (but not on the Yamanote Line) are at Asakusa (q.v.; linked in the plan to the subcenter at Ueno), Kinshichō-Kameido, Tachikawa, Ōme, Hachiōji, Machida, and Tama New Town (q.v.). There is also a subcenter being developed in Tokyo Bay (q.v.) called the Waterfront Subcenter or "Seaside City Subcenter" (see WATERFRONT DEVELOPMENT). Among the approximately 20 subcenters that have been designated outside Tokyo Metropolis are the downtown of Yokohama (q.v.), Yokohama's Minato Mirai 21 (see YOKOHAMA), Makuhari (Chiba Prefecture), the business center of Narita city (see NEW TOKYO INTERNATIONAL AIRPORT), and Tsukuba Science City (q.v.).

SUBWAYS *(chikatetsu)*. An extremely important network of commuter transportation lines underneath central Tokyo. There are 12 subways lines in all. Lines operated by the Tokyo Metropolitan Subways system (the "Toei Lines") are the Toei Asakusa Line, the Toei Mita Line, the Toei Shinjuku Line, and the new Toei No. 12 Line, still under construction. Subway lines operated by the Teito Rapid Transit Authority are the Chiyoda Line, Ginza Line, Hanzōmon Line, Hibiya Line, Marunouchi Line, Namboku Line, Tōzai Line, and Yūrakuchō Line. The total length of the subway system increases each year because of construction, and now adds up to at least 230.3 kilometers (143.1 miles). The usual number of passengers served exceeds eight million each day. Many of the commuters to central Tokyo arrive on trains from outlying residential areas and transfer to the subway system at interchange stations such as Shinjuku, Shibuya, Ueno, Asakusa (qq.v.), and others. (see COMMUTING)

The first subway line was the Ginza Line. It opened in 1927 and connected Ueno and Asakusa (2.2 kilometers; 1.4 miles). It has since been extended from Ueno to the central business district of Tokyo and then west to Shibuya. The Marunouchi Line was the next to be constructed, connecting Shinjuku and residential areas to the west with downtown Tokyo. Construction began in 1951. Construction is underway at present on the No. 12 Line under central Tokyo, as well as an extension of the Yūrakuchō Line to reclaimed land in Tokyo Bay (q.v.).

SUI (See IKI)

SUMIDA RIVER *(Sumidagawa)*. An important river in the eastern part of Tokyo. It originates in the Kantō Mountains and flows for 23.5 km (14.6 miles) to Tokyo Bay (q.v.). Its lower reaches are near the original site of Tokyo. The river flows through the *shitamachi* (q.v.) area of Tokyo, and it is associated strongly with Tokyo (or Edo; q.v.) history, notable historic bridges, and traditional leisure activities such as boating, cherry blossom viewing along the banks, and displays of fireworks.

SUMITOMO. One of Japan's most powerful business combines, now organized as an enterprise group *(keiretsu)* with some 80 member firms. Most of them have headquarters in either Tokyo or Osaka and maintain offices in both cities. Some of the largest members of the group include Sumitomo Bank, Sumitomo Corporation (a general trading company), Sumitomo Heavy Industries, and Sumitomo Realty and Development Company. The Sumitomo empire was founded in the early 17th century by Sumitomo Masatomo (1585–1652). Its early growth came from supplying copper to the Tokugawa Shogunate (q.v.) from its mines in Besshi, in what is now Ehime Prefecture. In the Meiji Period (q.v.), the company expanded into numerous other fields, especially various branches of manufacturing. As a result, it grew to become one of the three largest *zaibatsu* (q.v.) in the country. Like the other *zaibatsu,* it was disbanded during the post-World War II Occupation of Japan by U.S. forces (see OCCUPATION). It was reconstituted in its present form in the 1950s.

SUNSHINE CITY. A large, multifunction commercial development in the Ikebukuro (q.v.) district of Toshima Ward. Opened in 1978 and operated by the Sunshine City Corporation, the project consists of a 60-story (240 meters; 787 feet) office tower called Sunshine 60, a 37-story hotel, a convention and exhibition center, a popular aquarium, and a shopping center named Alpa with approximately 220 stores. The Sunshine 60 building features an observatory on the top floor.

SUZUKI SHUNICHI (1910–). Four-term (15 years) governor of Tokyo Metropolis (q.v.), member of the Liberal Democratic Party (LDP). He was first elected to the governorship on 23 April 1979 and was reelected for additional terms commencing on 23 April 1983, 23 April 1987, and 23 April 1991. On 1 December 1994 he announced publicly that he would retire from political life and would not seek a fifth term. He was succeeded as governor by Aoshima Yukio (q.v.) on 24 April 1995.

Suzuki was born in the Akishima neighborhood of Tokyo on 6 November 1910 and was graduated in 1933 from the Faculty of Law of Tokyo Imperial University (now Tokyo University; q.v.). In the same year he joined the Ministry of the Interior and worked in local government administration. In 1957 he became vice-minister in charge of Home Affairs, and in 1958 was named Deputy Chief Cabinet Secretary. While in the Interior Ministry, Suzuki's major achievement was passage of a law that increased self-determination for local governments in Japan. Because of this he has been called "the father of local government autonomy" in Japan. From 1959 to 1967 Suzuki was vice-governor of Tokyo. Other positions have included president of the Tokyo Expressway Public Corporation between 1971 and 1977 and president of the Finance Corporation of Local Public Enterprise in 1978–79. As governor of Tokyo, Suzuki promoted the internationalization of the city, and he improved social welfare services, cultural activities, and education. Even more so, he promoted Tokyo as a business center and supported the expansion of commercial districts, high-rise office buildings, hotels, and other large projects. In 1991 he moved the headquarters of Tokyo Metropolitan Government (q.v.) from Marunouchi (q.v.) to a new City Hall complex in Shinjuku (q.v.). Critics have referred to this structure, by design the tallest in Tokyo, as Governor Suzuki's monument to himself (see also TANGE KENZO). Suzuki has also favored enormous redevelopment projects along Tokyo Bay (q.v.). Near the end of his four terms he was an especially vocal

vatism and the rise of ultranationalistic forces and Japanese expansionism. Consequently, many historians dispute the term "Taishō Democracy."

The Emperor Taishō was born in 1879 as the third son of the Emperor Meiji. His personal name was Yoshihito. Because his health was poor, he was not particularly active in government. His son, Crown Prince Hirohito, took over as regent *(sesshō)* in 1921 and became emperor after Emperor Taishō died on 25 December 1926.

TAMA AREA *(Tama chiku)*. Also called Tama District. The western part of Tokyo Metropolis (q.v.). The name comes from the Tama River (q.v.) and the Tama Hills *(Tama kyūryō)*, both of which are located in this area. The term is often used to refer to those parts of Tokyo Metropolis that are west of the Tama River. Tama is also the name of a town on the Tama River in Tokyo Metropolis and of a large new housing development called Tama New Town (q.v.).

Formally, the term "Tama Area" refers to those parts of Tokyo Metropolis that are not within the 23 Wards section. Most of this area is to the west of the 23 Wards. The Tama Area extends to the boundary of Tokyo Metropolis with Yamanashi Prefecture and western Saitama Prefecture. The far west of this area is mountainous and is generally referred to as *Oku-Tama* ("Deep Tama"). In certain usages the Tama Area also includes two groups of small islands in the Pacific Ocean south of Tokyo that are administratively included in Tokyo Metropolis (see IZU ISLANDS; OGASAWARA ISLANDS), but this is part of a technical definition only. The term is not generally used to refer to these islands.

TAMAGAWA CANAL *(Tamagawa jōsui)*. One of the three main aqueducts that supplied drinking water to Edo (q.v.) during the time of the Tokugawa Shogunate (q.v.). It was completed in 1654 and ran from the Tama River (q.v.; *Tamagawa*) across the Musashino Plateau in what is now called the Tama Area (q.v.) of Tokyo Prefecture (q.v.) to a terminus at Yotsuya just west of Edo Castle (q.v.). From Yotsuya water was carried in a set of underground passageways into the castle and into various residential areas of Edo itself. In the Tama Area the canal supplied irrigation water for rice fields, thereby opening the area for agricultural settlement. The Tamagawa Canal remained in use until 1965.

TAMA NEW TOWN *(Tama nyū taun).* A large housing development begun in 1967 in the Tama Area of western Tokyo Metropolis (q.v.). It has over 150,000 residents and covers parts of four cities: Inagi, Hachiōji, Machida, and Tama. It is still being constructed. The projected total population is expected to be more than 300,000. Most of the development consists of planned clusters of apartment and condominium buildings, new commercial centers, industrial sites, universities, and other employment centers, as well as many recreation facilities. The principal commercial center is called Tama Center.

TAMA RIVER (TAMAGAWA). Important river in the Tama Area (q.v.), the western part of Tokyo Prefecture (q.v.). It originates in the Chichibu Highlands in Yamanashi Prefecture flowing through western Tokyo Metropolis to Tokyo Bay (qq.v.). Its lower reaches form the boundary between Tokyo Metropolis and Kanagawa Prefecture. The length of the Tama River is 126 kilometers (78 miles). The river supplies drinking water to the Tokyo area and is also a major recreation resource. (see LEISURE)

TANGE KENZO (1913–). Probably the best-known and most influential architect in Japan today; especially noteworthy for his work in Tokyo.

Tange was born in Imabari, Ehime Prefecture, and was educated at Tokyo University (q.v.), from which he graduated in 1938 with honors from the department of architecture. He did graduate work at the same university in 1942–1945 and accepted a professorship there in 1949. Tange was influenced substantially by the modern architecture and urban visions of Le Corbusier, Walter Gropius, and Sigfried Giedion. His first completed building was the Hiroshima Peace Center (1949–1955). In 1961 he organized Kenzo Tange and URTEC, a team of architects and urban planners that carried out important projects throughout Japan and other countries, including Taiwan, Yugoslavia (Skopje), Iran, the United States, and Saudi Arabia. He has won numerous awards and titles: Honorary Professor at the University of Buenos Aires (1978); Honorary Fellow, Architectural Institute of Japan; President, Japan Architect Association (1986); President, Japan Institute of Architects (1987); Order of Culture, Japan (1980); Commander dans l'Ordre des Arts et Lettres, France (1984); Grand Prize, Architectural Institute of Japan; and The Pritzker Architecture Prize (1987).

Tange's major works in Tokyo include the central offices for Tokyo Metropolitan Government (q.v.) in the Marunouchi (q.v.) section of the city (1952–1957); St. Mary's Cathedral (1964); the two Yoyogi National Gymnasium buildings for the Tokyo Olympics (q.v.; 1964); head office building for the Dentsu Corporation (1967); the Turkish Embassy (1977); Hanae Mori Building (1978), the Embassy of Saudi Arabia (1986); and the United Nations University (1992). Tange also prepared a major redevelopment plan for the Tsukiji (q.v.) area of Tokyo (1961–1964). The larger of the two Olympics buildings that Tange designed is regarded as particularly ambitious; at the time it had the largest suspended roof in the world. In 1991 Tange's Tokyo Metropolitan Government offices were replaced by a massive new complex of three interconnected buildings, also designed by Tange, in the Shinjuku (q.v.) area. Generally referred to in English as Tokyo's City Hall, it is Tange's biggest structure. Some critics regard it as a monument to himself and his political associates (see SUZUKI SHUNICHI). More recently, Tange has designed the Shinjuku Park Tower Building (1994) across from City Hall. Tange is also involved with planning for Tokyo Metropolis (q.v.) and has put forth ambitious proposals for new islands and futuristic urban centers in Tokyo Bay. (q.v.; see WATERFRONT DEVELOPMENT)

TATSUNO KINGO (1854–1919). Noted architect of the late 19th and early 20th centuries. He was a student of Josiah Conder (q.v.) in Tokyo and later of William Burgess in England. In 1883 he became a professor of engineering at Tokyo University. In 1903 he opened his own architectural firm. He is credited with designing many important buildings in Tokyo, most notably the Bank of Japan Building (1896) and Tokyo Station (1914; qq.v.).

TOBI. Roofers and construction workers who became the core of fire-fighting squads in Edo (q.v.) in the 1780s. Before then, the city's fires were fought by residents themselves. The skills of *tobi* in demolition work to create open spaces in advance of the spread of fires made them a superior force. (see FIRES)

TŌKAIDŌ. The longest and most important of the five highways (Gokaidō; q.v.) of central Japan in the Edo Period (q.v.). It ran along or close to the Pacific Coast for 488 km (303 miles) from Edo (q.v.) to Kyoto; there was also an extension to Osaka. Along the way there were 53 post-station towns (q.v.; *shukuba machi*), beginning with Shinagawa (q.v.) in Edo, that provided services to travelers. There were also inspection stations along the way called *sekisho*, the most important of which was at the Hakone Pass, considered to be the gateway to the Kantō Plain (q.v.) and to Edo. The post-station towns became celebrated in Japanese art and literature.

TŌKAIDŌ METROPOLIS. Term for the heavily urbanized region of Japan along the Pacific coast of Honshū from Tokyo to Osaka and Kobe, including the cities of Kyoto, Nagoya, Yokohama (q.v.), and Kawasaki. The region has approximately 45 percent of Japan's population. The name comes from the Tōkaidō (q.v.), the historic highway that connected Edo (q.v.) and Kyoto.

TOKUGAWA FAMILY *(Tokugawashi)*. The lineage that ruled Japan from its seat of government in Edo (q.v.) during the Edo Period (1603–1867; q.v.). It was a warrior family with roots in Mikawa Province (now part of Aichi Prefecture) going back to at least the early 15th century. The family achieved its power when Tokugawa Ieyasu (1543–1616; q.v.) rose to the position of *shōgun* (q.v.) in 1603. Ieyasu established the Tokugawa Shogunate (q.v.) as a family line that continued until the Meiji Restoration (q.v.) of 1867.

TOKUGAWA IEMITSU (1604–1651). The third *shōgun* of the Tokugawa family line (qq.v.; see also TOKUGAWA SHOGUNATE). He was the second son of Tokugawa Hidetada, the second *shōgun*, and he ruled from 1623 until 1651. He was known as a particularly authoritarian ruler who demanded extraordinary respect and sacrifice from his subjects. From an early age he demanded personal pleasure from women. Iemitsu's principal contribution to the shogunate was to improve its administration and to bring it to the peak of power. He did this by imposing controls over *daimyō* (q.v.), such as the *sankin kōtai* (q.v.) alternate attendance system, and by instituting a system of surveillance over potentially troublesome institutions or social ranks (see ŌMET-SUKE). He is also credited with finishing the construction of Edo Castle (q.v.) and with undertaking the construction of the sanctuaries at Nikkō at the tomb of Tokugawa Ieyasu (q.v.). Other aspects of Iemitsu's rule included persecuting Christians and secluding Japan from other nations.

TOKUGAWA IEYASU (1543–1616). The first Tokugawa *shōgun* and founder of the Tokugawa family line (qq.v.; see also TOKUGAWA SHOGUNATE). He was also the major builder of Edo (q.v.), now Tokyo, as he made it his capital and transformed what had been a neglected castle town into a huge and powerful center of government authority. (see EDO CASTLE)

Ieyasu was born in Okazaki Castle in the province of Mikawa, now located in Aichi Prefecture. His birth name was Matsudaira Takechiyo. He became a warrior chieftain and engaged in many battles for control of feudal domains during the time of Japan's warfare for national unification during the latter half of the 16th century. In 1567 he changed his name to Tokugawa Ieyasu, an ancestral family name, to signify independence from rivals who were also members of the Matsudaira clan. His power increased with successive military victories. After a decisive victory in 1590 against the Hōjō clan based in Odawara Castle, Ieyasu gained control over much of eastern Japan and claimed Edo as his capital. In 1600, as a result of the Battle of Sekigahara (q.v.), Ieyasu became military master of all Japan. Three years later his supremacy was confirmed with the title *seii tai shōgun*, "barbarian-subduing generalissimo."

Ieyasu ruled Japan from Edo. In doing so, he greatly transformed the city and turned it into an impressive symbol of his enormous power. The centerpiece of Edo was Edo Castle, which was reconstructed on Ieyasu's orders. It was notable for its imposing size and fortifications. Ieyasu also arranged the social geography of the city, designating specific sections of the map for residence by *daimyō*, others for *hatamoto*, and still others for *chōnin* (qq.v.). He rearranged physical geography as well. For example, he cut down Kanda Mountain and filled in the marshes near Tokyo Bay (q.v.) to create the district called *shitamachi* (q.v.), the low city. These and other public works projects that he initiated required the presence in Edo of many laborers, as well as many suppliers of materials for construction and many townspeople to provide consumer goods and services to this population. Thus, we can say that Ieyasu set in motion the rapid growth of population in Edo and is responsible for its becoming the giant city that it now is. Few individuals in history have ever had as much impact on the formation of a great city as Tokugawa Ieyasu had on Edo, or Tokyo.

Ieyasu resigned from office in 1605 in favor of his third son, Tokugawa Hidetada. However, he remained active in the affairs of government for several years thereafter. In 1614–1615 he led two successful attacks on Osaka Castle to put a bloody end to a long-standing feud with the Toyotomi family. He then issued a 13-point code of laws called *buke shohatto* ("Laws for Military Houses") that all *daimyō* were required to obey. Ieyasu retired not long after and died in 1616. His remains were taken to Nikkō (in what is today Tochigi Prefecture) where an ornate shrine and mausoleum were built in his honor.

TOKUGAWA SHOGUNATE *(Tokugawa bakufu).* The term given to the hereditary line of *shōguns* (q.v.) of the Tokugawa family (q.v.) that ruled over Japan from 1603 until 1867. This period is generally called the Edo Period (q.v.; also dated as 1600–1868) or the Tokugawa Period. The seat of power was Edo Castle in Edo (qq.v.).

The first *shōgun* was Tokugawa Ieyasu (1543–1616; q.v.), who ruled for two years until transferring power in 1605 to his son Tokugawa Hidetada (1579–1632) in order to establish a precedent for hereditary succession for the position. There were 15 Tokugawa *shōguns* in all, the last being Tokugawa Yoshinobu (q.v.; 1837–1913). The shogunate reached the height of its power in the 17th century when its authority was unchallenged and Japanese provinces were united under its rule. The Tokugawa Shogunate collapsed in 1867 due to internal financial difficulties, restlessness among *daimyō* (q.v.), and the pressures on Japan that began to build with the arrival in 1853 of Commander Matthew C. Perry (q.v.) and his squadron of American naval vessels. (see BAKUFU; MEIJI RESTORATION; PERRY, MATTHEW C.)

The Tokugawa Shogunate was the last of three warrior governments in Japanese history. The first was the Kamakura Shogunate from 1192 to 1333; the second was the Muromachi Shogunate (also called the Ashikaga Shogunate) based in Kyoto from 1338 to 1573. Of the three, the period of the Tokugawa Shogunate was the longest.

TOKUGAWA TSUNAYOSHI (1646–1709). The fifth *shōgun* of the Tokugawa family line (qq.v.; see also TOKUGAWA SHOGUNATE). He ruled from 1680 until 1709 during a time when the arts flourished in Edo (q.v.) and other cities, and when inflation undermined economic stability (see GENROKU ERA). He is thought to have been a rather weak and unenlightened ruler, being remembered mostly for a series of increasingly odd edicts called *Shōrui awaremi no rei* ("Edicts on Compassion for Living Things") that protected the lives of animals. The first edict was proclaimed in 1685 and banned falconry, which had been a popular sport among his predecessors and other members of the nobility. All other forms of hunting were restricted. Other edicts followed, including appointment of a special commissioner for living things *(shōrui bugyō)*.

Tsunayoshi was especially concerned with protecting dogs. He believed that in an earlier life he had taken the lives of many living things and that these actions were now causing him to experience difficulties fathering an heir. The special attention that he gave to dogs is traced to Tsunayoshi's birth in the Year of the Dog in the Chinese zodiac, and to instructions that he received from a Buddhist monk to whom he had turned for help with his problem. As a result, Tsunayoshi made it a capital offense to harm dogs and insisted that they be allowed to roam the city freely and be fed by the citizenry. Moreover, he proclaimed that dogs should be addressed in honorific terms. Such policies resulted in a canine population explosion in Edo that caused many annoyances for citizens, such as barking noises, dog fights, and dog waste. To protect the citizenry, Tsunayoshi's ministers soon set up large kennels in various suburbs of Edo. A kennel in the Nakano section of the urban area is reported to have had 100,000 dogs by the end of its first year of operation. Because of his obsession, Tsunayoshi was called "the dog *shōgun*" *(inu kubō)* by his subjects, and he is almost always referred to this way in the history books.

TOKUGAWA YOSHIMUNE (1684–1751). The eighth *shōgun* of the Tokugawa family line (qq.v.; see also TOKU-GAWA SHOGUNATE) who ruled from 1716 until 1745. He is remembered most by historians for being particularly involved in daily affairs of government and for austerity measures that he imposed on himself as well as other government officials in order to improve the financial situation of the *bakufu* (q.v.). Yoshimune reportedly ordered a list of the 50 most beautiful women in his court. Then he ordered that all of them be let go, explaining that the shogunate need not support them because they could easily find husbands. To reduce the cost of keeping up the fortifications of Edo Castle (q.v.), Yoshimune ordered that certain sections of palisades be replaced with pine trees.

His most singular achievement was the Kyōhō Reforms of 1716–1736, which were intended to bring financial stability to the government and to the *samurai (q.v.)* class. He also advanced martial arts and sports (riding, shooting, and falconry) as means of maintaining physical fitness and military readiness among the *samurai,* and for improving their morale. Another reform was a suggestion box system (see MEYASUBAKO) in which citizens of Edo (q.v.) could leave him complaints or suggestions. Yoshimune is also remembered by historians for such diverse improvements as a written judicial code; an astronomical observatory in Kanda (q.v.); a botanical garden in Koishikawa to advance science; a charitable hospital called the *Koishikawa yōjōsho* (q.v.); support for the study of foreign texts and for publication of a Dutch-Japanese dictionary and other books; a major flood control project for Edo that involved diverting local rivers; and advances in fireproof building technology for storehouses by using walls of earth and plaster. In the Kantō Plain (q.v.) near Edo, Yoshimune advanced agriculture by promoting sweet potatoes as a crop for fighting famine, as well as by promoting the cultivation of oranges, tobacco, and medicinal plants. New rice growing areas were opened as well, in addition to 80 new villages. For this reason Yoshimune was called the "rice *shōgun.*"

Yoshimune abdicated in 1745 in favor of his oldest son, who became *shōgun* with the name Tokugawa Ieshige. However, he continued to involve himself directly with government affairs until his death in 1751.

TOKUGAWA YOSHINOBU (1837–1913). The last of the *shōguns* of the Tokugawa family line (qq.v.; see also TOKUGAWA SHOGUNATE). He ruled for most of 1867. In spite of last-ditch attempts to bolster the weakening power of the *bakufu* (q.v.), he was forced to resign in the face of growing antishogunate sentiments among the leaders of Japan's feudal domains, as well as in response to calls for the restoration of imperial authority. Furthermore, a palace coup on 3 January 1868 caused

Yoshinobu to surrender the Tokugawa domains to the emperor's control (see MEIJI RESTORATION). After a brief civil war (the Boshin Civil War), in which forces loyal to the shogunate were defeated by the new imperial forces, Yoshinobu left Edo (q.v.) for quiet retirement in Sumpu (now Shizuoka city, Shizuoka Prefecture).

TOKYO (origin of the name). The word *Tōkyō* means "eastern capital." It is the name that was given to Edo (q.v.) in 1868, when the city was designated capital of Japan, and political power in the country was transferred from the shogunate to the emperor. (see RELOCATION OF THE CAPITAL)

TOKYO BAY. An inlet of the Pacific Ocean in the area of Tokyo, Kanagawa, and Chiba prefectures. It is bounded by the Miura and Bōsō peninsulas, and it has the Tokyo-Yokohama metropolis at its head (see YOKOHAMA). The channel to the open Pacific is called the Uraga Channel. Once the bay was rich in marine life, but pollution from coastal industries and urban development has severely damaged the environment and all but ended commercial exploitation (see ENVIRONMENTAL PROTECTION). There is considerable reclamation along the shoreline in order to create new land for urban expansion (see WATERFRONT DEVELOPMENT). Before 1868 Tokyo Bay was called Edo Bay.

TOKYO CITIZENS' DAY *(Tomin-no-hi)*. The date 1 October has been celebrated each year since 1898 as the day when local autonomy began for the City of Tokyo. Immediately before then, the government of the city was under a special exception to the national local autonomy law, and the city was administered as part of *Tōkyō-fu* (Tokyo Prefecture; q.v.).

TOKYO DISNEYLAND. Major amusement park near Tokyo

in Urayasu City, Chiba Prefecture. It opened in 1983 under license from the Disney Corporation in the United States, and is patterned after Disneyland in Anaheim, California. It is operated by the Oriental Land Company. The area is 82.6 hectares (204.1 acres) and has five theme parks. More than 10 million people visit this facility annually, including many foreign visitors from neighboring Taiwan and Korea. The success of Tokyo Disneyland has stimulated considerable development of hotels, restaurants, and other facilities for visitors in the adjacent area, especially along the waterfront near the facility. (see WATERFRONT DEVELOPMENT)

TOKYO DOME. An air-supported indoor stadium and concert facility in Bunkyō Ward, Tokyo. It was opened in 1988 and seats 56,000. The stadium is home for two professional baseball teams: the Yomiuri Giants (see SHŌRIKI MATSUTARŌ) and the Nippon Ham Fighters. Because of its shape it is sometimes called "Big Egg." (see LEISURE)

TOKYO EARTHQUAKE OF 1923 (See GREAT KANTŌ EARTHQUAKE)

TOKYO INSTITUTE ON MUNICIPAL RESEARCH (Tōkyō Shisei Chōsakai). A nonprofit foundation established in 1922 to promote the betterment of municipal government in Tokyo and other Japanese cities. It was the inspiration of Gotō Shimpei (q.v.), mayor of Tokyo between 1920 and 1923 and an ardent believer in the value of "scientific research" for solving problems related to urban administration and social welfare. Initial funding for the institute was provided through the will of Yasuda Zenjirō (q.v.), a powerful business leader who had died the previous year, and by smaller donations from two anonymous benefactors. An important model for the founding of the institute was the New York Bureau of

Municipal Research, a similar organization in the United States. The American historian Charles Austin Beard (q.v.), who had been working with the New York organization, was brought to Tokyo by Gotō to advise the newly established institute, and to help set its agenda. In May 1925 the Tokyo Institute on Municipal Research began publishing the journal *Toshi mondai* ("Municipal Problems").

TOKYO INTERNATIONAL AIRPORT *(Tōkyō Kokusai Kūkō)*. Also known as Haneda Airport. Opened in 1931, it served as Tokyo's chief airport until the opening of the New Tokyo International Airport (q.v.) in 1978. It is located in Ōta Ward along the shore of Tokyo Bay (q.v.) and is connected to the center of Tokyo by the Tokyo Monorail. Most of the traffic at this airport is domestic.

TOKYO METROPOLIS *(Tōkyō-to)*. The formally defined territorial unit that corresponds to what is called Tokyo. It was created in 1943 when the City of Tokyo and Tokyo Prefecture merged into a single unit. Its administrative status is similar to that of a prefecture (see TOKYO METROPOLITAN GOVERNMENT; TOKYO PREFECTURE). The area of Tokyo Metropolis is 2,168 square kilometers (837 square miles), while the population on 1 January 1995 totaled 11,810,709. The major parts of Tokyo Metropolis are 23 wards *(ku)* with 8,013,194 of the total population, plus 27 cities *(shi)*, one county *(gun)*, and four island administrative units *(sho-chō)*. The one county and the four island units contain 14 towns and villages *(chō, son)*. (see IZU ISLANDS; OGASAWARA ISLANDS; TAMA AREA)

TOKYO METROPOLITAN GOVERNMENT. The local public body that governs *Tōkyō-to* (Tokyo Metropolis; q.v.), the formally defined territorial unit that corresponds to what is called Tokyo. Tokyo Metropolitan Government was established in 1943 with the merger of *Tōkyō-fu* (Tokyo Prefecture; q.v.) and the City of Tokyo. It performs governmental functions similar to those of prefectures in Japan, as well as many of the functions that are commonly the responsibility of municipalities. Thus Tokyo Metropolitan Government has a dual character, functioning as both a prefectural government and a municipal government.

The administration of Tokyo Metropolitan Government has both an executive and a legislative branch. The chief executive is the governor of Tokyo Metropolis, under whom are numerous bureaus and commissions that oversee such areas of local government responsibility as transportation, waterworks, sewerage, public safety, education, local taxation and finance, and other functions. The main legislative unit is the Tokyo Metropolitan Assembly. Its 127 members are elected to four-year terms of service by direct popular vote.

TOKYO OLYMPICS. The 18th Summer Olympic Games were held in Tokyo (1–24 October 1964), the first Olympics ever held in Asia. More than 5,500 athletes from 94 countries participated. The Olympic Village was in Yoyogi Park (q.v.), located on the west side of central Tokyo in Shibuya Ward. Most of the sporting events were held in facilities nearby. Tokyo was supposed to have hosted the 12th Summer Olympics in 1940, but the plan was canceled due to war. The 1964 games were an opportunity for Japan to show off its progress in rebuilding after the devastation of World War II. Highlights were the high-speed bullet trains (q.v.; *shinkansen*) that were put into operation just in time for the arrival of Olympics visitors, a monorail line extending from Tokyo International Airport (q.v.; Haneda Airport) to the city center, and many new buildings and widened streets in Tokyo near the games themselves.

TOKYO PREFECTURE *(Tōkyō-fu)*. Unit of local government that was set up in 1868 when Edo (q.v.) was renamed Tokyo and old feudal-era fiefdoms were replaced by new administrative units called *fu* and *ken* (prefectures). Its structure was reformed or modified several times during its existence. In 1879 Tokyo Prefecture came to encompass the 15 wards and six counties that roughly corresponded to the previous limits of Edo plus surrounding territories. In 1889 the 15 wards were put under the administration of the City of Tokyo, although local autonomy was restricted, and the governor of Tokyo Prefecture continued to perform the functions local chief executive until 1 October 1898 (see TOKYO CITIZENS' DAY). Tokyo Prefecture was abolished in 1943 when it was consolidated with the City of Tokyo into *Tōkyō-to* (Tokyo Metropolis; q.v.). However, the term "Tokyo Prefecture" is still used somewhat casually in English to refer to Tokyo or *Tōkyō-to*.

"THE TOKYO PROBLEM." General term that occurs frequently in English-language literature about Tokyo to refer to a complex of urban problems and daily inconveniences that stem from the city's enormous population, excessive crowding, and high costs of land (see LAND PRICES). Thus, the term encompasses such problems as long-distance commuting (q.v.), peak hour crowding on subways (q.v.) and trains, traffic congestion, the high cost of housing, pollution (see ENVIRONMENTAL PROTECTION), and the lack of open space. The term also refers to the hazards that Tokyo faces from earthquakes (q.v.), and to the enormous human tragedy and economic chaos that would result if a massive earthquake should strike the city. One solution to "the Tokyo Problem" that is being discussed is relocating the capital (q.v.) of Japan to a place that would be both safer from disaster and less congested.

TOKYO STATION. The central rail station of Tokyo, located in Chiyoda Ward in the downtown area of the city. The original structure, now known as the Marunouchi Wing, was completed in 1914 and is considered to be an important historic landmark. It was designed by Tatsuno Kingo (q.v.), and is constructed of steel-reinforced red brick with white stone facing. It was badly damaged during the bombing raids of World War II and was rebuilt with modifications after the war. The other wing, known as the Yaesu Wing, was completed in 1968 and is a steel-and-glass structure. The station serves commuters, as well as passengers on Japan's bullet train (q.v.; *shinkansen*) system.

TOKYO STOCK EXCHANGE. Established in 1949 and located in Kabutochō, Chūō Ward, downtown Tokyo. It is an incorporated organization established in accordance with the Securities Exchange Law for the purpose of trading stocks, bonds, and futures options based on securities. Its membership is restricted to securities companies. In 1991 membership consisted of 99 Japanese and 25 non-Japanese securities companies. "Regular Members" receive orders from investors and forward them to the Exchange, while "*Saitori* Members" match, sell, and buy orders placed by the Regular Members.

TOKYO TELEPORT TOWN (See WATERFRONT DEVELOPMENT)

TŌKYŌ-TO (See TOKYO METROPOLIS)

TOKYO TOWER. A multipurpose transmission and reception tower for various television, radio, and communications broadcasts in Minato Ward, central Tokyo. Designed by Naitō Tachu, it opened in December 1958. It is 333 meters (1,093 feet) high from base to lightning rod and has public observation levels at 150 meters (492 feet) and 250 meters (673 feet). Construction took a year and a half, employed as many as 22,000 workers, and cost three billion yen. The tower has been an important landmark and symbol of Tokyo ever since it opened. In January 1995 the total number of visitors to visit Tokyo Tower since it opened topped 120 million.

TOKYO UNIVERSITY (*Tōkyō daigaku*; also called *Tōdai*). Prestigious university located in the Hongō area of Bunkyō Ward and in Meguro Ward, Tokyo. It was founded in 1877 with the merger of *Tōkyō Kaisei Gakkō* (the former Institute for the Investigation of Barbarian Books) that was established in 1855 by the Tokugawa Shogunate (q.v.) and Tokyo Medical School *(Tōkyō Igakkō)* (see BANSHO SHIRABESHO; KOISHIKAWA YŌJŌSHO). In 1886 it became the Imperial University. In 1897 after a second Imperial University was opened in Kyoto, the name was adjusted to Tokyo Imperial University. It was renamed Tokyo University in 1947. There are ten faculties in a wide variety of academic fields, as well as several research institutes in the sciences and social sciences. There are nearly 15,000 students. Admission is very competitive, as Tokyo University is widely regarded as an excellent base for starting careers in government and politics, business, medicine, education, and many other fields. In the late 1960s Tokyo University was the scene of large protest demonstrations and violent confrontations between discontented students and police. The conflicts culminated on 19 January 1969 with a major battle at a building on the Hongō campus called Yasuda Hall (q.v.). Another famous landmark on that campus is *akamon*, a "red gate" that dates back to 1827. It is a remnant of the Maeda family estate that had previously occupied the grounds of the campus.

TOSHIYORI. A word meaning "elders" or "those who have become old." It referred to senior officials and persons of high standing in Japan's authority structure during the Tokugawa Shogunate (q.v.) and earlier.

TOWNSPEOPLE (See CHŌNIN)

TOZAMA DAIMYŌ (See DAIMYŌ)

TRANSPORTATION (See COMMUTING; SUBWAYS; YAMANOTE LINE)

TSUKIJI. A district in Chūō Ward, Tokyo, near the waterfront that is best known for its large fish and produce market. It is built on reclaimed land, as the literal meaning of the word *"Tsukiji"* indicates (see WATERFRONT DEVEL-OPMENT). In 1867 the district was opened as a desig-nated settlement for foreigners (see YATOI). It was sepa-rated from the rest of the city by canals and gates, but access was not restricted. Two important institutions from missionary activity in the early settlement still sur-vive: St. Luke's Hospital and St. Paul's University (now Rikkyō University [q.v.], relocated in 1918 to Toshima Ward). Just outside the district were other institutions associated with the foreign settlement, a prominent hotel called the Hoterukan (q.v.), and the New Shimabara licensed quarter (q.v.). The wholesale market was opened in 1935. (see TSUKIJI MARKET)

TSUKIJI MARKET *(Tsukiji shijō)*. A large wholesale market in the Tsukiji area (q.v.) of Chūō Ward, Tokyo. It opened in 1935 in connection with the planned relocation of the previous market, which had been in the Nihombashi dis-trict (q.v.) of Chūō Ward and was badly damaged in the earthquake and fire of 1923 (see GREAT KANTŌ EARTHQUAKE). The market specializes in fish and other marine products but also sells produce. In recent years many tourists have come to see the early morning fish auctions.

TSUKUBA (See TSUKUBA SCIENCE CITY)

TSUKUBA SCIENCE CITY. A planned city at the outer edge of the Tokyo metropolitan area that was initially developed in the 1960s and 1970s as a research and academic center. It is in southwestern Ibaraki Prefecture, about 34 miles (approximately 55 kilometers) from the center of Tokyo, in what was once a farming area at the foot of Mount Tsukuba. The city is commonly referred to as simply "Tsukuba." It is the home of Tsukuba University, which was founded in 1973, and more than 40 public and private research institutions, most of them focusing on technology development. In 1985 an international science and technology fair known as Expo '85 was held in the city. The population is approximately 143,000 (1990).

TSUKUBA UNIVERSITY (See TSUKUBA SCIENCE CITY)

TWELVE STORIES (See ASAKUSA TWELVE STORIES)

– U –

UCHIKOWASHI. A word that means "smashing" and that refers to urban riots in the Edo Period (q.v.) in which hungry townspeople stormed the properties of wealthy businessmen. The riots occurred in various cities. In Edo (q.v.) the biggest riots occurred in 1733, 1787, and 1866. (see RICE RIOTS)

UENO. A major commercial district in Taitō Ward, just north of central Tokyo. Its train station is one of the busiest in Tokyo, and is a gateway to the city from the north. The area is also known for Ueno Park (q.v.), one of the city's premier recreation attractions. (see SUB-CENTERS)

UENO PARK. One of the largest public parks in Tokyo, comprising 131 acres (53.2 hectares). It was established in 1873 and is located in Taitō Ward next to the Ueno (q.v.) commercial district. The park is famous for its several museums, the Ueno Zoological Gardens, Shinobazu Pond, and the historic Kan'eiji (q.v.) temple. In the spring Ueno Park is a popular spot for veiwing cherry blossoms (see LEISURE). Nowadays, the park is also known for having one of the city's largest concentrations of homeless people.

UENO WAR (See SHŌGITAI)

UKIYO-E. The word means "pictures of the floating world" and refers to a genre of art, especially the woodblock print, that was popular in Japan during the Edo Period (q.v.). Many of the prints were produced in Edo (q.v.), and depicted the life of the townspeople (see CHŌNIN). Specific subjects included entertainment and brothel districts such as Yoshiwara (q.v.), women, *kabuki* theater and famous actors, and urban scenes such as commercial streets, artisans' districts, and famous bridges. Initially the prints were monochromatic, but eventually bright, multicolored prints called *nishiki-e* were developed. They were printed in large numbers as single sheets, greeting cards, and illustrations for books. They were distributed widely. A particular type of woodblock print was called *namazu-e* (q.v.). Some of the most prolific and most popular artists were Andō Hiroshige (1797–1858), Katsushika Hokusai (1760–1849), Utagawa Kuniyoshi (1798–1861), Kitagawa Utamaro (1753–1806), Suzuki Harunobu (1725–1770), and Torii Kiyonobu (1664–1729).

– W –

WASEDA UNIVERSITY *(Waseda Daigaku).* Large private, coeducational university with more than 40,000 students located in Shinjuku Ward, Tokyo. It was founded in 1882 as *Tōkyō Semmon Gakkō* (Tokyo College) by Ōkuma Shigenobu (q.v.) and was renamed Waseda University in 1902. It has earned a reputation as one of Japan's leading institutions of higher learning. Its faculties include those of political science and economics, commerce, law, letters, and engineering. There is also an international division where foreign students study.

WASHINGTON HEIGHTS. The name that was given by Americans to the old Yoyogi parade grounds in what is now Shibuya Ward, Tokyo, during the Occupation of Japan (q.v.). It is where family housing for Americans stationed in Tokyo during the Occupation was constructed. The site was returned to Japan in time for use during the 1964 Olympics (see TOKYO OLYMPICS; YOYOGI PARK). In exchange, housing for families of American military personnel still stationed in Japan was constructed in Chōfu City, in the Tama Area (q.v.) of Tokyo Prefecture (q.v.).

WATERFRONT DEVELOPMENT. The shoreline of Tokyo Bay (q.v.) is a major area of urban development and expansion. Reclamation projects date back to the earliest part of the 17th century when the shōgun Tokugawa Ieyasu (q.v.) ordered the marshes at the foot of Edo Castle (q.v.) filled in to create land where the city's commoners would live (see MACHIDOSHIYORI; SHITAMACHI). Reclamation has continued in every period of Tokyo's history since the early Edo Period (q.v.), with the result that many parts of the city's central business district are actually on land that was once part of the bay. Tsukiji (q.v.), a commercial district in Chūō Ward, is an excellent example; its name means "reclaimed land."

The Tokyo Metropolitan Government (q.v.) has promoted the waterfront as the city's "last frontier." The main area of development is a series of close-in islands that have been reclaimed from Tokyo Bay. While some of these islands (and stretches of adjacent shoreline) are given to industrial land uses, harbor facilities, and storage of commodities such as chemicals and lumber, emphasis is now being given to converting reclaimed land to commercial, residentia, and recreational land uses. The focus of such construction has been a multi-island area in Kōtō Ward known as the Aomi, Ariake, and Daiba districts after the names of specific artificial islands. The area has been designated as the site of a major new subcenter (q.v.) of the Tokyo Metropolis (q.v.) to be called Tokyo Teleport Town. Plans call for it to be a highly futuristic city with advanced telecommunications technology that provides outstanding links to business centers around the globe. This development is expected to have a working population of approximately 110,000 and a residential population of about 60,000. New rail lines and a new highway link this area to the rest of the city. However, a plan by the Tokyo Metropolitan Government to host a major international exhibition at the site in 1996 that would be called "World City Expo Tokyo '96" or "Tokyo Frontier" was canceled because of high costs. (see AOSHIMA YUKIO; SUZUKI SHUNICHI)

Another key waterfront development project is River City 21, a large, high-rise residential development that is being built on a close-in artificial island near the mouth of the Sumida River (q.v.) by the Tokyo Metropolitan Government and the national Housing and Urban Development Corporation in concert with various private developers. One of its main attractions is nearness to downtown Tokyo, thereby cutting down substantially on commuting (q.v.) time and costs for its residents. Other expansion of urban land, ranging from enhanced industrial and port facilities to new office districts and residential neighborhoods, is taking place along various other parts of the shoreline of Tokyo Metropolis and in neighboring Chiba and Kanagawa Prefectures (see

TOKYO DISNEYLAND; YOKOHAMA). Kasai Marine Park along the bayfront of Edogawa Ward is an example of land reclamation for urban recreation. (see LEISURE)

WATERS, THOMAS (1830–?). English architect who came to Japan during the early Meiji Period (q.v.) and designed Western style buildings. He was especially influential in the promotion of brick construction. His major projects were constructing Ginza Brick Town (q.v.) in Tokyo after the Ginza Fire of 1872, and the Osaka Mint. He is also credited with the introduction of modern water pipes and sewers to Tokyo.

WRIGHT, FRANK LLOYD (See IMPERIAL HOTEL)

– Y –

YAKUZA (See CRIME)

YAMANOTE. An area of Tokyo where feudal lords or *daimyō* (q.v.) built their sumptuous residences in the Edo Period (q.v.). Today it houses some of the city's more fashionable residential neighborhoods and commercial centers. It is also noted for many important institutions such as prestigious universities, foreign embassies, offices of the Japanese national government, and top-rated international hotels. It is a fairly large area mostly to the north and west of the historic center of the city, the site where Edo Castle once stood and where the Imperial Palace (qq.v.) is today. There are no formal boundaries, but the area can be said to cover all or part of the following wards: Bunkyō, Shinjuku, Shibuya, Minato, and Chiyoda (western part only). As suggested by the word *yamanote* itself, which is translated variously as "hills," "foothills," or "in the direction of the mountains," the *yamanote* area is defined by higher ground and more greenery than the city's other "side," *shitamachi* (q.v.) or "low city." Except where it goes through downtown Tokyo (such as the area closest to Tokyo Station), the Yamanote Line (q.v.) commuter rail loop runs through most of Tokyo's *yamanote* district.

YAMANOTE LINE *(yamanote-sen)*. One of the most important commuter rail lines in Tokyo. It is a loop of 34.5 kilometers (22 miles) that links many of the busiest commercial centers and passenger rail stations in central Tokyo and connects with most of Tokyo's train and subway (q.v.) lines. There are 29 stations along the route, including exceptionally busy stations at Tokyo, Shinagawa, Shibuya, Shinjuku, Ikebukuro, and Ueno (see SUBCENTERS). The complete circuit takes about 63 minutes. During peak periods, a train arrives at any station every 2.5 minutes. Each train is ten cars long; there are 677 trains scheduled each day. For much of the day, trains are jammed well beyond capacity, as the Yamanote Line is the most heavily used passenger line in the entire Tokyo area. The Yamanote Line opened in November 1925 when its last link, the one between Tokyo Station and Ueno, was completed. For most of its history the line was operated by Japan National Railways, but since privatization in 1987 the operator has been the East Japan Railway Company (*Higashi Nihon Ryokaku Tetsudō*). In terms of the color-coding scheme for commuter lines in the Tokyo area, the Yamanote Line's color is green. (see COMMUTING)

YANAKA. Historic district in northern Taitō Ward, Tokyo, just to the north of Ueno and Ueno Park (qq.v.). It is noted for its rows of old wooden houses and small shops, and for its many old temples and cemeteries. Development of Yanaka is traced to the aftermath of the Meireki Fire (q.v.) of 1657, when many of the temples of Edo (q.v.) were ordered to be relocated there. Because

Yanaka escaped the worst damage from the Great Kantō Earthquake of 1923 and the air raids of 1945 (qq.v.), it is one of the few places in Tokyo to offer authentic glimpses of what the historic city looked like.

YASUDA. The name of the financial empire that was founded in 1880 by Yasuda Zenjirō (q.v.) and that grew to become one of Japan's most powerful *zaibatsu* (q.v.). By 1919 it controlled 17 banks and at least 16 other companies through its Yasuda Hozensha Holding Company. Industrial investments were mostly through the Asano *zaibatsu*. By the time *zaibatsu* were dissolved in 1945 (see OCCUPATION), Yasuda holdings numbered more than 50 companies. The descendant of the empire now is an enterprise group *(keiretsu)* known as the Fuyō group. Its leading companies include Fuji Bank, Ltd; Yasuda Trust and Banking Company; and Yasuda Fire and Marine Insurance Company.

YASUDA HALL *(Yasuda Kōdō)*. The central administration building of Tokyo University (q.v.) at the Bunkyō Ward campus. It is distinguished by its large size and tall Gothic clock tower. The structure was endowed by Yasuda Zenjirō, founder of the Yasuda (qq.v.) business empire. In the late 1960s the building was the focus of a raucous student protest against authority in Japan. Students referred to Yasuda Hall as their "castle" and occupied the structure on two occasions in 1968, expelling the president from his office. On 19 January 1969 there was a violent battle involving more than 8,000 police and hundreds of police vehicles and other pieces of equipment to finally dislodge the barricaded students. The battle was the first event in Japan to be broadcast on live television.

YASUDA ZENJIRŌ (1838–1921). Powerful financier and businessman in Tokyo during the Meiji and Taishō Periods (qq.v.). He is best known as the founder of the Yasuda *zaibatsu*, a family-run business empire that emphasized banking and finance, as well as insurance, railways, and other enterprises (see YASUDA; ZAIBATSU). Among the large companies that he established were Yasuda Bank in 1880 (now Fuji Bank) and the forerunner of the Yasuda Fire and Marine Insurance Company in 1888. He was also a founding member and director of the Bank of Japan. (see BANK OF JAPAN BUILDING)

Yasuda began his career in finance with a small money-changing business that he established in 1864. This was soon after he had migrated to Edo (q.v.) from Etchū, a province in what is now Toyama Prefecture, where he was born. He made great profits at this business after the Meiji Restoration (q.v.) by buying paper currency at a discount and then reselling it at full value to the government. Before long he came to monopolize money changing in Tokyo. The first bank that he founded was the Third National Bank (*Daisan Kokuritsu Ginkō*) in 1876.

Yasuda was active in Tokyo's civic affairs. In 1879 he was elected to membership in the first Tokyo Prefectural Assembly and in 1889 became a member of the first Tokyo City Council. He contributed money to found the Tokyo Institute on Municipal Research (q.v.), for construction of Hibiya Public Hall in Hibiya Park (q.v.), and for Yasuda Hall (q.v.) on the campus of Tokyo University (q.v.). Yasuda was assassinated in 1921 by a right-wing fanatic at his country home in Ōiso.

YATOI. Word meaning "foreign employees." It refers to the many foreigners who came to Japan during the Meiji Period (q.v.) to work as instructors of Western culture and technology. In all there were some 4,000 *yatoi* employed in Japan, the largest number of them in Tokyo. About half were British, and most of the rest were French, German, or American. (see CHAMBERLAIN, B. H.; CONDER, J.; HOEHN, H. F.; WATERS, T.)

YEBISU GARDEN PLACE. A large, multiple-use urban rede-velopment complex in Meguro and Shibuya Wards, Tokyo, near Ebisu Station on the Yamanote Line (q.v.); an important commuter rail loop in inner Tokyo. It was opened in 1994 on the site of a brewery operated by Sapporo Breweries, and features a new shopping center, a 39-story office building, the head office of Sapporo Breweries in another building, a Westin Hotel, two high-rise residential buildings, a museum about beer, and the Tokyo Metropolitan Museum of Photography. There are many restaurants and a beer garden as well. Yebisu Garden Place is a good example of a shift in Tokyo's economy and land uses from manufacturing to services. It has come to be a popular attraction for families and couples on Sundays and other days off from work or school. (see LEISURE)

YOKOHAMA. Large city near Tokyo in neighboring Kana-gawa Prefecture, on Tokyo Bay (q.v.). The distance from central Yokohama to downtown Tokyo is approximately 17 miles (about 27.2 kilometers). The city ranks third in size in Japan and has a population of approximately 3.2 million (1995).

Yokohama was originally a small fishing village. It developed into a major city after the signing of the Harris Treaty in 1858 (see HARRIS, TOWNSEND), which opened Japan to foreign trade after a long period of isolation under the Tokugawa Shogunate (q.v.). The landing of Commodore Matthew C. Perry (q.v.) in the city in 1854 is regarded as one of the key events leading to the transformation of Japan from a feudal state to a modern industrial power. Japan's first railroad line was constructed between Yokohama and Tokyo in 1872 (see SHIMBASHI) and contributed to developing the city and its waterfront into a major manufacturing zone.

Yokohama is now Japan's largest port, an enormous-ly important industrial center, a prefecture capital, and a fast-developing concentration of high-rise office buildings, busy shopping centers, and other commerce. Its principal industries include steel, automobiles and automobile parts, electronics equipment, petrochemicals, and food processing. Electronics and other high-technology fields are growing rapidly, particularly in Yokohama's suburbs in Kanagawa Prefecture. Popular attractions for visitors to the city include Yamashita Park along the waterfront, a shopping district named Motomachi, the Chinatown district, the Silk Center and Silk Museum, and Sankaien, a beautiful Japanese garden. A major redevelopment project at the waterfront named Minato Mirai 21 is both a popular attraction and a new direction for the Yokohama economy, emphasizing services instead of manufacturing. Its centerpiece is the 70-story Landmark Tower, Japan's tallest building, a combination office building, international hotel, and multilevel shopping mall.

YOKOYAMA GENNOSUKE (1871–1915). Journalist who wrote widely about the problems of poor people in Japan during a time of rapid industrialization and social change. Much of his writing was for the newspaper *Mainichi shimbun,* for which he worked starting in 1894. He covered such groups as slum dwellers in Tokyo, factory workers, and poor farmers. His major work is *Nihon no kasō shakai* (Japan's Lower Classes), which was published in 1899. The book is still highly regarded and is credited with having alerted the contemporaneous Japanese public to some of the country's most important social problems.

YOSHIWARA. The largest and most famous of Tokyo's early licensed quarters or regulated districts for prostitution. It was founded in 1617 by Shōji Jin'emon, who had received a license to operate it from the shogunate. Yoshiwara thrived for the remainder of the Edo Period (q.v.) and for some years thereafter. It declined in the 20th century and was finally closed in 1958, after adoption of the Prostitution Prevention Law of 1957.

Yoshiwara was originally established in a marshy area close to Edo Castle (q.v.), in what is now a part of the Nihombashi (q.v.) district of Tokyo's downtown. The word "Yoshiwara," which is now written in characters that mean "auspicious plain," was written at the time to mean "reed *(yoshi)* plain" because of the reeds growing at the site. The quarter was destroyed in the 1657 in the Meireki Fire (q.v.), and a new Yoshiwara (formally called *Shin* ["new"] *Yoshiwara*) was opened north of the center of the city, in what is now a part of the Senzoku district of Taitō Ward. Even before the fire there had been a search for a new site because it was thought that prostitution should be moved from the center of the city. It is the new site that survived as a pleasure quarter until the middle of the 20th century. After the opening of Shin Yoshiwara, the original location came to be referred to as *Moto* ("original") *Yoshiwara*.

The area of Shin Yoshiwara was eight hectares (20 acres). It was enclosed by walls and moats to prevent customers from leaving without paying and to keep the prostitutes (mostly females) from escaping. The streets were laid out in a grid pattern and were lined with teahouses called *hikite-jaya* where assignations were arranged and crowded houses where prostitutes and other workers lived. The number of prostitutes at any one time was generally between 2,000 and 3,000, and the number of establishments was about 200. There was a Great Gate *(Ōmon)* that controlled almost all access, as well as a drawbridge over a moat, *Ohaguro-dobu*, the "Ditch of Black Teeth" (so named because of a cosmetic fashion that was popular among many women). The main street that ran the length of the quarter from the Great Gate was called Naka-no-Machi. In the early years of Shin Yoshiwara, the distance from the center of Edo was considered to be quite great. Consequently, business was bad until boat service was provided along the Sumida River (q.v.) and a local waterway called San'yabori.

Yoshiwara was a complex social world. There were many levels of prostitutes and brothels, and a variety of established procedures for obtaining their services. High-class prostitutes *(tayū)* were accorded considerable respect, and they were often distinguished for their skills in various arts as well personal services. There were also various categories of male customers in Yoshiwara. The most respected was the *tsū*, or "citizen of the quarter." He was a sophisticated regular who knew the ways of Yoshiwara well, and was always in touch with changes in fashion and fads in entertainment, as well as the proper etiquette for any situation. The entertainment that was available at Yoshiwara was not limited to sexual pleasure. During its heyday in the 18th and early 19th centuries, the district was also a lively center of innovation in music, art, and literature, and played a vital role in developing the cultural life of Edo. The women of Yoshiwara and the various forms of entertainment that were practiced in this district were popular subjects for woodblock prints (*ukiyo-e,* q.v.) by artists such as Kitao Masanobu and Kitagawa Utamaro.

YOYOGI PARK (*Yoyogi Kōen*). A large public park in Shibuya Ward between the business centers of Shibuya and Shinjuku (qq.v.) and adjacent to the Meiji Shrine (q.v.). It opened in 1967 and comprises 54 hectares (133 acres). Before World War II the area was used as a parade ground (*Yoyogi rempeijō*) by the Japanese military. During the postwar Occupation (q.v.), it was an area of residential barracks for American troops and was known as Washington Heights (q.v.). After the land was returned to Japan in 1964, it became the site for the Tokyo Olympics (q.v.). The park is especially crowded on Sundays. In recent years one of the streets through the park *(Inokashira-dōri)* has become a Sunday gathering place for thousands of young rock music fans and their favorite bands, as well as for many foreigners in the city. (see LEISURE)

YUSHIMA SEIDŌ. Historic Confucian shrine in southeastern Bunkyō Ward. It originated in 1632 in what is now Ueno Park as a school for the study of Confucian classics, and was moved to the present site in 1691 by the fifth *shōgun*, Tokugawa Tsunayoshi. The school was called *Shōheizaka Gakumonjo* (the Shoheizaka Institute for Higher Learning) or simply *Shōheikō*. Throughout the Edo Period (q.v.), Yushima Seidō enjoyed prestige as the center for Confucian learning by the Tokugawa elite. The main hall, built in 1691, was destroyed in 1923 by the Great Kantō Earthquake (q.v.). The present structure, constructed in a traditional style, dates to 1965. It has a statue of Confucius. An old gate named *Nyūtokumon* survived the earthquake and still stands. Yushima Seidō is operated as a historic shrine by a private organization on behalf of the government.

– Z –

ZAIBATSU. Giant industrial and financial combines that dominated the Japanese economy from their inception in the Meiji Period (q.v.) until the period shortly after World War II, when they were dissolved by the American Occupation (q.v.) of Japan. The term is applied especially to the so-called Big Four *zaibatsu*, Mitsui, Mitsubishi, Sumitomo, and Yasuda (qq.v.), but may also include a second grouping of companies called *shinkō zaibatsu* (new *zaibatsu*) that had risen to similar prominence by the 1930s. Until the 1920s and 1930s, when public shareholding in subsidiary companies was permitted for the first time, the *zaibatsu* were entirely family owned and controlled. Control was exercised through powerful holding companies that directed member companies and operated them as units.

While *zaibatsu* operations such as manufacturing plants and mines were scattered in all parts of Japan and in Japanese colonial possessions abroad, the headquarters of member companies and the holding companies themselves were invariably in central Tokyo. This location pattern facilitated close ties to the leadership of national government and enhanced the power and influence of the *zaibatsu*. Furthermore, concentration of *zaibatsu* headquarters in Tokyo forms the basis of the city's role as Japan's premier corporate center.

ZŌJŌJI. Historic Buddhist temple of the Jōdo sect in the Shiba district of Minato Ward, Tokyo. Its origins date back to the 9th century, when it was known as Kōmyōji. Affiliation with Jōdo Buddhism began in 1393 under the influence of an abbot named Shōsō (1366–1440). In 1590 Tokugawa Ieyasu (q.v.) is said to have stopped at the temple for a rest when he and his retinue were entering Edo (q.v.) for the first time. At that time Zōjōji was located west of Edo Castle (q.v.), in what is today called the Kōchimachi district. The land in Shiba was given to the temple by Ieyasu in 1598. Throughout the Edo Period (q.v.), the temple protected the city from evil that would approach from the south, thought to be an especially dangerous direction. It was also distinguished as the Tokugawa family temple and burial ground. Moreover, Zōjōji came to be a major seminary of the Jōdo sect, with as many as 48 subsidiary temples, 100 other buildings, and 3,000 novices in residence at one time on the site.

Zōjōji's prestige declined after the Meiji Restoration (q.v.) in 1868 and most of the subsidiary buildings were lost in the years after that. The main temple building was destroyed in 1873 by arsonists. Another fire in 1909 destroyed its replacement. The temple was destroyed again in the air raids (q.v.) of 1945. The present temple building was completed in 1974. A surviving structure from the early Edo Period is a grand gate to Zōjōji. Known as Sanmon, or Triple Gate, because of its three portals, it was built in 1622 and has been designated as an Important Cultural Property. In addition to being a place for worship, the Zōjōji complex is also a significant sightseeing attraction. Because it is adjacent to Tokyo Tower (q.v.), photographers have used Zōjōji to illustrate contrasts between traditional and modern aspects of the city.

BIBLIOGRAPHY

INTRODUCTION

This bibliography is intended for English language readers who want to learn more about Tokyo. I believe that it is the most detailed bibliography in English about the city; I hope that it is helpful. I have concentrated on published material that can be obtained at or through most better libraries and on material that is relatively recent. While I have tried to include as many relevant sources as possible, it is inevitable that some key entries have been overlooked.

I have organized the bibliography alphabetically by topic. The topics flow from those that are more general to those that are more specific, and from topics that are historical to those that are more contemporary. The first group of references is about works that offer general descriptions of Tokyo and cover many topics in presenting a profile of the city. This is followed by works that are primarily reference sources about the city, such as atlases and yearbooks. Next come guidebooks, such as those that are written mostly for use by tourists. Sources about Tokyo history cover more pages than any other classification in this bibliography. They include items that are about the general history and development of the city, as well as those that look specifically at a particular period or event. The next section after "History" lists sources about historic preservation and historic districts in Tokyo. After that is a section about Tokyo's economy. It looks primarily at the present (or recent times). The section after "Economy" is a list of sources that look at specific districts of the city or neighborhoods, particularly in terms of their present (or recent) characteristics. Many of these sources come from English language publications that are printed in Japan, such as the magazine *Look Japan*, which once featured a series of neighborhood profiles written by foreign residents of Tokyo.

After "Neighborhoods and Districts" is a section called "Planning and Land Development." This is a special interest of mine that relates to my own teaching, so this section is longer than some of the others. Quite a few of the sources therein are publications in English by Tokyo Metropolitan Government. A section about "Politics and Government" is next, followed by "Social Conditions and Problems," "Urban Design and Architecture," and "Environmental Hazards and Earthquakes." The last section of the bibliography is about "Cultural Life" and lists sources about the arts in Tokyo, people's daily routines, and historic traditions that are vanishing from the contemporary scene. Sources are listed only once in the bibliography, even though some overlap with more than one topic area. Therefore, readers are urged to browse widely in search of references to topics that interest them.

I am often asked to recommend readings about Tokyo. The best sources about the history of the city, both in terms of the information they contain and the enjoyable style of writing, are the two books by Edward Seidensticker, *Low City, High City* (1983) and *Tokyo Rising* (1990). The former looks at the city during its period of rapid modernization and westernization of 1867-1923, while the latter focuses on the city's development since the Great Kantō Earthquake (q.v.) of 1923. Noel Nouet's *The Shogun's City: A History of Tokyo* (1990) is an excellent complement; it focuses on Edo (q.v.) during the time of the *shōguns* (q.v.) between 1603 and 1868. I also recommend the books by Paul Waley: *Tokyo Now and Then: An Explorer's Guide* (1984) and *Tokyo: City of Stories* (1991).

They too are rich in information and well written. Professor Yasuo Masai's bilingual atlas, *Atlas Tokyo: Edo/Tokyo through Maps* (1986), is a wonderful resource that shows how the old city was laid out.

There are few books that offer a comprehensive portrait of Tokyo and include both history and present characteristics.

Waley's *Fragments of a City: A Tokyo Anthology* (1992) is a welcome addition to this literature. I also recommend Peter Popham's *Tokyo: The City at the End of the World* (1985) as an especially enjoyable book with many memorable passages and some striking photographs. Readers have told me that my own book, *Tokyo: The Changing Profile of an Urban Giant* (1991), is a helpful profile of the city. I now know too many of that book's shortcomings to be totally enthusiastic, but I am thankful that reviewers have recommended it nonetheless. I am working on a revision of that book, including considerable updated information. Readers should look for it sometime in 1997. The revised edition will be published by John Wiley and Sons.

There are several guidebooks about Tokyo. In terms of general information for the tourist or business traveler, I recommend both *Tokyo*, edited by M. Rivas-Micoud, J. Zanghi, and M. Hirokawa and published by APA Publications (1991), and *Tokyo: City Guide* put together by C. Taylor and published by Lonely Planet Publications (1993). The best guidebooks for exploring the city by walking around its neighborhoods are those by Sumiko Enbutsu, especially her most recent *Old Tokyo: Walks in the City of the Shogun* (1993). *Tokyo Museums* by T. Flannigan and E. Flannigan (1993) is an excellent guide to the city's many museums. I also think highly of Elizabeth Kiritani's *Vanishing Japan: Traditions, Crafts and Culture* (1995). It is listed in the "Cultural Life" section of the bibliography, and it is a beautifully illustrated guide to the many old ways that can still be seen in Tokyo but are, unfortunately, fast disappearing.

Finally, I want to recommend a particular encyclopedia as an excellent source of additional information about Tokyo: the two-volume *Japan: An Illustrated Encyclopedia* published in 1993 by Kodansha. It looks at the country as a whole, but many of its entries deal with Tokyo specifically, including entries about important individuals in the life of the city, key events, famous districts, and prominent landmarks. The encyclopedia is totally authoritative, well written, and nicely illustrated with color photographs and maps. It is a "must" for any library about Tokyo (or Japan as a whole). I have found it to be an invaluable resource for checking facts and resolving conflicts of interpretation that arise from other readings.

GENERAL

Cybriwsky, R. *Tokyo: The Changing Profile of an Urban Giant.* London: Belhaven; Boston: G. K. Hall, 1991.

——. "Tokyo." *Cities: The International Journal of Urban Policy and Planning* 10, no. 1 (February 1993): 2–11.

Graves, W., and W. Parks. "Tokyo: The Peaceful Explosion." *National Geographic* 126, no. 4 (October 1964): 445-87.

Hall, P. *The World Cities.* London: Weidenfeld and Nicolson, 1984.

Honjo, H. "Tokyo: Giant Metropolis of the Orient." In *World Capitals: Toward Guided Urbanization,* edited by H. W. Eldredge, 340-87. Garden City: Anchor Press/Doubleday, 1975.

Inouchi, N. *Tokyo.* Tokyo: International Society for Educational Information, 1987.

Ishii, K. K. *Tokyo.* Tokyo: Tokyo Metropolitan Government, 1971.

Isomura, E. "Tokyo: An International City." *New Japan* 12 (1960): 26-28.

Kato, H. "Tokyo Comes of Age." *Japan Echo* 14 (Special Issue 1987): 8–11.

Kornhauser, D. *Japan: Geographical Background to Urban-Industrial Development.* London and New York: Longman, 1982.

Miyamoto, K. "Japan's World Cities: Osaka and Tokyo Compared." In *Japanese Cities in the World Economy,* edited by K. Fujita and R. C. Hill, 53-83. Philadelphia: Temple University Press, 1993.

Morris, J. *Traveler from Tokyo.* New York: Sheridan House Publishers, 1944.

Mutsu, J., and O. D. Russell. *Here's Tokyo.* Tokyo: Tokyo News Service. 1953.

Nakamura, H., and J. White. "Tokyo," In *The Metropolis Era: Mega-Cities, Volume 2,* edited by M. Dogan and J. D. Kasarda, 123-56. Newbury Park, Calif.: Sage Publications, 1988.

Nishida, K. *Storied Cities of Japan.* Tokyo: Weatherhill, 1963.

Popham, P. *Tokyo: The City at the End of the World.* Tokyo: Kodansha International, 1985.

Smith, H. D., II. "Tokyo and London: Comparative Conceptions of the City." In *Japan: A Comparative View,* edited by A. M. Craig, 49-99. Princeton: Princeton University Press, 1979.

Tokyo Metropolitan Government. *Sizing Up Tokyo.* Tokyo: TMG Municipal Library No. 3, 1969.

——. *Plain Talk about Tokyo.* Tokyo: Tokyo Metropolitan Government, 1984.

——. *Plain Talk About Tokyo.* Tokyo: Tokyo Metropolitan Government, 1987.

——. *Tokyo: Yesterday, Today, and Tomorrow.* Tokyo: Tokyo Metropolitan Government, 1989.

Tokyo Municipal Office. *Tokyo.* Tokyo: Tokyo Municipal Office, 1934.

Waley, P. *Fragments of a City: A Tokyo Anthology.* Tokyo: The Japan Times, 1992.

ATLASES, YEARBOOKS, ETC.

Masai, Y. *Atlas Tokyo: Edo/Tokyo through Maps.* Tokyo: Heibonsha, 1986.

Tokyo: A Bilingual Atlas. Tokyo: Iris, 1987.

Tokyo Metropolitan Atlas. Tokyo: Shobunsha, 1991.

Tokyo Metropolitan Government. *Tokyo Metropolis: Facts and Data.* Tokyo: Tokyo Metropolitan Government, 1994.

Tokyo Statistical Yearbook, 1982. Tokyo: Tokyo Statistical Association, 1982.

Tokyo Statistical Yearbook, 1987. Tokyo: Tokyo Statistical Association, 1987.

Tokyo Statistical Yearbook, 1994. Tokyo: Tokyo Statistical Association, 1994.

GUIDEBOOKS, TOURIST INTEREST

A Look into Tokyo. Tokyo: Japan Travel Bureau, 1988.

Boardman, G. R. *Living in Tokyo.* Camden, N.J.: Thomas Nelson, 1970.

Brand, J. *Tokyo Night City.* Rutland, Vt., and Tokyo: Charles E. Tuttle, 1993.

Clemens, S. L. *Tokyo Pink Guide.* Tokyo: Yenbooks, 1993.

Connor, J., and M. Yoshida. *Tokyo City Guide.* Tokyo: Ryuko Tsushin, 1984.

Edo-Tokyo Museum. *Guide to Edo-Tokyo Museum* (English Edition). Tokyo: Foundation Edo-Tokyo Historical Society, 1995.

Enbutsu, S. *Discover Shitamachi: A Walking Guide to the Other Tokyo.* Tokyo: The Shitamachi Times, 1984.

Enbutsu, S. *Old Tokyo: Walks in the City of the Shogun.* Rutland, Vt. and Tokyo: Charles E. Tuttle, 1993.

Flannigan, T., and E. Flannigan. *Tokyo Museums.* Rutland, Vt. and Tokyo: Charles E. Tuttle, 1993.

Fodor's Tokyo. New York: Fodor's Travel Publications, 1993.

Hall, C. *Tokyo Dining Out.* Tokyo: The Japan Times, 1992.

Kami, R. *Tokyo: Sights and Insights.* Rutland, Vt. and Tokyo: Charles E. Tuttle, 1992.

Kennedy, R. *Good Tokyo Restaurants.* Tokyo: Kodansha International, 1993.

Kennedy, R. *Little Adventures in Tokyo: 39 Thrills for the Urban Explorer.* Berkeley: Stone Bridge, 1992.

Kennerdell, J. *Tokyo Journal's Tokyo Restaurant Guide.* Tokyo: Yohan Publications, 1994.

Kinoshita, J., and N. Palevsky. *Gateway to Tokyo.* Tokyo: Kodansha International, 1993.

Kirkup, J. *Tokyo.* London: Phoenix, 1966.

Martin, J. H., and P. G. Martin. *Tokyo: A Cultural Guide to Japan's Capital City.* Rutland, Vt. and Tokyo: Charles E. Tuttle, 1996.

Miyao, S. and F. Dunbar. *Tokyo: Past and Present.* Osaka: Hoikusha Publishing, 1984.

Moriyama, T. *Tokyo Adventures: Glimpses of the City in Bygone Eras.* Translated by B. Gavey and R. Gavey. Tokyo: Shufunotomo, 1993.

Morton, D., and N. Tsunoi. *The Best of Tokyo.* Rutland, Vt. and Tokyo: Charles E. Tuttle, 1989.

Pearce, J. *Foot-Loose in Tokyo: A Curious Traveler's Guide to the 29 Stages of the Yamanote Line.* New York and Tokyo: Weatherhill, 1983.

Richie, D. *Introducing Tokyo.* Tokyo: Kodansha International, 1987.

Rivas-Micoud, M., J. Zanghi, and M. Hirokawa, eds. *Tokyo.* Singapore: APA Publications, 1991.

Schilling, M. *Tokyo After Dark.* Tokyo: The Japan Times 1992.

Taylor, C. *Tokyo: City Guide.* Hawthorn, Victoria, Australia: Lonely Planet Publications, 1993.

Usami, M., and C. Hon-Cheung. *Tokyo*. Secaucus, N.J.: Chartwell Books, 1978.

Wurman, R. S. *TokyoAccess*. New York: AccessPress, 1984.

HISTORY

Allinson, G. D. "Japanese Cities in the Industrial Era." *Journal of Urban History* 4, no. 4 (1978): 443–76.

Barr, P. *The Deer Cry Pavilion: A Story of Westerners in Japan, 1868–1905*. New York: Harcourt, Brace and World, 1968.

Bennett, J. W., and S. B. Levine. "Industrialization and Urbanization in Japan: The Emergence of Public Discontent." *Habitat* 2, nos. 1-2 (1977): 205–18.

Bureau of Reconstruction and the Tokyo Institute for Municipal Research. *The Outline of the Reconstruction Work in Tokyo and Yokohama*. Tokyo: Sugitaya, 1929.

Busch, N. F. *Two Minutes to Noon*. New York: Simon and Schuster, 1962.

Center for Urban Studies, ed. *Tokyo: Urban Growth and Planning, 1868–1988*. Tokyo: Tokyo Metropolitan University Center for Urban Studies, 1988.

Coaldrake, W. H. "Building a New Establishment: Tokugawa Iemitsu's Consolidation of Power and the Taitokuin Mausoleum." In *Edo and Paris: Urban Life and the State in the Early Modern Era*, edited by J. L. McCain, J. M. Merriman, and K. Ugawa, 153-72. Ithaca and London: Cornell University Press, 1994.

Daniels, G. "The Great Tokyo Air Raid, 9–10 March 1945." In *Modern Japan: Aspects of History, Literature and Society*, edited by W. G. Beasley, 113-31; 278-79. Berkeley and Los Angeles: University of California Press, 1977.

Elisonas, J. "Notorious Places: A Brief Excursion into the Narrative Topography of Early Edo." In *Edo and Paris: Urban Life and the State in the Early Modern Era*, edited by J. L. McCain, J. M. Merriman, and K. Ugawa, 253-91. Ithaca and London: Cornell University Press, 1994.

Guillain, R. *I Saw Tokyo Burning: An Eyewitness Narrative from Pearl Harbor to Hiroshima.* Translated by W. Byron. Garden City, N.Y: Doubleday, 1981.

Hatano, J. "Edo's Water Supply." In *Edo and Paris: Urban Life and the State in the Early Modern Era,* edited by J. L. McCain, J. M. Merriman, and K. Ugawa, 234-50. Ithaca and London: Cornell University Press, 1994.

Hayashi, R. "Provisioning Edo in the Early Eighteenth Century: The Pricing Policies of the Shogunate and the Crisis of 1733." In *Edo and Paris: Urban Life and the State in the Early Modern Era,* edited by J. L. McCain, J. M. Merriman, and K. Ugawa, 211-33. Ithaca and London: Cornell University Press, 1994.

Ishida, Y. "Ougai Mori and Tokyo's Building Ordinance." In *Tokyo: Urban Growth and Planning, 1868–1988,* edited by Center for Urban Studies, 83-86. Tokyo: Tokyo Metropolitan University Center for Urban Studies, 1988.

Ishizuka, H. "Amusement Quarters, Public Squares and Road Regulations of Tokyo in the Meiji Era." In *Tokyo: Urban Growth and Planning, 1868–1988,* edited by Center for Urban Studies, 71-75. Tokyo: Tokyo Metropolitan University Center for Urban Studies, 1988.

Jones, H. J. *Live Machines: Hired Foreigners and Meiji Japan.* Tenterden: Paul Norbury Publications, 1980.

Kelley, W. W. "Incendiary Actions: Fires and Firefighting in the Shogun's Capital and the People's City. In *Edo and Paris: Urban Life and the State in the Early Modern Era,* edited by J. L. McCain, J. M. Merriman, and K. Ugawa, 310-31. Ithaca and London: Cornell University Press, 1994.

Longstreet, S., and E. Longstreet. *Yoshiwara: The Pleasure Quarters of Old Tokyo.* Rutland, Vt., and Tokyo: Yenbooks, 1988.

Kato, T. "Governing Edo." In *Edo and Paris: Urban Life and the State in the Early Modern Era,* edited by J. L.

McCain, J. M. Merriman, and K. Ugawa, 41-67. Ithaca and London: Cornell University Press, 1994.

Kojiro Y. "Edo: The City on the Plain." In *Tokyo: Form and Spirit,* edited by Mildred Friedman, 37-53. Minneapolis: Walker Art Center; New York: Harry N. Abrams, 1986.

McClain, J.L. "Edobashi: Power, Space, and Popular Culture in Edo." In *Edo and Paris: Urban Life and the State in the Early Modern Era,* edited by J. L. McCain, J. M. Merriman, and K. Ugawa, 105-31. Ithaca and London: Cornell University Press, 1994.

McClain, J. L., J. M. Merriman, and K. Ugawa, eds. *Edo and Paris: Urban Life and the State in the Early Modern Era.* Ithaca and London: Cornell University Press, 1994.

McClain J. L., and J. M. Merriman. "Edo and Paris: Cities and Power." In *Edo and Paris: Urban Life and the State in the Early Modern Era,* edited by J. L. McCain, J. M. Merriman, and K. Ugawa, 3-38.

McClain, J. L., and K. Ugawa. "Visions of the City." In *Edo and Paris: Urban Life and the State in the Early Modern Era,* edited by J. L. McCain, J. M. Merriman, and K. Ugawa, 455-64. Ithaca and London: Cornell University Press, 1994.

Masai, Y. "Tokyo: From a Feudal Million City to a Global Supercity." *Geographical Review of Japan* 63 (Ser. B), no. 1 (1990): 1–16.

Moriya, K. "Urban Networks and Information Networks." In *Tokugawa Japan: The Social and Economic Antecedents of Modern Japan,* edited by C. Nakane and S. Ōishi, 97-123. Translated by C. Totman. Tokyo: University of Tokyo Press, 1990.

Naito, A. "Planning and Development of Early Edo." *Japan Echo* 14 (Special Issue 1987): 30–38.

Nakamura, H. "Urban Growth in Prewar Japan." In *Japanese Cities in the World Economy,* edited by K. Fujita and R. C. Hill, 26-49. Philadelphia: Temple University Press, 1993.

Noguchi, K. "Construction of Ginza Brick Street and Conditions of Landowners and House Owners." In *Tokyo: Urban Growth and Planning, 1868–1988,* edited by Center for Urban Studies, 76-82. Tokyo: Tokyo Metropolitan University Center for Urban Studies, 1988.

Nouet, N. *The Shogun's City: A History of Tokyo.* Translated by J. Mills and M. Mills. Sandgate, Folkestone, England: Paul Norbury Publications, 1990.

Rozman, G. *Urban Networks in Ch'ing China and Tokugawa Japan.* Princeton: Princeton University Press, 1973.

Seidensticker, E. *Low City, High City: Tokyo from Edo to the Earthquake.* Rutland, Vt., and Tokyo: Charles E. Tuttle, 1983.

——. *Tokyo Rising: The City since the Great Earthquake.* New York: Alfred A. Knopf, 1990.

Shōji, S. "Enzō Ohta and Reconstruction Work after the Great Kantō Earthquake." In *Tokyo: Urban Growth and Planning, 1868–1988,* edited by Center for Urban Studies, 92-95. Tokyo: Tokyo Metropolitan University Center for Urban Studies, 1988.

Smith, H. D., II. "Edo-Tokyo Transition: In Search of a Common Ground." In *Japan in Transition: From Tokugawa to Meiji,* edited by M. B. Jansen and G. Rozman, 347-74. Princeton: Princeton University Press, 1986.

——. "The History of the Book in Edo and Paris." In *Edo and Paris: Urban Life and the State in the Early Modern Era,* edited by J. L. McCain, J. M. Merriman, and K. Ugawa, 332-52. Ithaca and London: Cornell University Press, 1994.

Takeuchi, M. "Festivals and Fights: The Law and the People of Edo." In *Edo and Paris: Urban Life and the State in the Early Modern Era,* edited by J. L. McCain, J. M. Merriman, and K. Ugawa, 384-406. Ithaca and London: Cornell University Press, 1994.

Tokyo Metropolitan Government. *Twenty-Five Tales in Mem-*

ory of Tokyo's Foreigners. Tokyo: TMG Municipal Library No. 23 (supplement), 1989.

Tokyo Metropolitan Government. *Tokyo: The Making of a Metropolis.* Tokyo: TMG Municipal Library No. 27, 1993.

Wagatsuma, H., and G. A. DeVos. "Arakawa Ward: Urban Growth and Modernization." *Rice University Studies* 66, no. 1 (1980): 201–24.

Waley, P. *Tokyo Now and Then: An Explorer's Guide.* New York and Tokyo: Weatherhill, 1984.

——. "Twelve Storys—Asakusa's Towering Cultural Achievement." *The Japan Times,* 24 January 1989.

——. *Tokyo: City of Stories.* New York and Tokyo: Weatherhill, 1991.

Walthall, A. "Edo Riots." In *Edo and Paris: Urban Life and the State in the Early Modern Era,* edited by J. L. McCain, J. M. Merriman, and K. Ugawa, 407-28. Ithaca and London: Cornell University Press, 1994.

Wildes, H. E. *Typhoon in Tokyo: The Occupation and Its Aftermath.* New York: Macmillan, 1954.

Yazaki, T. *Social Change and the City in Japan: From Earliest Times through the Industrial Revolution.* Tokyo: Japan Publications, 1968.

Yoshima, S. "Industrial Expositions in Modern Japan: A Gauge of the Changing City." Paper presented at the annual meeting of the Association for Asian Studies, Los Angeles, 25-28 March 1993.

HISTORIC PRESERVATION, HISTORIC DISTRICTS

Cybriwsky, R. "Historic Preservation in Tokyo." *Proceedings of the New England/St. Lawrence Valley Division of the Association of American Geographers* 21 (1991): 58–62.

Fujimoto, K. "Trying to Save Tokyo Station." *The Japan Times,* 15 November 1987, p. 8.

Gill, T. "Sanbancho's Last Stand." *Tokyo Journal* 9, no. 11 (February 1990): 82–86.

Kingston, J. "Artist Captures the Charm of Old Tokyo." *The Japan Times,* 18 December 1988, p. 5.

Ma, K. "Parking Lot or Pond?" *The Daily Yomiuri,* 11 September 1989.

Symposium Executive Committee, ed. *Symposium on Proposed Construction of Shinobazu Pond Underground Parking Lot, March 3, 1990 (proceedings).* Tokyo: Symposium Excecutive Committee, 1990.

Waley, P. "Remaining Nagaya Serve as Reminders of a Poorer Life." *The Japan Times,* 3 September 1989, p. 12.

ECONOMY

Fujita, K. "A World City and Flexible Specializtion: Restructuring of the Tokyo Metropolis." *International Journal of Urban and Regional Research* 15, no. 2 (1991): 269–84.

Fujita, K. "Women Workers and Flexible Specialization: The Case of Tokyo." *Economy and Society* 20, no. 3 (1991): 260–82.

Fujita, K., and R. C. Hill, eds. *Japanese Cities in the World Economy.* Philadelphia: Temple University Press, 1993.

Itakura, K., and A. Takeuchi. "Keihin Region." In *An Industrial Geography of Japan,* edited by K. Murata and I. Ota, 47-65. New York: St. Martin's Press, 1980.

Kiyonari, T. "Restructuring Urban-Industrial Links in Greater Tokyo: Small Producers' Responses to Changing World Markets." In *Japanese Cities in the World Economy,* edited by K. Fujita and R. C. Hill, 141-56. Philadelphia: Temple University Press, 1993.

Kosai, Y. *The Era of High-Speed Growth: Notes on the Postwar Japanese Economy.* Tokyo: University of Tokyo Press, 1986.

Lewis, M. "How a Tokyo Earthquake Could Devastate Wall Street and the World Economy." *Manhattan, Inc.,* June 1989, 69–79.

Machimura, T. "The Urban Restructuring Process in Tokyo in the 1980s: Transforming Tokyo into a World City." *International Journal of Urban and Regional Research* 16, no. 1 (1992): 114–28.

———. *The Structural Change of a Global City: Urban Restructuring in Tokyo.* Tokyo: University of Tokyo Press, 1994.

Murata, K., and I. Ota, eds. *An Industrial Geography of Japan.* New York: St. Martin's Press, 1980.

Sassen, S. *The Global City: New York, London, Tokyo.* Princeton: Princeton University Press, 1991.

Tatsuno, S. *The Technopolis Strategy; Japan, High Technology, and the Control of the Twenty-first Century.* New York: Prentice Hall, 1986.

Tokyo Metropolitan Government. Tokyo Industry, 1990: *A Graphic Overview.* Tokyo: Tokyo Metropolitan Government, 1990.

Tokyo Metropolitan Government, Bureau of Labor and Economic Affairs. *Industry and Labor in Tokyo 1996.* Tokyo: Tokyo Metropolitan Government, 1996.

NEIGHBORHOODS AND DISTRICTS

Betros, C. "Tsukiji: Afishionados." *Look Japan* 34, no. 391 (1988): 54–55.

Brown, A. "Black Mischief." *Tokyo Journal* 13 (April 1993): 24–31.

Chapman, C. "Denenchōfu: An Oasis of Spacious Living." *Look Japan* 33, no. 377 (1987): 38–39.

Cybriwsky, R. "Shibuya Center, Tokyo." *Geographical Review* 78, no. 1 (1988): 48–61.

———. "Takadanobaba: The Shogun and the Show Girl." *Look*

Japan 34, no. 392 (1988): 38–39.

Eastham, K. "Requiem for a Neighborhood." *Tokyo Journal,* October 1995, 33-36.

Fujimori, T. "Shitamachi, In Tokyo's Left Hand" *Japan Quarterly* 34, no. 4 (October/December 1987): 410–17.

Gluck, P. "Shinjuku." *Architectural Record* 162 (September 1977): 101–4.

Kawamoto, S. "Ōkubo: Ethnic Melting Pot." *Japan Echo* 14 (Special Issue 1987): 73–76.

Kennerdell, J. "Golden-Gai." *Tokyo Journal* 8, no. 4 (supplement 1988): 13.

Masler, D. "Tsukudajima: An Island in Time." *Look Japan* 33, no. 237 (1987): 38–39.

Normile, D. "Electric City: Postcards from Akihabara." *Popular Science* 242, no. 1 (January 1993): 82–84.

Simmons, D. "Asakusa: Into the Twilight Zone" *Look Japan* 33, no. 386 (1988): 38–39.

Spivak, M. "Kichijōji: What More Could You Want?" *Look Japan* 33, no. 378 (1987): 38–39.

Takeuchi, H. "The Two Faces of Shinjuku." *Japan Echo* 14 (Special Issue 1987): 69–72.

Tanzer, A. "Techie Heaven." *Forbes* 148, no. 6 (1991): 184–85.

Van Hook, H. "Prime Time in Kabuki-Chō." *Tokyo Journal* 9, no. 3 (1989): 4–9, 12–17.

Wade, D. "Shibuya: Old Dog, New Sticks." *Look Japan* 34, no. 393 (1988): 38–39.

Waley, P. "Fukagawa: Memories of Edo." *Look Japan* 33, no. 373 (1987): 38–39.

——. "The Shinjuku Story." *Tokyo Journal* 8, no. 4 (supplement 1988): 14–15.

——. "The Ginza Story." *Tokyo Journal* 8, no. 9 (supplement 1988): 5–7.

Whitin Kiritani, E. "Nezu: A Quiet Haven." *Look Japan* 33, no. 380 (1987): 38–39.

PLANNING AND LAND DEVELOPMENT

Alden, J. "Metropolitan Planning in Japan" *Town Planning Review* 55, no. 1 (1984): 55–74.

——. "Some Strengths and Weaknesses of Japanese Urban Planning." *Town Planning Review* 57, no. 2 (1986): 127–34.

Alden, J. D., and H. Abe. "Some Strengths and Weaknesses of Japanese Urban Planning." In *Planning for Cities and Regions in Japan,* edited by P. Shapira, I. Masser, and D. W. Edgington, 12-24. Liverpool: Liverpool University Press, 1994.

Alden, J. D., M. Hirohara, and H. Abe. "The Impact of Recent Urbanisation in Inner City Development in Japan." In *Planning for Cities and Regions in Japan,* edited by P. Shapira, I. Masser, and D. W. Edgington, 33-58. Liverpool: Liverpool University Press, 1994.

Arisue, T., and E. Aoki. "The Development of Railway Network in the Tokyo Region from the Viewpoint of the Metropolitan Growth." In *Japanese Cities: A Geographical Approach,* edited by S. Kiuchi et al., 191-200. Tokyo: The Association of Japanese Geographers, 1970.

City Planning Association of Japan, ed. *City Planning in Japan.* Tokyo: Sugitaya Printing, 1969.

Crowell, T. "Tokyo of the Future: Dazzling Ideas That Will Reshape City Life." *Asia Week,* 1 May 1994, 34–35, 38, 40–44, cover.

Doi, T. "Japan Megalopolis: Another Approach." *Ekistics* 26, no. 152 (July 1968): 96–99.

Douglass, M. "The Transnationalization of Urbanization in Japan." *International Journal of Urban and Regional Research* 12, no. 3 (1988): 425–54.

———. "The 'New' Tokyo Story: Restructuring Space and the Struggle for Place in a World City." In *Japanese Cities in the World Economy*, edited by K. Fujita and R. C. Hill, 83-119. Philadelphia: Temple University Press, 1993.

Fujii, N. "Directions for Growth." *Japan Echo* 14 (Special Issue 1987): 12–19.

Fujimori, T. "Urban Planning in the Meiji Era." *Japan Echo* 14 (Special Issue 1987): 45–49.

"Future City on the Sea." *Tokyo Municipal News* 37, no. 3 (1987): 1–3.

Haberman, C. "Tokyo Aims to Reshape Itself as a 'World Class City,'" *The New York Times*, 8 February 1987, p. 14.

Hanes, J.E. "From Megalopolis to Megaroporisu." *Journal of Urban History* 19, no. 2 (1993): 56–94.

Hattori, K., N. Sugimura, and S. Higuchi. "Urbanization and Commercial Zones." In *Geography of Japan*, edited by Association of Japanese Geographers, 320-46. Tokyo: Teikoku-Shoin, 1980.

Hebbert, M. "Sen-biki amidst Desakota: Urban Sprawl and Urban Planning in Japan." In *Planning for Cities and Regions in Japan*, edited by P. Shapira, I. Masser, and D. W. Edgington, 70-91. Liverpool: Liverpool University Press, 1994.

———. "Urban Sprawl and Urban Planning in Japan." *Town Planning Review* 57, no. 2 (1986): 141–58.

Hirose, M. "Development of Tokyo Metropolitan Area and Countermeasures against Congestion of Commuting Traffic, 1960–1980." In *Tokyo: Urban Growth and Planning, 1868–1988*, edited by Center for Urban Studies, 125-28. Tokyo: Tokyo Metropolitan University Center for Urban Studies, 1988.

Holloway, N. "Tokyo: Time to Tame the Monster of the Capital." *Far Eastern Economic Review* 16 (June 1988): 53–55.

Hovinen, G. R. "The Search for Quality of Life in Japanese Planned Communities." *Proceedings of the Middle States Division of the Association of American Geographers* 21 (1988): 47–56.

Ishida, Y. "Chronology on Urban Planning in Tokyo, 1868–1988." In *Tokyo: Urban Growth and Planning, 1868–1988,* edited by Center for Urban Studies, 37-68. Tokyo: Tokyo Metropolitan University Center for Urban Studies, 1988.

Ishizuka, H., and Y. Ishida. "Tokyo, the Metropolis of Japan and Its Urban Development." In *Tokyo: Urban Growth and Planning, 1868–1988,* edited by Center for Urban Studies, 3-35. Tokyo: Tokyo Metropolitan University Center for Urban Studies, 1988.

Isomura, E. "A New Proposal for the Relocation of the Capital." *Japan Interpreter* 8, no. 3 (1973): 292–303.

Ito, M. "Coming to Terms with the Tokyo Problem." *Japan Echo* 15, no. 3 (1988): 50–54.

Itoh, S. "Land Problems in the Tokyo Region: The Existing Situation and Land Policy." In *The Cities of Asia: A Study of Urban Solutions and Urban Finances,* edited by J. Wong, 47-70. Singapore: Singapore University Press, 1976.

Itoh, T. "Design and Layout of Bridges and Parks in Reconstruction Project after the Great Kantō Earthquake: A Comparative Study of Tokyo and Yokohama." In *Tokyo: Urban Growth and Planning, 1868–1988,* edited by Center for Urban Studies, 96-101. Tokyo: Tokyo Metropolitan University Center for Urban Studies, 1988.

Jinnai, H. "Can the Tokyo Waterfront Be Revitalized?" *International Social Science Journal* 42, no. 3 (1990): 379–86.

Katoh, H. "Development of Housing Areas by Mitsui Trust Company." In *Tokyo: Urban Growth and Planning, 1868–1988,* edited by Center for Urban Studies, 106-11. Tokyo: Tokyo Metropolitan University Center for Urban Studies, 1988.

Kirwan, R. M. "Fiscal Policy and the Price of Land and Housing in Japan." *Urban Studies* 24 (1987): 345–60.

Kishi, N. "On the Waterfront." *Business Tokyo* (May 1987): 18–21, 25.

Kuroda, T. "Urbanization and Population Distribution Policies in Japan." *Regional Development Dialogue* 11, no. 1 (1990): 112–29.

Kurokawa, K. "New Tokyo Plan, 2025." *The Japan Architect* 367-78 (1987): 46–63.

Kurokawa, N. "Getting Serious About Land Prices." *Japan Quarterly* 37, no. 4 (1990): 392–401.

Mammen, D. "Toward an Urban Policy for Central Tokyo." *Japan Quarterly* 37, no. 4 (1990) 402–14.

Masai, Y. "Metropolitanization in Densely Populated Asia: The Case of Tokyo." In *The Asian City: Processes of Development, Characteristics and Planning,* edited by A. K. Dutt, et al., 119-29. Dordrecht: Kluwer Academic Publishers, 1994.

———. "Urban Development of Edo, Tokyo and the Tokyo Region." Rissho University offprint, no. 10, 20 March 1994.

Matsuda, K. "A Bold Plan to Remodel Tokyo's Business Center" *Japan Echo* 15, no. 2 (1988): 28–30.

My Town Concept Consultative Council. *Tokyo Tomorrow.* Tokyo: Tokyo Metropolitan Government, 1982.

Nagashima, C. "Megalopolis in Japan." *Ekistics* 24, no. 140 (1967): 6–14.

———. "Japan Megalopolis: Part 2, Analysis." *Ekistics* 26, no. 152 (1968): 95.

Nussbaum, S. P. *The Residential Community in Modern Japan: An Analysis of a Tokyo Suburban Development.* Ph.D. diss., Cornell University, 1985.

Onishi, T. "A Capacity Approach for Sustainable Urban Development: An Empirical Study." *Regional Studies* 28, no. 1 (1994): 39–51.

Ōtani, K. "Makuhari New Town." *Japan Quarterly* 37, no. 4 (1990): 451–58.

Phalon, R. "Land Poor." *Forbes,* 14 November 1988, 56–62.

Robertson, J. "Affective City Planning in Kodaira City (Tokyo)." Unpublished paper prepared for the annual meeting of the Association of American Geographers, Portland, Oregon, 22-26 April 1987.

——. *Native and Newcomer: Making and Remaking a Japanese City.* Berkeley and Los Angeles: University of California Press, 1991.

Sato, M. "Shinkawa: A City Center is Born." *Japan Echo* 15, no. 2 (1988): 31–33.

Shapira, P., I. Masser, and D. W. Edgington, eds. *Planning for Cities and Regions in Japan.* Liverpool: Liverpool University Press, 1994.

Smith, C. "Paying for Past Neglect." *Far Eastern Economic Review* 16 (June 1988): 49–51.

——. "Tokyo: Retain the City, but Shift the Functions." *Far Eastern Economic Review* 16, (June 1988): 55–56.

——. "Japan's Regions: Solving the Development Imbalance." *Far Eastern Economic Review* 16 (June 1988): 56.

Suzuki, E. "Makichō Avenue Project and Excess Condemnation." In *Tokyo: Urban Growth and Planning, 1868–1988,* edited by Center for Urban Studies, 87-91. Tokyo: Tokyo Metropolitan University Center for Urban Studies, 1988.

Suzuki, S. "Urban Planning in Tokyo during the 1960s." In *Tokyo: Urban Growth and Planning, 1868–1988,* edited by Center for Urban Studies,120-24. Tokyo: Tokyo Metropolitan University Center for Urban Studies, 1988.

Takami, M. "A Myriad of Projects in the Offing." *The Japan Times,* 4 February 1988, p. 16.

Tamura, A. "Deconcentrating Tokyo, Reconfiguring Japan" *Japan Quarterly* 34, no. 4 (1987): 378–83.

Tanaka, K. *Building a New Japan: Remodeling the Japanese Archipelago*. Tokyo: Simul Press, 1972.

Tange, K. "A Plan for Tokyo, 1986–." *The Japan Architect* 367-68 (1987): 8–45.

"Tokyo Frontier." *Tokyo Municipal News* 40, no. 1 (1990): 1–3.

"Tokyo in Torment: The Disoriented City." *The Economist,* 9 April 1988, 21–24.

Tokyo Metropolitan Government. *Tokyo's Housing Problem*. Tokyo: TMG Library No. 5, 1972.

——. *Tokyo for the People: Concepts for Urban Renewal*. Tokyo: TMG Municipal Library No. 6, 1972.

——. *Planning of Tokyo, 1985*. Tokyo: Tokyo Metropolitan Government, 1985.

——. *The Fiscal Outlook for the Metropolis of Tokyo*. Tokyo: Tokyo Metropolitan Government, 1986.

——. *Second Long-Term Plan for the Tokyo Metropolis*. Tokyo: Tokyo Metropolitan Government, 1987.

——. *Planning of Tokyo, 1988*. Tokyo: Tokyo Metropolitan Government, 1988.

——. *The Fiscal Outlook for the Metropolis of Tokyo*. Tokyo: Tokyo Metropolitan Government, 1989.

——. *Planning of Tokyo, 1990*. Tokyo: Tokyo Metropolitan Government, 1990.

——. *The 3rd Long-Term Plan for the Tokyo Metropolis*. Tokyo: Tokyo Metropolitan Government, 1991.

——. *The Tokyo Metropolitan Housing Master Plan*. Tokyo: Tokyo Metropolitan Government, 1991.

——. *Planning of Tokyo, 1994*. Tokyo: Tokyo Metropolitan Government, 1994.

——. *Tokyo Teleport Town: Metropolitan Waterfront Subcenter*. Tokyo: Tokyo Metropolitan Government, 1994.

——. *Urban White Paper on Tokyo Metropolis, 1994*. Tokyo:

Tokyo Metropolitan Government, 1994.

Udagawa, H. "Tokyo Reaches the Outer Limits." *Tokyo Business Today* (April 1988): 34–37.

Wegener, M. "Tokyo's Land Market and Its Impact on Housing and Urban Life." In *Planning for Cities and Regions in Japan,* edited by P. Shapira, I. Masser, and D. W. Edgington, 92-112. Liverpool: Liverpool University Press, 1994.

Witherick, M. E. "Tokyo." In *Urban Problems and Planning in the Developed World,* edited by M. Pacione, 120-56. New York: St. Martin's Press, 1981.

Yamaga, S. "Urbanization in the Northern Suburbs of Tokyo." In *Japanese Cities: A Geographical Approach,* edited by S. Kiuchi, et al, 73-78. Tokyo: Association of Japanese Geographers. 1970.

Yasuoka, N. "Slum Clearance in the Prewar Days of Showa." In *Tokyo: Urban Growth and Planning, 1868–1988,* edited by Center for Urban Studies,112-15. Tokyo: Tokyo Metropolitan University Center for Urban Studies, 1988.

Yawata, K. "Why and Where to Relocate the Capital." *Japan Quarterly* 35 (1988): 127–32.

Zetter, J. "Challenges for Japanese Urban Policy." In *Planning for Cities and Regions in Japan,* edited by P. Shapira, I. Masser, and D. W. Edgington, 25-33. Liverpool: Liverpool University Press, 1994.

——. "Challenges for Japanese Urban Policy." *Town Planning Review* 57, no. 2 (1986): 135–40.

POLITICS AND GOVERNMENT

Allinson, G. D. *Japanese Urbanism: Industry and Politics in Kariya, 1972–1972.* Berkeley: University of California Press, 1975.

——. Suburban *Tokyo: A Comparative Study in Politics and Social Change.* Berkeley and Los Angeles: University of California Press, 1979.

Beard, C. A. "Goto and the Rebuilding of Tokyo." *Our World* 5 (April 1924): 11–21.

———. "Japan's Statesman of Research." *Review of Reviews* 68 (September 1923): 296–98.

Gordon, A. "The Crowd and Politics in Imperial Japan: Tokyo 1905–1918." *Past and Present* 121 (1988): 141–70.

Hayase, Y. *The Career of Goto Shinpei: Japan's Statesman of Research, 1857–1929.* Ph.D. diss., Florida State University, 1974.

Lockheimer, F. R. "The People's Choice: Ryokichi Minobe." *East Asia Series (American University Field Staff)* 14, no. 4 (Japan 1967): 1–18.

Narita, R. "Toshihiko Sakai in the Transition Period of Urban Structure: His Participation in the Tokyo City Assembly Member Election in 1929." In *Tokyo: Urban Growth and Planning, 1868–1988,* edited by Center for Urban Studies, 102-5. Tokyo: Tokyo Metropolitan University Center for Urban Studies, 1988.

Robinson, M. "Trial by Fire: The Political Education of Yukio Aoshima." *Tokyo Journal,* November 1995, 32-37.

Steiner, K. *Local Government in Japan.* Stanford: Stanford University Press, 1965.

Tokyo Metropolitan Government. *An Administrative Perspective of Tokyo, 1970.* Tokyo: Tokyo Metropolitan Government, 1970.

———. *Tokyo Metropolis: Organization.* Tokyo: Tokyo Metropolitan Government, 1994.

SOCIAL CONDITIONS AND PROBLEMS

Allinson, G. D. "Japanese Urban Society and Its Cultural Context." In *The City in Cultural Context,* edited by J. A. Agnew, J. Mercer, and D. E. Sopher, 163-185. Boston: Allen and Unwin, 1984.

Allison, A. *Nightwork: Sexuality, Pleasure and Corporate Masculinity in a Tokyo Hostess Club.* Chicago and London: University of Chicago Press, 1994.

Bedford-Numata, Y. "Recent Trends in Japan's Population Movement," *Michigan Academician* 3, no. 2, (Fall 1970): 85–94.

Bestor, T. C. *Neighborhood Tokyo.* Stanford: Stanford University Press, 1989.

——. "Tokyo no Daidokoro: Research on the Tsukiji Wholesale Fish Market." *Japan Foundation Newsletter* 17, no. 4 (1989): 17–21.

——. "Tokyo Mom-and-Pop." *Wilson Quarterly* 14, no. 4 (Autumn 1990): 27–33.

——. "Tradition and Japanese Social Organization: Institutional Development in a Tokyo Neighborhood." *Ethnology* 24, no. 2 (1985): 121–35.

Betros, C. "Down and Out in Tokyo." *Japananlysis* 1–2 (February 1980): 20–21.

——. "The Shepherds of Sanya" *Asahi Evening News,* 25 January, 1985, p. 3.

Blake, S. L. *Spatial and Social Structures of Tokyo's Ethnic Communities.* Ph.D. diss., University of Tokyo, 1995.

Caldarola, C. "The Doya-Gai: A Japanese Version of Skid Row." *Pacific Affairs,* 41, no. 4 (1968–69): 511–25.

de Bary, B. "Sanya: Japan's Internal Colony." In *The Other Japan: Postwar Realities,* edited by E. P. Tsurumi, 112-18. Armonk, N.Y. and London: M. E. Sharpe, 1988.

Dore, R. P. *City Life in Japan: A Study of a Tokyo Ward.* Berkeley and Los Angeles: University of California Press, 1958.

Fallows, J. "The Other Japan" *The Atlantic* 261, no. 4 (April 1988): 16–18, 20.

——. "Tokyo: The Hard Life" *The Atlantic* 263, no. 3 (March

1989): 16–26.

Guzewicz, T. D. "A New Generation of Homeless." *Japan Quarterly* 43, no. 3 (1996): 43-53.

Hamabata, M. M. "Ethnographic Boundaries: Culture, Class, and Sexuality in Tokyo." *Qualitative Sociology* 9, no. 4 (1986): 354–71.

———. *Crested Kimono: Power and Love in the Japanese Business Family.* Ithaca: Cornell University Press, 1990.

Hanayama, Y. "Urban Land Prices and the Housing Problem." *Developing Economies* 10, no. 4 (December 1972): 468–78.

Hane, M. *Peasants, Rebels and Outcastes: The Underside of Modern Japan.* New York: Pantheon Books, 1982.

Imamura, A. E. *Urban Japanese Housewives: At Home and in the Community.* Honolulu: University of Hawaii Press, 1987.

Ishimizu, T., and H. Ishihara. "The Distribution and Movement of Population in Japan's Three Major Metropolitan Areas." In *Geography of Japan,* edited by Association of Japanese Geographers, 347-78. Tokyo: Teikoku-Shoin, 1980.

Kamo, Y. "Husbands and Wives Living in Nuclear and Stem Family Households in Japan." *Sociological Perspectives* 33, no. 3 (1990): 397–417.

Kato, H. "Comparative Study of Street Life: Tokyo, Manila, New York." *Occasional Paper No. 5.* Tokyo: Gakushuin University for Oriental Cultures, 1979.

Kauffman, R. "Tokyo's Housing Dilemma: Who's Paying the Price?" *Tokyo Journal* 8, no. 1 (1988): 78–83, 104.

Kim, M. *The State, Housing Producers, and Housing Consumers in Tokyo and Seoul.* Ph.D. diss., Brown University, 1993.

Kondo, D. K. *Crafting Selves: Power, Gender, and Discourses of Identity in a Japanese Workplace.* Chicago: University of Chicago Press, 1990.

Kurasawa, S. *Social Atlas of Tokyo.* Tokyo: University of Tokyo Press, 1986.

Lee, C., and G. DeVos. *Koreans in Japan: Ethnic Conflict and Accommodation.* Berkeley and Los Angeles: University of California Press, 1981.

Louis, L. *Butterflies in the Night: Mama-sans, Geishas, Strippers and the Japanese Men They Serve.* New York and Tokyo: Tengu Books, 1992.

Nakazawa, M. "Tattered Lives." *Tokyo Journal* (March, 1993): 34–39.

Ohshima, S., and C. Francis. *Japan Through the Eyes of Women Migrant Workers.* Tokyo: Japan Women's Christian Temperance Union, 1989.

Okamoto, K. "The Quality of Life in Metropolitan Suburbs of Japan: The Availability of Private Cars and the Daily Activities of Married Women." *The Journal of the Faculty of Letters,* Nagoya University 122 (March 1995): 155–65.

Rauch, J. *The Outnation: A Search for the Soul of Japan.* Boston: Harvard Business School Press, 1992.

Seymour, C. "A Look at the Other Japan: Sanya's Dying Mavericks." *The New Leader* 74, no. 12 (November 1991): 8–10.

Suginohara, J. *The Status Discrimination in Japan: Introduction to Buraku Problem.* Kobe: The Hyogo Institute of Buraku Problem, 1982.

Suzuki, K. "Equal Job Opportunity for Whom?" *Japan Quarterly* 43, no. 3 (1996): 54-60.

Taira, K. "Urban Poverty, Ragpickers, and the `Ants' Villa' in Tokyo." *Economic Development and Cultural Change* 17, no. 2 (1969): 155–77.

Tanaka, A. *Tokyo as a City of Consumption: Space, Media and Self-Identity in Contemporary Japan.* Master's thesis, University of British Columbia, 1994.

Ventura, R. *Underground in Japan.* London: Jonathan Cape, 1992.

Vogel, E. F. *Japan's New Middle Class: The Salary Man and His Family in a Tokyo Suburb.* 2d ed. Berkeley and Los Angeles: University of California Press, 1971.

Wagatsuma, H., and G. A. DeVos, *Heritage of Endurance: Family Patterns and Delinquency Formation in Urban Japan.* Berkeley and Los Angeles: University of California Press, 1984.

Yamamuro, B. "Alcoholism in Tokyo." *Quarterly Journal of Studies on Alcohol* 34, no. 3, part A (September 1973): 950–954.

Yazaki, T. *The Japanese City: A Sociological Analysis.* San Francisco and Tokyo: Japan Publications Trading Company, 1963.

——. *The Socioeconomic Structure of the Tokyo Metropolitan Complex.* Translated by M. Matsuda. Honolulu: University of Hawaii, Social Science Research Institute, 1966.

Yoshino, I. R., and S. Murakoshi. *The Invisible Visible Minority: Japan's Burakumin.* Osaka: Buraku Kaiho Kenkyusho, 1977.

URBAN DESIGN AND ARCHITECTURE

Ashihara, Y. "Chaos and Order in the Japanese City." *Japan Echo* 14 (Special Issue 1987): 64–68.

——. *The Hidden Order: Tokyo through the Twentieth Century.* Tokyo and New York: Kodansha, 1989.

Coaldrake, W. H. "Order and Anarchy: Tokyo from 1868 to the Present." In *Tokyo: Form and Spirit* edited by M. Friedman, 63-75. Minneapolis: Walker Art Center; New York: Harry N. Abrams, 1986.

——. "Edo Architecture and Tokugawa Law." *Monumenta Nipponica* 36, no. 3 (1981): 256–61.

Coaldrake, W. H. *Architecture and Authority in Japan.* London: Routledge, 1996.

Cybriwsky, R. "Tokyo Moves Westward: A Geography of New Landmarks and New Symbols of the City." *Middle States Geographer* 26 (1993): 108–14.

Fawcett, C. "Tokyo's Silent Space." In *Tokyo: Form and Spirit,* edited by Mildred Friedman, 179-91. Minneapolis: Walker Art Center; New York: Harry N. Abrams, 1986.

Friedman, M., ed. *Tokyo: Form and Spirit.* Minneapolis: Walker Art Center; New York: Harry N. Abrams, 1986.

Gallery-Ma, ed. *The Architectural Map of Tokyo.* Tokyo: Toto Shuppen, 1994 (in Japanese with some in English).

Golany, G. S., and T. Ojima. *Geo-Space Urban Design.* New York, John Wiley and Sons, 1996.

Greenbie, B. B. *Space and Spirit in Modern Japan.* New Haven and London: Yale University Press, 1988.

Isoda, K. "Tokyo and the Mythology of Modernity." *Japan Echo* 14 (Special Issue 1987): 59–63.

Jinnai, H. *Tokyo: A Spatial Anthropology.* Translated by K. Nishimura. Berkeley and Los Angeles: University of California Press, 1995.

——. "Tokyo Then and Now: Keys to Japanese Urban Design." *Japan Echo* 14 (Special Issue 1987): 20–29.

——. *Ethnic Tokyo.* Tokyo: Process Architecture, 1988.

——. "The Spatial Structure of Edo." In *Tokugawa Japan: The Social and Economic Antecedents of Modern Japan,* edited by C. Nakane and S. Ōishi, 124-46. Translated by C. Totman. Tokyo: University of Tokyo Press, 1990.

——. "Parks and Squares in the Scheme of Tokyo's Urban Spaces." Paper presented at the annual meeting of the Association for Asian Studies, Los Angeles, 25-28 March 1993.

Levy, D., L. Sneider, and F. B. Gibney. *Kanban: Shop Signs of*

Japan. New York and Tokyo: Weatherhill, 1983.

Ojima, T. *Imageable Tokyo: Projects by Toshio Ojima* (Tokyo: Process Architecture, 1991).

Osborne, C. "Space for Thought." *Tokyo Journal,* March 1994, 22–29.

Phillips, D. P. "The Ginza Brick District: Japan's First Experiment with Urban Design." Paper presented at the annual meeting of the Association for Asian Studies, Los Angeles, 25-28 March 1993.

Shimizu, A. *Sexism in Tokyo's New Public Art: Results from Field Research and Opinion Surveys,* Master's thesis, Temple University, 1994.

Smith, H. D., II. "Sky and Water: The Deep Structures of Tokyo." In *Tokyo: Form and Spirit,* edited by M. Friedman, 21-35. Minneapolis: Walker Art Center; New York: Harry N. Abrams, 1986.

Takashima, S. "Tokyo: Creative Chaos." *Japan Echo* 14 (Special Issue 1987): 2–6.

Takatani, T. "Tokyo Street Patterns: A Historical Analysis" *Japan Echo* 14 (Special Issue 1987): 39–44.

ENVIRONMENTAL HAZARDS AND EARTHQUAKES

Hadfield, P. *Sixty Seconds That Will Change the World: The Coming Tokyo Earthquake.* London: Pan Books, 1992.

Huddle, N., and N. Stiskin. *Island of Dreams: Environmental Crisis in Japan.* New York and Tokyo: Autumn Press, 1975.

Short, K. "Tokyo Bay: An Ecosystem in the Clutches of Development," *The Japan Times,* 24 February 1988, p. 16.

Stanley, T. A. "Tokyo Earthquake of 1923." In *Kodansha Encyclopedia of Japan.* Tokyo: Kodansha, 1983, 8: 66.

Swinbanks, D. "Conflicting Views on Extent of Earthquake Threat to Tokyo." *Nature,* 15 December 1988, 609.

——. "Builders Look to `Anti-Quake' Device." *Nature,* 15 December 1988, 609.

Tokyo Metropolitan Government. *Tokyo Fights Pollution.* Tokyo: Tokyo Metropolitan Government Municipal Library, no. 4, 1971.

Tokyo Metropolitan Government. *Tokyo and Earthquakes.* Tokyo: TMG Municipal Library No. 29, 1995.

Ueda, T. "Be Prepared!" *Look Japan* 35, no. 407 (1990): 26–27.

"When the Great Quake Comes to Tokyo." *Business Tokyo* 3, no. 7 (1989): 5–10.

CULTURAL LIFE

Akai, T. "The Common People and Painting." In *Tokugawa Japan: The Social and Economic Antecedents of Modern Japan.* Edited by C. Nakane and S. Ōishi, 167-91. Translated by C. Totman. Tokyo: University of Tokyo Press, 1990.

Barthes, R. *Empire of Signs.* London: Jonathan Cape, 1982.

Bornoff, N. *Pink Samurai: Love Marriage and Sex in Contemporary Japan.* New York: Pocket Books, 1991.

Brannen, M. Y. "`Bwana Mickey': Constructing Cultural Consumption at Tokyo Disneyland." In *Re-made in Japan: Everyday Life and Consumer Taste in a Changing Society,* edited by J. J. Tobin, 216-35. New Haven: Yale University Press, 1992.

Creighton, M. "The Depato: Merchandising the West While Selling Japaneseness." In *Re-made in Japan: Everyday Life and Consumer Taste in a Changing Society,* edited by J. J. Tobin, 42-57. New Haven: Yale University Press, 1992.

Gunji, M. "Kabuki and Its Social Background." In *Tokugawa Japan: The Social and Economic Antecedents of Modern Japan,* edited by C. Nakane and S. Ōishi, 192-211. Translated by C. Totman. Tokyo: University of Tokyo Press, 1990.

Hakuhodo Institute of Life and Living. *Young Adults in Japan: New Attitudes Creating New Lifestyles*. Tokyo: Hakuhodo Institute of Life and Living, 1985.

Hulme, D. "Godzilla Stamps His Approval." *Asian Business,* December 1994, 80.

Kawazoe, N. "The Flower Culture of Edo." *Japan Echo* 14 (Special Issue 1987): 53–58.

Kennedy, R. *Home, Sweet Tokyo: Life in a Weird and Wonderful City*. Tokyo and New York: Kodansha International, 1988.

Kiritani, E. *Vanishing Japan: Traditions, Crafts and Culture*. Rutland, Vt.: Charles E. Tuttle, 1995.

Littleton, S. "The Organization and Management of a Tokyo Shrine Festival." *Ethnology* 25 (1986): 195–202.

Meech-Pekarik, J. *The World of the Meiji Print: Impressions of a New Civilization*. New York and Tokyo: Weatherhill, 1986.

Richie, D. *A Lateral View: Essays on Contemporary Japan*. Tokyo: The Japan Times, 1991.

Robertson, J. "A Dialectic of Native and Newcomer: The Kodaira Citizens' Festival in Suburban Tokyo." *Anthropological Quarterly* 60, no. 3, (1987): 124-36.

Sadler, A. "Carrying the Mikoshi: Further Field Notes on the Shrine Festival in Modern Tokyo." *Asian Folklore Studies* 31 (1972): 89–114.

Seigle-Segawa, C. *Yoshiwara: The Glittering World of the Japanese Courtesan*. Honolulu: University of Hawaii Press, 1993.

Shibusawa, K. *Japanese Life and Culture in the Meiji Era*. Translated by C. S. Terry. Tokyo: Ōbunsha, 1958.

Smith, H. D., II. "The Tyranny of Tokyo in Modern Japanese

Culture." *Studies on Japanese Culture* 2 (1973): 367–71.

———. "Tokyo as an Idea: An Exploration of Japanese Urban Thought Until 1945." *The Journal of Japanese Studies* 4, no. 1 (1978): 45–80.

Sugiura, N. "The Urbanization of Nostalgia: The Changing Nature of Nostalgic Landscape in Postwar Japan." Paper prepared for the annual meeting of the Association of American Geographers, Portland, Oregon, 22-26 April 1987.

Takeuchi, M. "Edo Style and the Aesthetic of Iki." *Japan Echo* 14 (Special Issue 1987): 50–52.

Tobin, J. J. ed. *Re-made in Japan: Everyday Life and Consumer Taste in a Changing Society.* New Haven: Yale University Press, 1992.

APPENDIX ONE
AREA AND POPULATION OF TOKYO'S WARDS AND
MUNICIPALITIES
1 FEBRUARY 1994

	Area (sq. km.)	Population	Households
TOKYO PREFECTURE	**2,186.61**	**11,816,703**	**4,950,440**
All wards	621.00	8,019,938	3,487,537
All cities	733.03	3,681,634	1,424,306
Towns and villages	426.86	83,417	25,179
All islands	45.72	31,714	13,418
ALL WARDS	**621.61**	**8,019,938**	**3,487,537**
Chiyoda	11.64	33,849	13,639
Chūō	10.15	64,945	28,027
Minato	20.31	147,296	66,145
Shinjuku	18.23	276,527	132,868
Bunkyō	11.31	172,660	76,265
Taitō	10.08	155,421	67,415
Sumida	13.75	218,161	88,006
Kōtō	39.10	372,817	149,259
Shinagawa	22.69	330,132	150,297
Meguro	14.70	243,296	114,475
Ōta	59.46	637,644	273,809
Setagaya	58.08	778,980	356,527
Shibuya	15.11	189,465	92,028
Nakano	15.59	311,291	154,685
Suginami	34.02	522,015	251,343
Toshima	13.01	250,427	125,229
Kita	20.59	339,448	146,538
Arakawa	10.20	181,287	75,181
Itabashi	32.17	515,180	223,600

	Area (sq. km.)	Population	Households
Nerima	48.16	633,630	259,589
Adachi	53.15	629,473	241,955
Katsushika	34.84	425,588	167,357
Edogawa	49.86	590,406	233,300
ALL CITIES	**733.03**	**3,681,634**	**1,424,306**
Hachiōji	186.31	495,939	183,239
Tachikawa	24.38	156,099	60,643
Musashino	10.73	135,286	62,464
Mitaka	16.50	165,381	72,532
Ōme	103.26	136.868	45,450
Fuchū	29.34	216,127	87,550
Akishima	17.33	108,337	40,109
Chōfu	21.53	197,922	85,142
Machida	71.64	360,120	129,101
Koganei	11.33	108,061	46,311
Kodaira	20.46	170,865	66,599
Hino	27.53	167,338	66,939
Higashi Murayama	17.16	136,539	49,410
Kokubunji	11.48	105,032	45,158
Kunitachi	8.15	66,655	27,948
Tanashi	6.80	75,046	29,940
Hoya	9.05	98,405	39,128
Fussa	10.24	61,173	23,573
Komae	6.39	74,391	32,552
Higashi Yamato	13.54	76,779	26,866
Kiyose	10.19	68,292	24,216
Higashi Kurume	12.92	113,114	40,610
Musashi Murayama	15.37	67,702	23,718
Tama	21.08	148,571	55,055
Inagi	17.97	62,358	23,113
Akikawa	22.44	53,897	16,628
Hamura	9.91	55,337	20,312

	Area (sq. km.)	Population	Households
TOWNS AND VILLAGES	**832.58**	**115,131**	**38,597**
WESTERN TAMA AREA	426.86	83,417	25,179
Mizuho (town)	16.83	32,857	10,559
Hinode (town)	28.08	16,751	4,577
Itsukaichi (town)	50.90	21,899	6,433
Hinohara (village)	105.42	3,623	1,020
Okutama (town)	225.63	8,287	2,550
ISLANDS	**405.72**	**31,714**	**13,418**
OSHIMA	141.82	15,453	6,202
Oshima (town)	91.06	9,657	4,085
Toshima (village)	4.12	309	156
Niijima Honson (village)	27.77	3,219	1,228
Kozushima (village)	18.87	2,268	733
MIYAKE	76.08	4,150	1,905
Miyake (village)	55.50	3,870	1,750
Mikurajima	20.58	280	155
HACHIJŌ	83.41	9,451	4,072
Hachijō (town)	72.62	9,244	3,959
Aogashima (village)	5.98	207	113
OGASAWARA	104.41	2,660	1,239
Ogasawara (village)	104.41	2,660	1,239

APPENDIX TWO
LISTS

TOKYO'S CHIEF EXECUTIVES

MAYORS OF TOKYO (years of service)
1. Matsuda Hideo (6 October 1898–16 June 1903)
2. Ozaki Yukio (29 June 1903–12 September 1908)
3. Ozaki Yukio (30 September 1908–29 June 1912)
4. Sakatani Yoshiro (12 July 1912–25 February 1915)
5. Okuda Yoshito (15 June 1915–21 August 1917)
6. Tajiri Inajirō (5 April 1918–27 November 1920)
7. Gotō Shimpei (17 December 1920–27 April 1923)
8. Nagata Hidejirō (29 May 1923–8 September 1924)
9. Nakamura Zenkō (8 October 1924–8 June 1926)
10. Izawa Takio (16 July 1926–23 October 1926)
11. Nishikubo Hiromichi (29 October 1926–12 December 1927
12. Ichiki Otohiko (7 January 1928–14 February 1929)
13. Horikiri Zenjirō (24 April 1929–12 May 1930)
14. Nagata Hidejirō (30 May 1930–25 January 1933)
15. Ushizuka Toratarō (10 May 1933–9 May 1937)
16. Kobashi Ichita (28 June 1937–14 April 1939)
17. Tamonogi Keikichi (24 April 1939–19 February 1940)
18. Ōkubo Tomejirō (12 May 1940–22 July 1942)
19. Kishimoto Ayao (3 August 1942–30 June 1943)

SECRETARIES OF TOKYO METROPOLIS (years of service)
1. Ōtachi Shigeo (1 July 1943–22 July 1944)
2. Nishio Shuzō (25 July 1944–23 August 1945)

3. Hirose Hisatada (23 August 1945–15 January 1946)
4. Fujinuma Shōhei (15 January 1946–8 June 1946)
5. Matsui Haruo (8 June 1946–23 July 1946)
6. Yasui Seiichirō (23 July 1946–13 March 1947)
7. Iinuma Kazumi (13 March 1947–14 April 1947)
8. Yasui Seiichirō (14 April 1947–3 May 1947)

GOVERNORS OF TOKYO METROPOLIS (years of service)
1. Yasui Seiichirō (3 terms: 3 May 1947–18 April 1961)
4. Azuma Ryōtaro (2 terms: 27 April 1961–22 April 1967)
6. Minobe Ryōkichi (3 terms: 23 April 1967–22 April 1979)
9. Suzuki Shunichi (3 terms: 23 April 1979–22 April 1995)
12. Aoshima Yukio (23 April 1995–present)

TOKUGAWA SHŌGUNS (years of rule)
1. Ieyasu (1603–1605)
2. Hidetada (1605–1623)
3. Iemitsu (1623–1651)
4. Ietsuna (1651–1680)
5. Tsunayoshi (1680–1709)
6. Ienobu (1709–1712)
7. Ietsugu (1713–1716)
8. Yoshimune (1716–1745)
9. Ieshige (1745–1760)
10. Ieharu (1760–1786)
11. Ienari (1787–1837)
12. Ieyoshi (1837–1853)
13. Iesada (1853–1858)
14. Iemochi (1858–1866)
15. Yoshinobu (1867)

APPENDIX THREE
TOKYO'S TALLEST BUILDINGS

1. Tokyo Metropolitan Government (Building Number 1)
   Ward: Shinjuku   *Floors: 48*   *Height: 243.0 m.*

2. Sunshine 60 Building
   Ward: Toshima   *Floors: 60*   *Height: 226.2 m.*

3. Shinjuku Center Building
   Ward: Shinjuku   *Floors: 54*   *Height: 223.0 m.*

4. Shinjuku Sumitomo Building
   Ward: Shinjuku   *Floors: 52*   *Height: 212.0 m.*

5. Shinjuku Nomura Building
   Ward: Shinjuku   *Floors: 52*   *Height: 209.9 m.*

6. Shinjuku Mitsui Building
   Ward: Shinjuku   *Floors: 55*   *Height: 209.4 m.*

7. Yasuda Fire & Marine Insurance Building
   Ward: Shinjuku   *Floors: 43*   *Height: 200.0 m.*

8. Keiō Plaza Hotel
   Ward: Shinjuku   *Floors: 47*   *Height: 169.3 m.*

9. Toshiba Building
   Ward: Minato   *Floors: 40*   *Height: 165.1 m.*

10. KDD Building
    Ward: Shinjuku   *Floors: 32*   *Height: 164.4 m.*

11. Tokyo Metropolitan Government (Building Number 2)
    Ward: Shinjuku   *Floors: 34*   *Height: 163.0 m.*

12. Tōhō Life Insurance Building
    Ward: Shibuya   *Floors: 31*   *Height: 156.5 m.*

13. Mitsui Kasumigaseki Building
    Ward: Chiyoda   *Floors: 36*   *Height: 147.0 m.*

14. Daiichi Kangyo Building
     Ward: Chiyoda   *Floors: 35*   *Height: 142.5 m.*

15. Hotel New Ōtani, New Building
     Ward: Chiyoda   *Floors: 39*   *Height: 139.1 m.*

16. Akasaka Prince Hotel
     Ward: Chiyoda   *Floors: 39*   *Height: 138.9 m.*

17. Keiō Plaza Hotel (South Building)
     Ward: Shinjuku   *Floors: 35*   *Height: 138.7 m.*

18. Shinjuku NS Building
     Ward: Shinjuku   *Floors: 30*   *Height: 133.7 m.*

19. Tokyo Hilton Hotel
     Ward: Shinjuku   *Floors: 38*   *Height: 130.2 m.*

20. Sunshine City Prince Hotel
     Ward: Toshima   *Floors: 38*   *Height: 130.0 m.*

ABOUT THE AUTHOR

Roman Cybriwsky is professor of Geography and Urban Studies at Temple University. He divides his time between the university's campuses in Philadelphia and Tokyo, and teaches courses about Asian geography, Japan, and world cities, among others. He received a Ph.D. in geography from The Pennsylvania State University in 1972. His most recent books include *Tokyo: The Changing Profile of an Urban Giant* (Belhaven Press and G. K. Hall, 1991) and *Japan* (McDonald & Woodward Publishers, 1994). He has also written about American cities. His hobbies are watching college football, shooting pool, distance running, travel, and writing poetry.